BEN BUCHANAN

# The Cybersecurity Dilemma

*Hacking, Trust, and Fear Between Nations*

OXFORD
UNIVERSITY PRESS

# OXFORD
UNIVERSITY PRESS

Oxford University Press is a department of the
University of Oxford. It furthers the University's objective
of excellence in research, scholarship, and education
by publishing worldwide.

Oxford    New York

Auckland    Cape Town    Dar es Salaam    Hong Kong    Karachi
Kuala Lumpur    Madrid    Melbourne    Mexico City    Nairobi
New Delhi    Shanghai    Taipei    Toronto

With offices in

Argentina    Austria    Brazil    Chile    Czech Republic    France    Greece
Guatemala    Hungary    Italy    Japan    Poland    Portugal    Singapore
South Korea    Switzerland    Thailand    Turkey    Ukraine    Vietnam

Oxford is a registered trade mark of Oxford University Press
in the UK and certain other countries.

Published in the United States of America by
Oxford University Press
198 Madison Avenue, New York, NY 10016

Library of Congress Cataloging-in-Publication Data is available
Ben Buchanan.
The Cybersecurity Dilemma: Hacking, Trust, and Fear Between Nations.
ISBN: 9780190665012

Printed in India on acid-free paper

# CONTENTS

# CONTENTS

# LIST OF ACRONYMS

| | |
|---|---|
| APT | Advanced Persistent Threat |
| BIOS | Basic Input/Output System |
| CERTs | Computer Emergency Response Teams |
| CCNE | Counter-Computer Network Exploitation |
| C-OPE | Cyber Operations in Preparation of the Environment |
| DARPA | Defense Advanced Research Project Agency |
| GCHQ | Government Communications Headquarters |
| NIST | National Institute for Standards and Technology |
| NSA | National Security Agency |
| NATO | North Atlantic Treaty Organization |
| OPM | Office of Personnel Management |
| RAM | Random Access Memory |
| SALT | Strategic Arms Limitation Talks |
| SQL | Structured Query Language |

# INTRODUCTION

Every year, on the last Saturday in January, many of the political and business elite of the United States meet in Washington, DC for an evening of drinks and jokes known as the Alfalfa Club Dinner. Presidents frequently address this gathering, and the newly elected Barack Obama took his turn in 2009. During his tech-savvy campaign, much had been made of the candidate's obsession with his BlackBerry and the many security precautions he would need to take with his government device while in office. On stage, Obama brought up the issue of who was able to communicate digitally with him.

"It's a very exclusive list," he told the well-heeled crowd. "How exclusive? Everyone look at the person sitting on your left. Now look at the person sitting on your right. None of you have my e-mail address."[1]

The Alfalfa Club crowd did not get the president's email address that night. But, approximately six years later, Russian spies did. In fact, they reportedly did more than just obtain the address; they read the content of Obama's emails. The Russians also gained access to a White House communication system that staffers used for legislative affairs, personnel developments, presidential scheduling, correspondence with diplomats overseas, and more.

The operatives used computer hacking to copy these secrets. The White House breach, which came to light at a time of renewed geopolitical tension over Crimea and Ukraine, was a part of a series of major network intrusions into a variety of important targets within the American government. The foreign intruders also penetrated the Pentagon, the Joint Chiefs of Staff, the State Department, and others.

1

The series of breaches was "one of the most sophisticated we've ever seen," according to a senior government official, and prompted a major response. White House responders met nearly every day for several weeks after uncovering the hackers in their network. They recognized that intrusions were a modern form of espionage and that sensitive data would likely make its way back to a potential adversary. "It's the Russian angle to this that's particularly worrisome," another senior official said.[2]

The clearest statement on the digital break-ins came from Secretary of Defense Ash Carter. While he did not address the White House breach, the secretary gave a major speech in which he described a Russian intrusion into Pentagon networks and the United States government's rapid efforts to root them out.[3] A journalist later asked Carter about the case: what were the hackers' intentions? Carter acknowledged twice that the investigators were unable to determine the intruders' goals. Even so, the risk posed by the foreign presence was too high to leave unchecked, he said. The United States had to act, reaffirming its strength and rapidly expelling the hackers from the network. To some degree, once the government found an intruder, intentions did not matter. Carter asserted the importance of unwavering protection of America's computer systems and articulated a core organizing principle in cybersecurity: "[It] can't be good," he said, "for anybody to be inside of our networks—whatever their motivation."[4]

This case prompts a two-part practical question: why do nations (or, in the jargon of international relations scholars, states) break into the important computer networks of other states; and what happens when those intrusions are discovered? On the face of it, and with a glance at the headlines, the question seems straightforward. States penetrate the networks of one another to steal secrets, to manipulate data, or to attack computer systems. In so doing, states can gain insight into the political leadership of their potential adversaries, understand their potential adversaries' capabilities, and perform counterintelligence. Intelligence agencies and militaries can copy intellectual property, lay the groundwork for further operations, and change the conditions under which future conflict or competition will take place. In short, getting one's own malicious code into an adversary's computer systems can result in real gains for a state. Even a state that merely wants to develop options for future offensive action has strong incentives to launch intrusions in advance.

Conversely, suffering a network intrusion can result in real losses. Cognizant of the danger, states that detect an intrusion into strategically important networks[5] will feel threatened, even if the intrusion did not seem to do any immediate harm. To guard against this risk, states spend large amounts of money and time trying to prevent and detect intrusions into their important systems. As part of this protective effort, some states will break into the networks of other states, gathering intelligence on the threat. Defensive goals can therefore also motivate intrusions.

A conceptual question emerges as a result: what are the broader effects when states have reasons to intrude into the networks of one another to achieve gains or prepare offensive capabilities but also to build their defenses? If the intentions of an intrusion are hard to determine and if the potential effects of an intrusion are threatening, states will adjust their decision-making in response. This will affect when they feel tension towards other states and when they choose to escalate towards conflict.

These two ideas—the potential offensive and defensive value of launching a network intrusion, and the many dangers of suffering one—can combine to answer both the conceptual and the practical question. Together these building blocks form this book's main argument: To assure their own cybersecurity, states will sometimes intrude into the strategically important networks of other states and will threaten—often unintentionally—the security of those other states, risking escalation and undermining stability. This concept is hereafter referred to as the cybersecurity dilemma.

This proposition and the name that goes with it derive from the concept of the security dilemma. The security dilemma is the long-standing notion that states inevitably, though not deliberately, induce fear in other states as they secure themselves.[6] As a result, these other states are likely to respond, seeking to reaffirm their own security but in the process unintentionally threatening others and risking still further escalation. The core tenet has proven robust and applicable to a wide range of circumstances throughout history. In each case to which the security dilemma applies, from nuclear war[7] to non-state ethnic conflict,[8] scholars examine a number of key ideas. Primarily, they seek to uncover what structural factors drive the escalatory cycle of the security dilemma and what states might do to foster stability.

Typically, the security dilemma occurs with the development or deployment of forces. One state might invent a powerful new tank capable of outclassing other armor or might position its forces on the border of a neighboring state. In the state's own view, such moves are clearly defensive, merely assuring that its military will have the strength and flexibility to meet whatever comes its way. Yet potential adversaries are unlikely to share this perspective. They will see the new tank's potential for attack or will worry about the way in which the repositioned forces can now cross their border with greater ease. The potential adversaries will fear what comes next. They will consider taking measures to stop it, such as the development of their own capabilities or the repositioning of their own forces. This in turn can prompt a response from the first state, which is likely to perceive its own behavior as appropriate and defensive and the other state's actions as aggressive and unprovoked. The net effect is the real prospect of escalation and serious risk to the stability of the system. This danger is real even if neither state sought conflict in the first place.

This book contends that the security dilemma concept also holds great relevance in cybersecurity, where it can explain fear caused by network intrusions between states. The argument consists of five steps: considering intrusions, defenses, threats, failed mitigations, and further amplifications. Each part of the argument unpacks a key aspect of the cybersecurity dilemma and each is the subject of a chapter that follows.

The first part of the argument considers intrusions. States have evolved to try to set some limits on the use of conventional forces. National borders limit the degree to which weapons can be deployed, as a state can position its forces right up to the line, but not over. Borders also denote a symbolically important outer limit of a buffer zone. Often, the hardest part of many conventional operations comes after intruders cross these symbolic thresholds. A state may be able to send its intruding troops across a neighbor's border, but it should expect a major fight before those units reach the capital or accomplish strategic goals. The net effect is that in most cases a state will not actually invade until it is fully committed to the conflict that will follow.

# INTRODUCTION

For network intrusions, however, the dynamic is in some ways reversed. Given enough operational capacity, states can perform many hard parts of a cyber operation in secret and in advance, generating future options without locking in decision-makers to one course of action—thereby increasing the appeal of launching network intrusions. Chapter Two's study of the art of network intrusion reveals that some of the more technically challenging parts of many network intrusion efforts come earlier in the process. Gaining privileged access to an adversary's strategically important computer networks is usually harder than figuring out how to cause some basic level of damage once inside. Further, once intruders get in, they can often evade detection. They need not cause damage until the moment is right, provided that they have the resources and capability to ensure continual access. States can simply lie in wait until the situation calls for them to act. They can develop a persistent presence, try to maintain their capabilities, and bide their time. In addition, breaking into a foreign network rarely jeopardizes any lives, so such operations might seem less risky. States that might desire offensive options in the future thus have great incentive to launch intrusions early, well in advance of conflict.

Since the presence of a surreptitious adversary can be damaging in the long run, states also have strong incentive to ensure that other states have not intruded into their important networks. They need strong network protections, the topic of Chapter Three. To begin, most states will do their best to secure the perimeters of their important computer networks. This digital border security will keep out a great proportion of would-be intruders, but certainly not everyone. Therefore, well-functioning states will also actively look within their own networks for the presence of adversaries who slipped past the first level of defenses. They will look for deviations from baseline network behavior, examine the memory of computers for malicious code, and try to simulate attacks on their own systems so as to improve understanding of their weaknesses. Yet even all these efforts will not be enough to detect some adversaries who have broken in. States will sometimes have to, or will think they have to, get information to detect threats more effectively and to ensure their own network security. This intelligence can make defense easier.

One effective way to get this intelligence is by breaking into the networks of other states. This leads to an important point: even defensive-minded states that do not seek to threaten others have an incentive to launch intrusions against important networks of other states, especially—but not exclusively—potential adversaries. These intrusions can gather valuable information on what malicious code a potential adversary has deployed, what malicious code is under development, and which targets might be next. The intrusions can obtain specific intelligence that improves network defenses. Some of this information is quite likely very difficult to obtain using other methods. For many non-governmental organizations and some self-restraining states, developing intrusion capabilities—even for defensive purposes—is illegal, unwise, or impossible.[9] Yet for some states with network intrusion capabilities, it could be one of the final pieces in the cybersecurity puzzle.

But states have difficulty evaluating cybersecurity threats. If a state does detect an intrusion in one of its vital networks and if that intrusion looks to be from another state, what should the state suffering the intrusion conclude? On the one hand, it might be a defensive-minded intrusion, only checking out the intruded-upon state's capabilities and providing reassuring intelligence to the intruding state. This might seem unsettling but not necessarily threatening, presuming the state suffering the intrusion was not developing capabilities for attack or seeking conflict. On the other hand, the intrusion might be more nefarious. It could be a sign of some coming harm, such as a cyber attack or an expanding espionage operation. The state suffering the intrusion will have to decide which of these two possibilities is correct, interpreting limited and almost certainly insufficient amounts of data to divine the intentions of another state.

Thus Chapter Four's argument is vitally important: intrusions into a state's strategically important networks pose serious risks and are therefore inherently threatening. Intrusions launched by one state into the networks of another can cause a great deal of harm at inopportune times, even if the intrusion at the moment of discovery appears to be reasonably benign. The intrusion can also perform reconnaissance that enables a powerful and well-targeted cyber attack. Even operations launched with fully defensive intent can serve as beachheads for future attack operations, so long as a command and control mechanism is set up. Depending on its target, the intrusion can collect information that provides great insight into the communications and strategies of policy-makers. Network intrusions can also pose serious counterintelligence risks, revealing what secrets a state has learned about other states and provoking a damaging sense of paranoia. Given these very real threats, states are likely to view any serious intrusion with some degree of fear. They therefore have significant incentive to respond strongly, further animating the cybersecurity dilemma.

In past instances of the security dilemma, states and scholars have devised means of mitigation.[10] These mitigations seek to address the structures of the dilemma, shaping the international system in such a way that promotes stability and minimizes states' perceived threats. States have worked together to curtail the security dilemma by providing perceived advantages to defenders and by better differentiating offensive weapons from defensive ones. This makes the defensive position more desirable and requires attackers to spend more time and money. A perception of defense-dominance reassures states that they can capably maintain their own security while assuming a non-aggressive posture. Increased differentiation between offensive and defensive technologies helps states know when to feel threatened and when not to worry. This makes it easier to interpret the actions of others.

Unfortunately, however, these and other traditional mitigations do not work well when applied to the cybersecurity dilemma, as Chapter Five outlines. The overriding consensus is that the offensive side possesses a significant advantage in cyber operations, particularly for missions that do not seek a tailored physical effect. Intruders have a myriad of possible ways to make entry to networks, while defenders face many challenges. Much of what naturally provides advantages to defenders in conventional conflict, such as the ability to place stabilizing defensive fortifications at geographic chokepoints, lacks obvious parallels in cybersecurity. Similarly, it is quite difficult to distinguish between defensive and offensive network intrusions, especially since intrusions that begin as defensive in nature can morph reasonably quickly to suit offensive aims. Further, intruders sometimes use strong encryption to obscure their targets and obfuscate the malicious capabilities of their code, making interpretation of intentions harder still. Without additional nuance, past solutions to the security dilemma will not overcome the cybersecurity dilemma.

The situation gets still more concerning. As Chapter Six argues, two important factors that are frequently assumed to be constants in the traditional security dilemma models are in fact variables in cybersecurity. In most other security dilemma discussions, each actor sees the moves of its potential adversaries and must determine the intentions behind those moves. In cybersecurity, the distribution of information is vastly more asymmetric, which increases risk and uncertainty for decision-makers. With proper tradecraft, many actions, including the development of powerful capabilities and the launching of significant intrusions, often remain out of view to others. Thus, unlike in many historical and theoretical textbook cases, in cyber operations not only must states potentially fear what they see, but they must potentially fear what they do not see as well. Defensive-minded intrusions that resolve this uncertainty thus seem still more appealing.

Similarly, in the traditional security dilemma model there is almost always some status quo of shared expectations. This implicit or formal consensus of behavior provides significant guidance about which activities the involved parties consider normal and non-threatening. The potential for escalation in this model occurs only when this shared vision of normalcy breaks. In cybersecurity, however, there is only a nascent status quo. Without a common conception of appropriate national behavior, the probability of dangerous misinterpretation increases.

Building on these five steps to the argument, the final two chapters of the book are somewhat different in kind. Chapter Seven pauses to consider three objections to the cybersecurity dilemma logic and how they might constrain the argument. The first objection is that states are not capable of attributing the source of a network intrusion, short-circuiting any security dilemma. The second objection is that the danger posed by network intrusions does not pose an existential risk and so the cybersecurity dilemma is not a major concern. The third and final objection is that cyber capabilities are unevenly distributed; strong states are more likely to possess cyber capabilities than weak ones, but, the objection argues, this is true of all military weapons and so cyber capabilities are not significant. In responding to these objections, this chapter establishes the boundaries of the cybersecurity dilemma argument.

Chapter Eight addresses ways in which states can begin to approach the cybersecurity dilemma. The chapter outlines mechanisms through which states can encourage greater stability by signaling to other states that their intentions are benign. It first examines the central role that baseline defenses—protections that do not rely on intelligence collected from foreign networks—play in simplifying the problem. Next, it introduces ways in which the strongest states, the ones that are most at risk of doing the most damage in unintended conflict, can build trust with one another through bilateral action. Similarly, it examines the unilateral actions states can potentially perform to secure all states and send strong signals about their peaceful intentions. Lastly, it outlines a security posture that states can adopt to provide a mechanism which will contribute towards a stable status quo.

## The Approach

Computer hacking is now part of international relations. There is ample evidence that network intrusions serve as tools of statecraft, as means of attack and of intelligence collection. Simply put, those who study the actions of states and explain the course of international events will increasingly need to understand the nuances of cyber operations and their effect on the international system.[11]

But the long-established tools of international relations scholarship also retain their value when applied to cyber operations.[12] Given the reported scope of state-launched or state-sponsored intrusions, it is easy to assume that states are, and will always be, motivated by greed and mistrust. This work goes beyond such assumptions, however, and seeks insight into the fundamental possibilities and limitations at the intersection of statecraft and cybersecurity. Such an analysis draws on and sheds light on what states do, but more important is what these actions, once contextualized, reveal about future possible prospects. Long-run international aspirations, like trust and stability in the computing ecosystem, are unachievable without careful examination of the structural underpinnings of cybersecurity practice, of what states fear, of what they do to assuage those fears, and why they do it. The security dilemma is a proven means to get at these foundational elements.

Applying the security dilemma to cyber operations has another important benefit: it can help determine which cybersecurity concepts are most important for the non-cybersecurity specialist. Much of cybersecurity is deeply technical, but if particular ideas are relevant to the core themes of the security dilemma—the operational and strategic interplay of trust, fear, and cooperation—then these areas are worth examination. In effect, the security dilemma can serve as a roadmap through the sometimes opaque practice of cybersecurity. It is a method of identifying the most important trees and ultimately of understanding the forest.

The cybersecurity-focused portions of the text distill the most important technical ideas and link them to broader themes. The primary sources for these sections are often professional reports on noteworthy intrusions written by computer forensic analysts. In addition, these discussions draw on more abstract models of offensive and defensive operations put forth by research institutes, scholars, and practitioners. Because of their specialist nature, these reports and models are often overlooked. These sources prove to be of great value in understanding the known cyber operations of states and in presenting important cases. One cannot credibly claim to understand states' current approaches to cyber operations without examining this detailed evidence of actual behavior.

In reading these reports, context is vital. Splashy report covers, sometimes replete with custom logos, demonstrate that marketing is an ancillary purpose for some of these files. Nonetheless, some characteristics are common to high-quality products.[13] A document's technical foundation is vital, including the degree to which its authors publish forensic artifacts for other security researchers to examine (a kind of peer review process in the information security community). For documents advancing a particular claim, an analysis of competing hypotheses is similarly important. For documents that seek to illuminate broader trends in cybersecurity, the analysis must draw on an appropriately large and well-sampled collection of data, which usually requires carefully conducted surveys or data from a significant installed customer base. Used carefully, these technical sources can serve to aggregate key ideas or present new cases in a way that advances the study of statecraft.

Some important parts of the discussion of cybersecurity practice cannot rely upon intrusion reports, however. This is largely because some malicious code samples and case studies are not in the public domain. For discussion of these cases and concepts, this book examines policy documents and other internal files. These documents discuss intrusions and indicate how policy-makers conceive of future possible operations. Some of this material comes from revelations by Edward Snowden, a former contractor to the National Security Agency who provided a trove of highly classified files to journalists. Among the documents made public, those raising civil liberties concerns have attracted the most attention elsewhere. This book instead draws primarily on the often-overlooked documents that discuss cyber operations missions and techniques; Snowden's revelations provide a glimpse into how the cybersecurity dilemma can play out in practice.

Whatever one's views of Snowden's actions, there is no credible indication that anything he provided is inauthentic. Additional reporting has confirmed many of the claims in documents he provided.[14] Further, American officials have implicitly or explicitly acknowledged the accuracy of many points in the Snowden files, either as part of policy review commissions or in clarifying statements.[15] Even if one believes that some of the less technical documents overstate the efficacy of particular operations for reasons of internal marketing,[16] the Snowden files still provide a glimpse into how the cybersecurity dilemma can play out in practice. They are therefore valuable as one piece of a broader analytical puzzle.

## Definitions and Limitations

There are three vital definitional points. First, the argument focuses on states. This further situates the discussion within a long tradition of international relations scholarship, in which for decades the basic unit of analysis has been the state.[17] An emphasis on states also corresponds to real world practice. Although non-state actors are quite important in cybersecurity and quite active in performing network intrusions, for the most part the most sophisticated capabilities still belong to states, or those actors, such as contractors, serving the interests of a state.[18] Not all states, however, choose to invest in intrusion capabilities; this work concentrates on those major states that do.

Second, the argument limits itself to a state's "strategically important networks." While there are some common traits in the networks truly important enough to meet this standard, there is nevertheless a sizable amount of variance. For example, networks that support critical infrastructure—power, water, transportation, and so on—are of vital importance in virtually every country. Also strategically important are networks that are of enormous commercial significance, such as stock markets or financial systems. Within a government, some networks are vital for internal communications, for carrying out military and intelligence operations, or for storing classified secrets. A network intrusion reaching this threshold of importance need not be against another government directly, nor always against infrastructure, but rather against a target of deep strategic significance.

Third, this work draws a distinction between exploitation, which is the usually unauthorized collection of information from a computer network, and attack, which is the destruction or manipulation of data on a computer network. A wide variety of sources recognize this distinction,[19] with the possible exception of popular media reporting. As Chapters Two and Four will show in substantially more detail, exploitation and attack share similar operational foundations, but there are important differences. The relationship between these two concepts is at the core of the cybersecurity dilemma.

This work also has two important overarching limitations worth stating at the outset. Most significantly, it relies on information that is in the public domain. While the past few years have seen tremendously increased scrutiny and coverage of cyber operations, this restriction to public domain information is still a problematic constraint on analysis. Even with the revelations of the Snowden documents, a great deal of information on cyber operations remains secret. The security dilemma framework can suggest theoretical possibilities for action and intrusion analyses and leaks of classified documents can broadly confirm those possibilities, but it would be naïve to think that the public domain viewpoint is fully comprehensive and authoritative. Nonetheless, this constraint has long existed in intelligence studies.[20]

A second limitation follows. Because of the Snowden documents and Western nations' democratic systems, the United States' and United Kingdom's official policy perspectives are more transparent than those of other major states, such as China or Russia. For example, the evidence indicates that the United States and its signals intelligence partners in the so-called Five Eyes[21] perform intrusions for defensive reasons, among other motivations. But from professional forensic reports, it is clear only that other states employ intrusion capabilities, not whether they sometimes do so for defensive purposes. Given the ways in which states must cooperate to overcome the security dilemma completely, this will be an avenue worth exploring in the future, should more data emerge.

1

# THE SECURITY DILEMMA

*Overview*

The thirteen days from 16 to 28 October 1962 were some of the most tense of the Cold War. For almost two weeks, the United States and the Soviet Union engaged in fierce brinksmanship over the deployment of Soviet ballistic missiles in Cuba. The widely recounted case is a classic tale of international politics. It began with the American discovery of Soviet missile site construction, continued with diplomatic confrontation and denial, the risky American naval blockade, secret ad hoc negotiations, and ended with the missiles' eventual removal. The stakes could not have been higher, as the very real threat of escalation to nuclear war permeated every twist and turn.

One alarming sub-plot is often overlooked, hidden behind high levels of classification for many decades. On 27 October, at the height of the crisis, the United States Air Force flew an air-sampling mission over the North Pole. This air-sampling mission, like the ones that had preceded it, sought to gather information on possible Soviet atmospheric nuclear tests. It was a routine effort, not something ordered in response to the crisis in Cuba. But, through a stroke of bad luck, this particular mission went awry at the worst possible time. Blinded by the Northern Lights, the American U-2 pilot strayed into Soviet territory. The Soviets scrambled fighter jets to intercept the spy plane, prompting the American aviator to radio for assistance. The Alaskan Air Command mobilized fighters armed with air-to-air nuclear missiles to defend the U-2. What began as a regular mission instead quickly escalated: American and Soviet planes seemed on a collision course for atomic conflict during a geopolitical moment that was already filled with nuclear tension.

This case neatly condenses, at an operational level, the security dilemma and its dangers. The United States carried out what it thought was a benign defensive activity, but the Soviets, as a result of their fear and the American pilot's seemingly aggressive flight path, could only view it as a serious threat. Even though neither side took intentionally provocative action, the specter of nuclear conflict already made real by the Cuban Missile Crisis loomed even larger. As the incident unfolded, then-Secretary of Defense Robert McNamara quickly recognized the mortal danger of misperception and misinterpretation. When aides informed him of the U-2's accidental presence in Soviet airspace, he "turned absolutely white, and yelled hysterically, 'This means war with the Soviet Union.'"

Skillful piloting averted that fate. The U-2 aviator eventually oriented himself and evaded his Soviet pursuers. Neither the American nor Soviet fighter planes fired a shot. But afterwards both sides acknowledged the horror of what could have been. Soviet Premier Nikita Khrushchev bluntly warned President Kennedy of the dangers of such a mission and of misunderstandings. The Soviets could "easily" have thought the U-2 was "a nuclear bomber," he said, "which might push us to a fateful step."[1] The message was clear: operational misinterpretation can cause a conflict, even a nuclear one, which no one wants.

The security dilemma dynamics are laid barest in a fast-burning crisis like this one. But the security dilemma also animates the course of international events more generally, guiding strategic as well as operational thought. Throughout the Cold War, the United States and Soviet Union each had to provide for their own security. Each feared the existential risk posed by the other and its arsenal of nuclear weapons. In response, the two nations built and deployed potent military capabilities and collected intelligence, sometimes by employing intrusive methods. And although they often did not recognize it, each side had to grapple with the possibility of dangerous misunderstanding in high-stakes decisions, their own and their counterpart's.

This short first chapter argues that the security dilemma is an important tool for approaching cybersecurity and state decision-making since it has previously proven applicable to a wide range of international interactions. Each of the elements that governed the Cold War case and many others—the anarchic nature of the international system, the need for states to prepare capabilities and collect intelligence, and the ever-present risk of misinterpretation and escalation—holds enormous relevance in cybersecurity. While the cybersecurity dilemma has some unique and even vexing characteristics, it is more tractable when considered in the broader context of international relations history and theory. This approach resists the temptation to treat everything in cyber operations as new and unprecedented.

The chapter's argument has three parts. The first section outlines how the nature of international relations creates the security dilemma. This section gives greater nuance to the concept and contextualizes this book within the broader world of international relations scholarship. The chapter's second section narrows the focus to examine how intelligence operations affect the security dilemma. This tie to intelligence, which became apparent only with data from the Cold War, provides important insights for understanding the cybersecurity dilemma. The chapter's conclusion sets the stage for the transition to cybersecurity, where intelligence again plays a significant role.

## International Relations, Anarchy, and the Security Dilemma

The ancient Greek writer Thucydides is widely considered the world's first historian. In his best-known work, *The History of the Peloponnesian War*, he recounts a stand-off between the military forces of Athens and the rulers of the island of Melos. The Athenians demanded that the Melians, who were far less prepared for battle, join Athens' alliance and pay economic tribute. The Melians refused, pointing out that they were neutral in Athens' major war with Sparta and that it would be unjust for the Athenians to compel payment. The Athenians ignored these protests. When Melos did not pay, the Athenians lay siege to Melos and executed every adult male. Before they did so, they offered an unvarnished lesson into the brutal and sometimes counterproductive nature of international politics and conflict: "the strong do what they can and the weak suffer what they must."[2]

# THE CYBERSECURITY DILEMMA

The Peloponnesian War illustrates a concept known as anarchy that has become the centerpiece of international relations scholarship. The units in an anarchic system, such as the Greek city-states, are not under the power of any external arbiter or governing authority. There are no boundaries on what they can conceivably do, provided that they are strong enough.[3] In a true crisis, each entity must fend for itself. Strength and self-sufficiency are therefore extremely important, usually far more so than morality or justice. Trust and cooperation are hard to come by. As a result, life under anarchy is, in the words of the English political theorist Thomas Hobbes, "solitary, poor, nasty, brutish, and short."[4]

Hobbes favored an absolute sovereign to bring order. But John Locke, another English philosopher, offered a different answer that might seem more familiar to both the ancient Greeks and to the modern observer: governments.[5] Empowered by a social contract with its citizens, a government could be strong enough to protect rights, but separation of powers within a state would prevent the abuse of authority. Locke's approach is in wide use. Governments seek to create order and stability within their borders by establishing and enforcing laws, with varying degrees of success.[6] Effective government keeps anarchy at bay.

But, as Thucydides relayed, what happens between governments is another matter. Modern states themselves exist in an anarchic system that still has no external authority.[7] In such circumstances, each state must provide for its own security. There are no real restrictions on what it can try to do in service of that goal. Even if the state does not aspire to conquer others, it must always be wary of what others might do.

This anarchy facilitates the security dilemma. John Herz, a political scientist, first coined the term in 1950, and Herbert Butterfield, a historian, independently advanced a similar concept not long after.[8] States, since they have to provide for their own security, will seek to acquire a great deal of power to minimize the risks posed by other states. As it strengthens itself, though, a state's growing capabilities will inevitably, even if inadvertently, threaten other states. Those other states will recognize their own relative weakness and fear attack. Usually unable to turn to an external arbiter they will need to develop their own forces and provide for their own security, beginning a potentially dangerous sequence of events.[9]

# THE SECURITY DILEMMA

The security dilemma is what many international relations scholars call a structural problem. It is an outgrowth of the character of geopolitics. The individual attributes of the involved states—type of government, nature of economy, and the like—mean comparatively little.[10] All states must fear the worst, since assuming the best of other governments is sometimes a dangerous proposition. They must either prepare to kill or risk being killed.[11] But such fear is not conducive to stability. As Herz put it, "ultimately, somewhere, the conflicts caused by the security dilemma are bound to emerge among political units of power."[12] Such conflict might not be the fault of any given actor, although certainly states with expansionist intentions can be particularly destabilizing.[13] Even states seeking to avert war and preserve peace are subject to the security dilemma. They still must worry about their own safety in an unpredictable and dangerous world.

The security dilemma is also a psychological problem. Misinterpretation animates its danger, as states unintentionally threaten other states with their actions. They do so because they are frequently unable to understand how others who do not know their intentions will perceive their behavior.[14] Butterfield wrote that "It is the peculiar characteristic of the situation I am describing—the situation of what I should call the Hobbesian fear—that you yourself may vividly feel the terrible fear you have of the other party, but you cannot enter into the other man's counter-fear, or even understand why he should be particularly nervous."[15] When states must make wrenching decisions about escalation, anxiety and even panic are often the dominant emotions.

The psychology of the security dilemma often acquires a moral undertone. Each actor tends to view itself as morally right and the other as morally wrong. This perspective further animates the dilemma, as states convinced of their own superior moral position find it easier to act on their fears—and harder to appreciate that others might do the same.[16] Cold War policy-making, for example, at times took on a normative character. President Eisenhower's Secretary of State, John Foster Dulles, adopted a so-called "bad faith model" of interpreting Soviet decisions. He believed that every Soviet action reflected Communism and an ideological opposition to America.[17] A few decades later, President Reagan's remark that the Soviet Union was an "evil empire" cast the bilateral tension in similarly stark terms.[18]

These dangerous incentive structures and persistent challenges in perception can be cyclical and escalatory. There is no natural brake on intensification in a system characterized by fear and uncertainty. Each state will view its own actions, such as the development of new weapons or the movement of military forces, as defensive and unremarkable. But each state will also see the actions of many other states as a cause for concern. As states develop their capabilities and escalate their actions, the stakes of the security dilemma grow still higher.[19] The result is too often war that no party desires, what Butterfield called "the tragic dimension of human conflict."[20]

Modern security dilemma theorists have added additional nuance and structure to the original idea. They have divided the security dilemma into two halves, the dilemma of interpretation and the dilemma of response. The dilemma of interpretation occurs when states must decide about the underlying intentions of another state's actions. Other states may perform actions—such as developing military capabilities, deploying forces to a border, or increasing intelligence collection—for defensive reasons or as a prelude to an attack. But a state's interpretation of the other side's intent occurs without full information. Through intelligence collection, diplomacy, and careful observation, states can gain knowledge about each other, but these methods never yield the complete picture with complete confidence. This intrinsic ambiguity—which subsequent chapters will explore in much more depth as it relates to cyber operations—is at the root of the problem. Nonetheless, states must settle on an interpretation.[21]

The dilemma of response follows. Once decision-makers have determined how to understand the actions of another state, they must formulate an answer. Possibilities exist along a spectrum. On the one hand, states can signal reassurance. On the other, they can unleash a forceful rejoinder. Each approach has its dangers. If decision-makers threaten force in a case where the other state had only benign intentions, they risk causing hostilities in what would otherwise have been a peaceful situation. If decision-makers signal reassurance in response to aggressive intent, they risk remaining ill-prepared for a powerful attack by their adversary. Such an attack may rise to the level of existential threat.[22] Much, therefore, is at stake.

A key question emerges: can this problem be overcome? Can states secure themselves without unintentionally threatening one another and risking conflict? Security dilemma theorists have broken down the answer to this question into three broad categories: the "fatalist," "mitigator," and "transcender" approaches.[23] The fatalist view contends that states can never escape the security dilemma. According to this logic, a state providing for its own safety is before too long inevitably and unavoidably threatening to other states. Nevertheless, anarchy dictates that states must seek to grow their power, develop military might, and deploy intelligence capabilities. Even when states attain security, it is too often fleeting. Instead, states must always be on their guard, and possibly even always seeking to expand, regardless of what effect it might have on other states.[24] Norms, institutions, and international organizations are of little value in dampening this dangerous state of affairs.[25] This result is something more properly termed a "security paradox," in which the innate desire for security counterintuitively begets insecurity and instability.[26]

The mitigators are more hopeful. They premise their approach on the notion that states can meaningfully minimize the risks posed by the security dilemma, though not in any kind of permanent way. This view acknowledges that the anarchy in the international system and its associated dangers are here to stay. Nevertheless, states have a choice in how they manage the problem. Mitigators return to the root of the word "dilemma." A dilemma, as defined by the Greeks, is when an actor must choose between competing propositions, each of which could be true. As states approach the dilemma of interpretation, they need not always conclude that the action in question is threatening; as states decide on a response, they need not seek to escalate the situation in response to every serious threat.[27] If states make careful choices, the risk can be managed. Mitigators believe that some of the most destabilizing and dangerous aspects of relations between states can be curtailed, including arms racing, unintended conflict, and brinksmanship.[28] Different mitigators express different views on how this is best done.

Some mitigators argue that changing the incentive structures of operational and strategic decision-making can make the security dilemma less concerning.[29] Other mitigators place greater trust in the power of institutions, such the North Atlantic Treaty Organization or the United Nations, to mitigate the security dilemma. These mechanisms of collective defense and information sharing create a buffer that permits less fearful decision-making and promotes better risk management.[30] Though the practicalities of implementation differ, mitigators as a whole believe the dangers of the security dilemma can be partially managed.

The transcenders go well beyond this view. They base their approach on the empowering notion that humanity has a great deal of leeway to craft a new destiny, freeing itself from structures of escalation, fear, and conflict.[31] The means through which humanity can achieve this reinvention vary by thinker and approach.[32] Some writers in the transcenders camp, like Immanuel Kant, offered visions of an eternal peace based on federations, constitutions, and hospitality. Others, like Leo Tolstoy and Mahatma Gandhi, have advanced pacifist notions. Still others challenge the common view of anarchy in the international system, acknowledging its existence but contending that states are not bound to it. Instead, states can create norms and foster identities that limit which policy choices are acceptable.[33] Two constant themes recur throughout the wildly diverse transcender argumentation: the inclusion of politics, identity, and morality in the discussion of security and the idea that such a social reinvention must be universal. The transcender approach, by definition, looks beyond half-measures.[34]

In examining the cybersecurity dilemma, this book primarily explores the mitigator approach. Later chapters will apply previously successful mitigations to cybersecurity. In addition, these chapters will show how some past assumptions made by mitigators do not hold up in the digital domain. Since institutions and norms in cybersecurity are only nascent, the focus will be on state actions. Testing the applicability of mitigator ideas is important for evaluating the cybersecurity dilemma. If the cybersecurity dilemma is both serious and difficult to overcome, then it becomes more apparent that there are lasting structural obstacles to trust in cybersecurity, ones that states cannot easily surmount even if they seek cooperation. If the mitigator view fails, it may well prove the fatalist view correct as it applies to cybersecurity, though not necessarily. The transcender view, which is entirely embryonic in this area, is much more difficult as yet to evaluate.

## The Security Dilemma and Intelligence

The security dilemma is continually applied in new ways to suit changing times. Herz and Butterfield formally proposed it after World War

II, focusing on the bloodshed that results when states slide into conflict. Scholars focused on mitigation updated the idea several decades later in the midst of the Cold War, outlining how states could act to slow a slide towards violence and considering the role of nuclear weapons. As the Cold War waned, the study of tense but peaceful statecraft became one of historical perspective. Drawing on more information available on how the United States and Soviet Union perceived and acted towards one another, theorists and practitioners extended the security dilemma framework yet again.

Michael Herman served as a senior British signals intelligence officer during the Cold War. After a thirty-five-year career in a variety of posts, he turned to the academic analysis of intelligence collection. Herman's post-Cold War study concluded that the security dilemma applied beyond the development and deployment of military capabilities. Instead, it also applied to foreign intelligence operations in which one state sought to gather information on a potential adversary. In important respects, these collection efforts, and the potential adversary's perception of them if uncovered, lent themselves to the same dangerous cycles that Herz and Butterfield warned about in military affairs. On the one hand, the information gained can provide reassurance to the intelligence-collector seeking to ensure its own defense; on the other hand, the act of performing such collection can be intrusive and threatening to the states from which it is collected. The perception of a threat sometimes occurs even when the state that is collecting the intelligence has only benign intentions, paralleling the structure of the military-focused security dilemma.[35]

Intelligence collection can empower and secure states. Most obviously, good intelligence can guard against devastating surprise attacks. As the attacks on Pearl Harbor and on the World Trade Center have shown, intelligence collection is essential in peacetime as well as in war.[36] States must never get too comfortable about their own security. The collection and integration of intelligence from a wide range of disparate sources is a key part of efforts to detect and prevent unexpected dangers.

In addition, effective intelligence operations, including gathering insights about potential adversaries prior to conflict, can improve states' ability to fight wars against potential adversaries. A state with strong intelligence can develop its armed forces more efficiently and economically, preparing them better to exploit the weaknesses of their potential adversaries. Once in conflict, good intelligence can assist in deploying the forces where they are capable of having the greatest impact. Operating without high-quality intelligence has the reverse effect. States following misguided military development trajectories might find themselves preparing to wage the wrong fight and wasting resources on comparatively less valuable technology and equipment. Once in conflict, a lack of intelligence can be even worse. Without solid information, a military is open to feints and surprises and is likely to miss opportunities. Intelligence aids in the production, use, and conservation of power.[37]

In short, the right intelligence can lead to better and more rational policy-making. In a world full of many possible threats, contingencies, and opportunities, sound intelligence can help policy-makers prioritize objectives and tasks. Once focused, policy-makers rely on accurate information and analysis to guide their decisions, as no policy-maker can ever hope to know offhand all that he or she must about a potential adversary or a geopolitical event. Good intelligence can also sometimes act as a brake on unchecked ideology. Although policy-makers largely retain decision-making power, well-reasoned analysis can minimize the degree to which decisions rely on hunches, biases, and predispositions. By accurately and fairly framing issues, intelligence can ensure that reason has a place in government. This is a role long prized by some famous analysts.[38]

But intelligence collection can be threatening to the state targeted by the operation. States must bear additional costs to keep their operations secret. If a state fears that its communications are prone to interception, it will either limit the amount of information it communicates or establish additional protocols to try to secure its messages and technology. In peacetime, this need for security can delay weapons development and limit military training.[39] In wartime, such security measures can cripple operational speed and effectiveness; a notable example of this is the British experience during the desert warfare phases of World War II.[40] Fear of communication intercepts can remove military options, such as bold surprise attacks, from consideration.[41]

More broadly, a state may fear losing its secrets to a foreign intelligence service. Such suspicion can be deeply self-destructive, causing an intelligence agency to investigate or fire valuable employees, inhibiting the flow of information, and prompting an aversion to risk. Perhaps the most prominent American embodiment of this suspicion was James Jesus Angleton, the Central Intelligence Agency's controversial former head of counterintelligence. Angleton, who held his spy-catching role for almost two decades during the middle of the Cold War, was deeply worried about the Soviet penetration of the agency. Angleton's obsessive concern spawned in part from intelligence breaches. With this example in mind, Herman contended that "penetration—and the threat of it—constitutes a form of political action, putting a virus into the bloodstream of its intelligence target. It produces the special counterintelligence mentality: slightly paranoid, considering the possibility of manipulation and deception everywhere."[42] When fears of counterintelligence failure become overpowering, they can lead to paralysis that weakens a state's ability to operate its own intelligence service effectively.

Intelligence collection can also pose a direct threat. These efforts involve what is often known as "close access" and are most relevant for the discussion of the cybersecurity dilemma. Close access programs violate the sovereignty of another state, come alarmingly close to doing so, or are otherwise deeply intrusive. The state suffering the intrusion will likely interpret the actions as asserting hostile intent or advancing an aggressive power dynamic. The aerial incident that nearly boiled over into conflict during the Cuban Missile Crisis is the most significant example of a larger Cold War trend noted by Herman: "[American] airborne collection and other collection in Soviet backyards presumably appeared as a flexing of US muscle, touching on the [Soviet] regime's special sensitivity over secrecy and the defence of national territory; there were overtones of [the United States'] Strategic Air Command's nuclear threat, particularly when this was virtually unchallenged in the 1950s."[43] Even though the American planes sought only to gather intelligence, the operations deeply troubled the Soviets.

The consequence, intended or not, of such close access programs is to stoke doubt in the state suffering the intrusion (or near-intrusion, in the case of aircraft flights along borders). This state will fear the unwanted proximity of enemy forces and worry that future intruders might be attackers, rather than collectors. While this mindset was perhaps most vividly on display during the Cold War, in some important respects it has not faded. After discovering what seemed like increased Russian intelligence collection in northern Europe, a Swedish official said in 2015 that "We see Russian intelligence operations in Sweden … as preparation for military operations against Sweden." In security dilemma-like language, the official went on to note that "we can't interpret this any other way."[44] As Chapter Four will outline, the linkage between intelligence collection and attack is stronger still in cyber operations. It is thus significantly more threatening.

Sometimes the state performing close access intelligence does not wish to worry the state suffering the intrusion. But at other times a state will use the potential adversary's fear to gather valuable information in close access operations. One of the best ways to collect intelligence is to stimulate the potential adversary into a defensive reaction and carefully observe what happens next. During the Cold War, the United States used this technique to great effect as a means of supplementing its knowledge on Soviet military practice (the Soviets used similar, though slightly less provocative, techniques).

A noteworthy American program of this sort deliberately provoked the Soviets with fake air attacks. These efforts sought to awaken the Soviet anti-air defenses so that American intelligence could observe their function and communications. By varying the time, place, and manner of its provocations, the United States kept the Soviets on guard and probed for weaknesses.[45] As one American pilot said, "sometimes we would fly missions over the Black Sea … To tickle the Soviets a little and create more activity we would do a straight approach towards Sevastopol, turn and run out. Then we would listen to the racket."[46] This sort of incitement yielded a great deal of important intelligence, according to a former United States Department of Defense official: "First, we could understand the subordination of [the] Soviet command systems. Next, we could understand their strategy and tactics. We learned quite a bit of what is going on, from the locations of their radars … We learned how they reacted, and how promptly they reacted, to actions. Also the radar Order of Battle information was very useful."[47] The United States Navy ran a parallel effort at sea.[48]

As valuable as this information was to the Americans, the Soviets had little appreciation for the West's perspective. The operations "really got to them," according to one former United States Department of Defense overseer.[49] This again illustrates a broader trend: continued and repeated intrusive collection might yield prized intelligence for one side, but it almost certainly animates fears in the other side that a real attack will follow in the not too distant future. As with the Cuban Missile Crisis case, these aggressive techniques were not without their risks, especially when the operations were not performed as precisely as intended. Close access intelligence, though oftentimes necessary or seemingly necessary, is a dangerous game for all involved. When misinterpreted, the possibility of escalation into conflict is very real.

Another period of great Cold War anxiety, in 1983, showed how these operations could build tension. In the spring of that year, the United States Navy conducted a massive military exercise in the North Pacific Ocean, involving more than 23,000 sailors from three carrier battle groups. Included in the exercise, which took place near sensitive Soviet sites, was an attempt to provoke a Soviet reaction with flights on or over the border, so that naval intelligence could study the response.[50] In one mission, on 4 April, six United States planes directly overflew Soviet military installations on the Kurile Islands, outraging the Soviets and prompting an angry Soviet diplomatic response.[51] While there was no military exchange at the time, the incident built up significant anxiety on the Soviets' part.

Tension eventually led to tragedy. On 1 September 1983, Korean Air Lines Flight 007 from New York to Seoul inadvertently strayed into similar Soviet airspace. The civilian flight overflew the same Soviet intercontinental ballistic missile testing range which the United States Navy had approached a few months prior. The area was of great interest to the United States and was often surveyed by other American jets, including just a few hours before Flight 007 entered the area.[52] In response to the Korean Air flight, the Soviet air defense units scrambled fighters and eventually ordered the shootdown of the unknown intruding aircraft. Unlike in 1962, this time the Soviets were successful. A Soviet Su-15 interceptor fired air-to-air missiles, destroying the airliner and killing all of the 269 passengers and crew aboard. In explaining their decision to attack, the Soviets specifically blamed the repeated American overflights and their effect in increasing mistrust and suspicion. It is impossible to know for certain, but it seems likely that the

Soviets mistook the civilian airliner for an American military plane on an attack or intrusive collection mission.[53]

The incident, and less catastrophic ones of a similar origin, did little to resolve each side's security concerns. Each state assumed the worst about its adversary, viewing its suspicions as truth. Both the Americans and the Soviets were deeply concerned about the seemingly provocative actions of the other, from close access programs to human intelligence penetrations. On the other hand, each state remained convinced that its own actions were benign and necessary in the face of a looming threat.

Although neither state could prove its peace-seeking nature to the other, it remained baffled as to why its counterpart did not see things the same way.[54] During the 1983 tensions, President Reagan received intelligence about increased Soviet fears of American attack. He responded with puzzlement and surprise, saying, "Do you think they really believe that? I don't see how they would ... But it's something to think about."[55] Nor was Reagan alone. Secretary of Defense Casper Weinberger believed that "the Russians know perfectly well we will never launch a first strike on the Soviet Union," and Secretary of State George Shultz later wrote about how "incredible" the Soviet fears seemed to American policy-makers.[56] For his part, Mikhail Gorbachev acknowledged in his memoirs that he did not realize the fear that his actions sometimes caused in the United States.[57]

## Conclusion: The Stakes of the Security Dilemma

This chapter has shown both the adaptability and the relevance of the security dilemma. Throughout history, the security dilemma has proven useful to scholars in understanding how states relate to one another, how they cause fear in each other, and why they sometimes go to war. But it is not merely academic. Rather, the subject matter falls directly within the purview of national policy-makers. There is good reason to think, as the following chapters will argue, that the cybersecurity dilemma will be of similar relevance.

The security dilemma as it applies to intelligence is the most significant part of the foundation presented in this chapter. It is evident from history that there are high stakes in this kind of security dilemma, especially when there is also a closely linked threat of attack. A state collects intelligence in the service of reassurance and defense, but in doing so it often stimulates fear in a potential adversary. If the potential adversary ignores the fear, it risks the loss of its secrets, rendering it less capable in a time of conflict or competition. In an anarchic system, this is simply not a risk that most states are willing to take too frequently. If the potential adversary bolsters its own security by increasing its methods of secrecy and ratcheting up intrusive collection of its own—or by shooting back at the collectors—the first state will often feel a need to respond. To overcome its potential adversary's additional measures of security, the state will need still more intrusive collection.[58] The race to the bottom thus begins. This escalatory dynamic is perhaps even more concerning in cybersecurity.

2

# THE INTRUDER'S VIEW

## Overview

In 2010, a computer in Iran was acting strangely. It kept restarting, seemingly outside of the control of any operator. When cybersecurity specialists examined the machine, they found malicious code. And when they examined the malicious code, they found a number of unusual signs. The code spread itself between computers using previously unknown methods. It was much larger and more developed than was typical. It seemed to target industrial control systems in a very precise way. Investigators would eventually conclude that its purpose was covert sabotage of the Iranian nuclear program.

Investigators called the malicious code Stuxnet, a name derived from a combination of some of its files. Forensic examination and press leaks eventually revealed that the code was likely part of an American–Israeli operation. The digital attack on the Natanz Iranian nuclear facility stealthily destroyed approximately one thousand centrifuges processing nuclear material, almost one-fifth of all of Iran's uranium-enriching devices.[1] It did so in a slow and incremental fashion, manipulating centrifuges so that they broke apart over time with no apparent cause. As a result, the computer worm introduced doubt into the minds of Iranian scientists and engineers.[2] It even caused the Iranian authorities to arrest some of their own workers, accusing them of

31

espionage and treason.[3] Until the worm escaped the facility and eventually attracted attention with the strangely behaving computer, Stuxnet remained a highly classified secret.

But Stuxnet might only have been the beginning. American military planners reportedly feared that the attack would not be enough. The mission, which began during the Bush Administration and expanded under President Obama, destroyed centrifuges but did not resolve the broader concern. Iran's nuclear program continued to be a source of tension for the United States and in the Middle East. If the nuclear dispute led to a conflict between the United States and Iran, perhaps instigated by an Israeli military attack, there might be a need for something still more powerful. In such a scenario, the United States might desire a cyber capability—or rather, a series of cyber capabilities—that targeted Iranian infrastructure more broadly.

A part of the United States' contingency plan for this scenario was reportedly code-named NITRO ZEUS. Like Stuxnet, the operation was to be another cyber attack effort against Iran. Also like Stuxnet, NITRO ZEUS sought to have a physical, or kinetic, effect, destroying or disabling facilities by employing malicious computer code. This kind of effect is remarkable and exceedingly rare, even after Stuxnet had demonstrated the concept. But more remarkable still, and unlike Stuxnet, was NITRO ZEUS' extensive target list. Instead of focusing on the Iranian nuclear program, it cast a wide net. The victims included power plants, transport infrastructure, and air defenses all over Iran. Planners describe it as the largest combined cyber and kinetic effort the United States—and almost certainly the world—had ever conceived.

The plan required extensive unauthorized access to Iranian systems. The United States obtained this access through the efforts of thousands of American military and intelligence community personnel. It invested tens of millions of dollars and intruded into vital networks all across Iran. American operators checked in with their malicious code frequently, sometimes even nightly, to ensure access. Yet what was perhaps most remarkable was that the destructive part of the operation was never needed or employed. Instead, the United States and Iran reached a nuclear deal in 2015, forestalling the need for another round of damage wrought by cyber capabilities.[4]

This chapter argues that the operational processes of network intrusion, perhaps best exemplified in cases such as Stuxnet and NITRO

ZEUS, help create the cybersecurity dilemma. But to appreciate these cases and their implications, one must assume the view of an intruder. It is necessary to understand what a network intrusion is and how intruders carry them out. To do this, the first section of this chapter presents a model for intrusions, outlining the process in a non-technical and accessible fashion.

Next, it is important to recognize the operational and strategic implications of the network intrusion process. In essential respects, the dangerous incentive structure of the cybersecurity dilemma derives directly from this operational reality, as discussed in the chapter's second section. These incentives, many of which may be counterintuitive for those new to cyber operations, cause states to launch intrusions as a means of developing capabilities for possible later use. In short, states use intrusions to develop offensive options against other states well in advance of needing them. The chapter's conclusion links this concept back to the cybersecurity dilemma.

*An Intrusion Model*

Breaking into a computer network is a multifaceted process. The model that follows goes beyond the strategic objectives of network intrusions, such as destroying data or gathering information. But it is not a technical model focused on tactical techniques for performing the tasks of network intrusion.[5] Instead, drawing on examples and incident reports from cybersecurity professionals, this model focuses on operational concepts.[6] It outlines what intruders need to do in various stages of a cyber operation to achieve their strategic objective and considers very briefly how they might carry out these tasks. Cyber operations have more history and more constancy than is often assumed;[7] this model's concepts are relevant for some of the earliest cyber operations, such as the Cuckoo's Egg case of the late 1980s,[8] for the early state-on-state operations like Moonlight Maze in the late 1990s,[9] and for the most sophisticated modern operations. If the pattern holds, the concepts presented here will hold relevance into the future.

Figure 1

The model outlines eight concepts, or steps, common to most intrusions. These are *target acquisition*, *development*, *authorization*, *entry*, *establishing command and control*, *pivoting*, *payload activation*, and *confirmation*. In some operations, a given step may take on greater importance than in others, but the underlying theory behind this model is that each will be present to some degree in virtually all operations that attract the attention of national-level policy-makers. This simplified discussion presents these concepts in a linear fashion, but, as discussed later, several different operations can rely on shared foundational efforts.

Once the intruders know their intended victim, the first step is *target acquisition*. In this step, the would-be intruders determine which computer, server, or network is of interest to their mission. They learn what they can about this target, including its software and connectivity information. In some cases, this scoping process will be easy. In order to enable legitimate connections, systems will often be transparent about what software they are running, responding to requests for information with their configuration details. Because computers and servers do respond so frequently with information, however, it therefore becomes possible to send requests to many potential targets at once, gathering information in bulk.[10] Very frequently, these scans are portrayed as "attacks," often as part of a hyperbolic claim (for example, as will be discussed later, that hackers attack the Office of Personnel Management millions of times per month).[11] Such a framing is, intentionally or not, misleading. Target acquisition via scanning is, at most, only a part of the potential foundation for a later attack, rather than any sort of deeply destructive act.

Other operations can require more time-consuming forms of target acquisition than simple scanning. Operators who want to learn more about their specific target might rely on other sources, such as non-technical forms of open source intelligence like employee directories or organizational charts. Or they might compromise overarching or nearby networks—operations in and of themselves—before narrowing their focus. In rare cases, the process of target acquisition might rely on cooperation with non-technical actors, such as human intelligence assets or operators on the ground.[12] Regardless of how it is done, effective reconnaissance of the target is vital to operational success. The head of NSA's Tailored Access Operations unit, which conducts intrusions, attributed some of the organization's achievements to the fact that "In many cases we know networks better than the people who designed and run them."[13]

Next, intruders must dedicate time for *development*, in which they build or acquire the computer code that will enable them to get access to their target and perform malicious activity.[14] In this step, the intruders often first look for security vulnerabilities in the software employed by their target. These vulnerabilities can be oversights in design by the software's creators or flaws in implementation. Operators can target each vulnerability with malicious software known as an exploit. The exploit code takes advantage of the vulnerability to give the intruders greater control over the target. For example, exploits often enable remote code execution, meaning that an intruder can force (usually malicious) programs to run on the target computer without having physical access to the machine. At other times, exploits can target vulnerabilities to reveal sensitive information, like administrative passwords or user account information.[15] The vulnerability targeted by the exploit might exist in the code of a well-known application that the target knowingly uses, such as the Safari or Internet Explorer web browsers. It could also be in an extension or add-on, such as Adobe Flash, installed by the target to complement another piece of software, or it might lie within a subsidiary piece of code, often called a library, which enables certain functionality in software and is often shared between many programs.

Crucially, each exploit affects only a certain piece of software. Computers without that software are immune from the exploit. As a result, the most valuable exploits often affect widely-used pieces of software, such as popular operating systems, libraries, or authentication mechanisms. Different targets use different software, which underscores the importance of target acquisition.[16] There are many exploits already developed for use against virtually any software platform in existence, targeting a similarly wide range of vulnerabilities. Researchers and hackers often make these exploits publicly available in software packages, which enable them to be quickly readied for deployment.[17] But exploits that are already in use, while still frequently effective, are easier to prepare for and defend against.

For this reason, intruders seeking to maximize their chances of success and minimize the risk of detection will search for previously unknown vulnerabilities. In cybersecurity jargon, these previously unknown vulnerabilities are known as zero days. The software vendor, unaware of the existence of these flaws in its code, will not have issued a fix. Intruders who know of the vulnerability can more easily exploit the weakness in the software to gain access or perform unauthorized activity. Discovering these kinds of vulnerabilities and developing new exploits to take advantage of them can be time-consuming and can require a high level of expertise.[18] But the benefit is clear. Operations that use zero days on average remain undetected substantially longer than those that do not.[19]

The intruders also need to develop or obtain the malicious code they will deploy on the targeted machine once they gain access. This is the code that will actually carry out much of the activity throughout the rest of the intrusion model. For performing basic functions, such as stealing files or recording the target's keystrokes, some tools are publicly available, though states often develop their own tools that they re-use for many operations. But for more complex tasks, intruders must develop or customize software specifically for the mission.[20] This frequently requires time-consuming testing. To test, the developers often deploy their code in a simulation of the target environment. This is hardest, but most important, in attacks designed to have a physical effect, such as Stuxnet and the to-be-discussed attack on the power grid in Ukraine.[21] For Stuxnet, reports indicate that the American and Israeli operators went to extensive lengths to acquire the model of centrifuge used in Iran and even to construct a mock facility with the exact same configuration.[22]

The next step, *authorization*, will vary depending on an intruder's bureaucratic processes. Though authorization is presented here as one step for the purposes of simplicity, in reality it is embedded in many steps throughout the process. Political and legal decision-makers might authorize their cyber operators to make entry and perform basic reconnaissance on a target, but not to develop or deploy destructive code until they collect more information. Standing general orders might permit a certain range of development, intrusion, and collection activities, but specific steps beyond those orders could require further authorization. Regardless of the particulars, the authorization process might carry with it a delay for legal review, cost-benefit analysis, risk assessment, avoiding interference with other operations, consideration of blowback, the definition of mission objectives, and other inquiries and debates. Approval might be conditional on changes to the code. These changes might make the malicious code less likely to spread, less visible, or more carefully targeted.

Once again, the Stuxnet attack on Iran provides a good example of how evidence of this sort of political and legal review can show up at the operational and technical level. Before it executed any destructive code, Stuxnet verified its target against a detailed configuration checklist.[23] This verification process had the intended purpose of sharply narrowing what the code could damage. As the journalist Kim Zetter noted in her detailed history of Stuxnet:

> Embedded in the attack code was a detailed dossier describing the precise technical configuration of the [Programmable Logic Controllers][24] it sought. Every plant that used industrial control systems had custom configurations to varying degrees; even companies within the same industry used configurations that were specific to their needs. But the configuration Stuxnet was looking for was so precise that it was likely to be found in only a single facility in Iran or, if more than one, then facilities configured exactly the same, to control an identical process.[25]

For Richard Clarke, a former White House Cybersecurity Coordinator, these constraints were indicative of the United States' authorization procedures. Stuxnet, he said, "very much had the feel to it of having been written by or governed by a team of Washington lawyers."[26] Perhaps to reduce the role such verification mechanisms can play in attributing the source of an intrusion, some newer pieces of malicious code have encrypted their targeting information as a means of obfuscation.[27]

After development and at least preliminary authorization, the intruders must make *entry*. This involves finding a surreptitious way to get the malicious code to the target; the exploit cannot take advantage of the vulnerability if it is not delivered. As software security has improved, targeting gullible users has become a comparatively more effective means of making entry. Spear-phishing, the practice of sending socially-engineered messages to users so that they install a malicious program or download a malicious file, is one of the most prominent methods.[28] Intruders use this technique in more than two-thirds of cyber espionage operations,[29] including almost one-fifth of intrusions into the systems that manage physical devices.[30] Effective social engineering can also obviate the need for exploits if intruders can trick users to grant the intruders access, execute malicious code, or share their credentials.[31]

Another category of entry methods relies on compromising an intermediary trusted by the target, such as a website. When the target visits the infected site, the server loads malicious code via a vulnerability in the web browser; this process is called a watering hole attack, and can be especially useful in less targeted operations.[32] Illicit control over a certificate authority—a means of verifying identity on the internet—can also enable entry. Intruders used this latter technique against activists in Iran to gain access to the activists' email accounts, bypassing Google's security mechanisms.[33] Leaked files indicate that the United States and United Kingdom use a conceptual variant, known as a man-on-the-side attack, to intercept benign requests by targets and inject malicious exploits as a means of gaining entry.[34]

In response to these many ways of entry, defenders have built so-called airgaps into their networks. These airgaps are physical and logical means of separating the most valuable data and systems from less valuable ones. In theory, there is no communication between the two networks on either side of an airgap. If such protection is in place, intruders will need to get malicious code across an airgap in order to make entry, sometimes a time-consuming or challenging process. Crossing an airgap might require targeting a nearby internet-connected network and spreading via USB drives plugged into computers on both sides of the airgap by unwitting network users.[35] This was reportedly the case in intrusions that breached the United States military's airgapped classified networks in 2008.[36] A major version of Stuxnet, which began on the internet-connected networks of Iranian contractors and used up to eight different ways of propagation to make its way to the targeted Iranian nuclear facility, is another example of airgap crossing.[37]

An optional but common step follows making entry: the intruders can choose to *establish command and control* over the malicious code once it is inside the target network. Command and control is a means of communication between the intruders and the malicious code they have deployed. If there is no communication mechanism at all, then the rest of the steps from entry onward will have to be pre-planned in the code delivered to the targeted network.[38] In such circumstances, the verification procedures presented as part of the authorization concept above become even more important in achieving the desired effect. Such pre-planning of operations might be possible if the code is incredibly adaptive to its environment, if it is very broadly effective—which could lead to collateral damage—or if the intruders have excellent knowledge of their target in advance, either from previous operations or other sources. Given the difficulty in doing this, intruders tend to prefer using command and control mechanisms.

There are many different means through which the intruders can establish command and control. The fastest and easiest method is to communicate over the internet connection used in the target network, assuming there is one. But because defenders are more likely to spot this direct approach, sophisticated intruders have tried to find ways to hide their command and control instructions.[39] Other slower methods are useful when targeting networks not connected to the internet or ones where defenders heavily monitor internet connections for malicious communications. The NSA has explored ways to communicate information via delay-tolerant networking, which does not require a continuous connection to be effective, for "data exfiltration from isolated networks and denied areas."[40] Other documents indicate that the agency has communicated information from infected computers via small radios embedded in hardware devices. An accidental explosion in Iran prompted further suspicion that this technique was used there: what seemed to be an ordinary rock near a nuclear facility was in fact filled with electronic equipment that may have been relaying pilfered information or transmitting command and control instructions.[41]

After the intruders make entry, they must perform *pivoting*. First, the operators must verify that the intrusion is indeed of the correct target. Sometimes the methods of entry are broad-based, such as watering hole attacks, spreading to many irrelevant computers and networks.[42] Once the intruders confirm their target, they can load additional and more powerful malicious code onto the victim's machine; they are less likely to use this code without such confirmation, for fear of having it needlessly discovered. Intruders can also look within the targeted network to see what might be of interest. They can look broadly for machines of a certain type, like file or email servers. When doing reconnaissance, intruders can minimize the data they exfiltrate at first in order to avoid attracting unwanted attention.[43] If the intruders know the intended purpose of their mission, a more narrow and careful approach makes more sense. If they are on a general exploratory mission, they are more likely to turn over as many rocks as possible.

After intruders have a sense of the network, they can move laterally within it. To do so, they might need to deploy additional exploits targeted at other vulnerabilities. For example, once Stuxnet compromised the relevant Windows machines in Iran's nuclear facility, it pivoted to the Siemens Programmable Logic Controllers by targeting a different set of weaknesses.[44] Often, however, intruders move laterally by stealing the passwords of users on the networks.[45] In some cases, such as the intrusion at HBGary Federal, social engineering can aid this task. Those intruders first compromised an email account of the CEO and then emailed a request in his name to another employee asking for log-in credentials to a critical server.[46] They were successful—few people ignore such emails from the CEO.

Once the intruders have pivoted, they have at last reached their target. But just because they have done so, they need not immediately perform the next step, *payload activation*—actually executing the final part of the operation. Assuming they have some means of command and control over the malicious code, the intruders can establish such a position and then wait for the right moment to strike. If the intruders do not have command and control mechanisms in place, they can set the code to deliver or activate the payload at a pre-set moment in time. In either case, however, the intruders must be confident that the attack code will work when needed. Testing is important, as mentioned earlier, but even slight and sometimes unintentional changes in configuration within the target network can thwart well-tested code.[47] Former NSA Director Michael Hayden acknowledged this danger, warning, "Access bought with months if not years of effort can be lost with a casual upgrade of the targeted system, not even one designed to improve defenses, but merely an administrative upgrade from something 2.0 to something 3.0."[48] Maintaining access is doable, as NITRO ZEUS shows, but it takes resources.

Lastly, in order for network intrusions to serve as a tool of state-craft, some after-action analysis and verification of mission success is necessary. This is *confirmation*. It has many parallels in other forms of military and intelligence operations, from battle damage assessment to intelligence reviews. The analysis can also be time-consuming. In the case of espionage operations, appropriate intelligence community experts, usually distinct from the operators, will need to determine the value of the exfiltrated data. For attacks, verifying the intended effect is sometimes straightforward. This is the case with many of the attacks that have obvious effects and quickly gain public attention. In some other cases, however, confirmation may require other intelligence assets, diplomatic communications, or further cyber operations. Consider Stuxnet once more: understanding whether or not a subtle attack was functioning as intended in another state's secret underground facility could be difficult, likely requiring a range of intelligence resources. Nevertheless, the task of confirmation is an important one, and the information gained from it can be immensely useful in planning further operations. As such, this stage marks the conclusion of the intrusion model.

## How Operational Incentives Drive the Cybersecurity Dilemma

States adjust their operational behavior to achieve their strategic ends. Policy-makers shape their approach to network intrusions in response to the practicalities of carrying them out. To develop offensive capabilities, states have strong incentives to begin their operations early, well before they might need them. This is due to specific characteristics about the process of performing network intrusions. The model yields four interrelated ideas that spur states to intrude in advance of tension or conflict: the speed of a cyber operation varies by step; operational steps are linear but without strong momentum; persistence is powerful; and parts of operations can be prepared in advance. These operational incentives for intrusions create the first component of the cybersecurity dilemma, as they give states a reason to develop threatening capabilities before they appear necessary.

First, it is possible to read the preceding model with an eye towards the speed of cyber operations. In academic and public discussions, cyber operations are often envisioned as being lightning-fast, with speed as the decisive element. Former White House official Richard Clarke claimed that "cyberwar happens at the speed of light"[49] while former national security official Joel Brenner argued that "Speed, not secrecy, is the coin of the realm."[50] Former Director of the NSA, Keith Alexander, testified that "in terms of ... cyber attacks, it is over before you know what happened. These happen at lightning speed."[51] But the notion of tempo in cyber operations has important limits and nuances that are sometimes overlooked.

An examination of the intrusion model reveals that some parts of cyber operations take place at high speed, but not all. The computation of instructions, the execution of code, and the transmission of reasonable amounts of data all occur at fast rates. But there are many more steps that can be much less immediate. These include the finding of a zero day vulnerability and the development of an exploit, the development of new tools, the need for political and legal authorization, some ways of making entry to the target, some forms of command and control, and pivoting throughout the network. The model above notes the ways and reasons for these potential sources of delay. Compounded together, these delays mean that some complex operations, such as Stuxnet, took years to execute fully.

Increased automation of some of these steps is sometimes possible, though difficult.[52] Tool development can enable vastly more scalable operations. Reports indicate that the NSA has been working on ways to speed up the entry process[53] and in some sophisticated operations, like Stuxnet, a pre-planned sort of automation is overtly noticeable. But more automation also offers less granular control than in human-directed operations.[54] All told, though, the great number of individuals hired by military and intelligence agencies hints at a counterintuitive truth: cyber operations are still human operations, and many parts of them take place at human speed. Viewed in this way, cyber operations look less like a flashy silver bullet and more like other intelligence and military undertakings. They require time, discipline, patience, trained people, well-crafted tools, and careful advance planning. This means that states cannot wait until a crisis to begin building their capabilities or launching their intrusions.

Second, a concept closely associated with speed is momentum. In physics, this is the impetus gained by a moving object. To a layperson, it simply reflects the likelihood of continued movement in the same direction. In short, it takes effort to reverse momentum. In operations, momentum might be thought of as the structural incentive for immediately taking up the next step after operators achieve a particular step. Depending on the mission, traditional kinetic military operations have varying degrees of momentum. The momentum could even vary between stages of an operation. For example, it might be quite easy to call off a bombing run while the bombers wait on the runway, but slightly harder to do when the bombers have taken off and crossed into neutral airspace, and harder still once they have crossed into enemy territory and nearly made it to the target. At least if the enemy has any air defenses, the costs of making it that far and then turning back with nothing to show for it could be quite significant. Although a state will do its best to preserve military and intelligence options for as long as possible, at a certain point the increasing momentum between steps of many conventional operations can narrow the number of palatable options.

By contrast, cyber operations seem to have less momentum at a technical level. Cyber operations usually take place in something approximating the sequence shown in the model (with the possible exception of authorization and development). Nonetheless, cyber operations do not exhibit strong momentum between stages. Consider the beginning of a network intrusion effort: just because a state has performed target acquisition, which is for the most part a task that does not induce much risk, does not mean that the state needs to seek to breach that target. This is largely analogous to physical operations, in which drawing up secret plans to attack another state does not carry tremendous risk or momentum to act on those plans. But in the end-stages of a cyber operation, there is still a lack of momentum. Unlike in the foregoing bombing run example, with cyber operations a state may make entry and pivot to its target location, but never do damage. Indeed, it might never feel much pressure to do so, so long as it can remain hidden in place and ensure access. Intruders may choose to gain the desired level of access to the desired location, do their best to ensure continuous command and control, and attempt to maintain operational readiness without actually delivering or activating the payload.[55]

The NITRO ZEUS contingency plan against Iran appears to demonstrate this idea, but it is not just the United States that operates with this concept.[56] NSA Director Admiral Michael Rogers acknowledged that adversaries of the United States are also likely to launch intrusions well in advance of their desire to attack. "We have seen nation states spending a lot of time and a lot of effort to try to gain access to the power structure within the United States, to other critical infrastructure, and you have to ask yourself why," the admiral said, before answering his own question. "It's because in my mind they are doing this with a purpose, doing this as a way to generate options and capabilities for themselves should they decide that they want to potentially do something."[57] The lack of momentum means that states can launch intrusions early, overcoming the slower speeds of some operational phases, but take the final steps at a time of their choosing.

The lack of momentum works in both directions. Just because a defender has thwarted one late stage of the operation does not mean that the work of all previous steps is necessarily lost. This leads to a third idea: persistence is powerful. As intruders progress through the early stages of the operation, they can employ a variety of methods to ensure continual access, even if the operation goes awry at a later point. By doing this, the intruders can make it quite difficult for defenders to root them out and can create shortcuts for future operations. This drives the cybersecurity dilemma by giving states another reason to intrude early. If their presence in a foreign network is likely to endure, there is a greater chance that it will someday be of value.

Intruders can achieve persistence in a variety of ways. They sometimes modify the breached systems to make it easier for them to gain access in the future, to avoid having to go through the work of breaking in again. These modifications are usually hidden so well that it is unlikely that network defenders will find them by accident. One of the most famous examples of this kind of operation is a case known as the "Athens Affair," a significant operation conducted for the purposes of surveillance in 2004–5. In that effort, the operators—likely the NSA—modified an authentication system so that any user's command entered followed by six consecutive spaces would be automatically run with greater privileges.[58] The change saved time and enabled an easier way in for operators in the future.[59]

Another approach to achieving persistence relies on previously infected machines to serve a similar function. Given the importance of pivoting in intrusions, it is only natural that intruders often target a range of computers and servers along the way to their final destination. So long as they maintain access—usually through the presence of malicious code—these intermediate hops can also serve as fallback points.[60] Even if defenders block the intruders at the ultimate target of the operation, the intruders can simply pick up from one of the earlier stepping-stones. This was the case in a 2011 intrusion that targeted the United States Chamber of Commerce. The organization worked with the FBI to root out the intruders from the network. According to reports, however, "months later, the chamber discovered that Internet-connected devices—a thermostat in one of its corporate apartments and a printer in its offices—were still communicating with computers in China."[61] This concept was also seen in an operation called Duqu 2, which relied on computers within the targeted network to re-infect one another when required.[62]

Yet another method of developing persistence is related, but likely even more effective: intruders can burrow deeper into the layers of software that make computers and servers tick. Most intrusions occur on the surface levels, exploiting vulnerabilities in commonly run applications, or in the operating system that manages those applications. It is possible for malicious code to make its way to more obscure parts of computer systems, however. NSA documents outline parts of a broad effort by a group known as the "Persistence Division" that pursues these kinds of operations against a wide range of technologies.[63] To do this, they target the software that lies underneath the operating system, sometimes called the Basic Input/Output System (BIOS), using that to establish a deeply rooted presence in a network. This software is less familiar and public discussion of these sorts of attacks is somewhat rare, but there is solid evidence of significant vulnerabilities.[64] The NSA appears to have achieved such capabilities against Dell computers (and likely also others), dating back to at least 2007.[65] Burrowing this deep can make malicious code enormously difficult to remove, since most detection tools are unable to spot such a low-level presence.

Similar to targeting the BIOS, intruders can also achieve persistence by targeting the low-level software that runs individual hardware components of the computer. Known as firmware, this code is largely invisible to the operating system of the computer and is hard to access. As a result, if intruders do manage to develop a presence of this sort, it is virtually impossible to get them out. For example, even if incident-responders wipe a hard drive targeted in this way and install a fresh copy of the operating system, the malicious code will persist in firmware and re-infect the computer. Intruders who have gained firmware access also enjoy a position of privilege, often enabling them to decrypt communications more easily and exploit or attack the device. As a result, cybersecurity experts sometimes refer to the push for such persistence as "the race to the bare metal" of the machine.[66] Security researchers from Kaspersky Lab provided strong evidence that the United States has developed methods to perform this technique for hard drives made by virtually all of the world's leading manufacturers.[67] The principal security researcher of the Kaspersky study highlighted how impressive the American implementation of this technique is, saying, "This is an ultimate persistence mechanism, and it has the ultimate resilience to removal. This is a next level of persistence never seen before."[68]

The combination of a lack of speed, a lack of momentum, and the possibility of persistence leads to the fourth general overarching point: *intruders can prepare operational steps in advance.* Just as states can launch intrusions early, so can intruders begin parts of operations that will contribute to future capabilities. By starting early, states can get time-consuming tasks out of the way, leverage economies of scale for shared tasks between operations, and establish procedures for better results.

Some parts of the network intrusion model are particularly ripe for preparation in advance. Most obvious among the ones presented here is development. While some cyber operations, like Stuxnet, are against unique targets, most are not. There are dominant, or co-dominant, market leaders for almost every type of software, from operating systems, to mobile phones, to internet browsers, to word processing suites, and much more. A large number of a state's cyber operations will be against those computers and networks running popular software. States are therefore incentivized to look for and develop exploits against these systems well in advance of needing to use the exploits. They also have cause to develop the tools needed to perform the desired action once inside the network, such as stealing files, recording keystrokes, or wiping the targeted machine.

There is good evidence that those states with significant resources dedicated to cyber operations already do this. The United States, for example, has paid tens of millions of dollars in contracts to firms that provide it with zero day exploits.[69] American officials have also acknowledged that the United States also seeks out and uses such vulnerabilities for law enforcement and intelligence purposes.[70] Some of the NSA's systems for automating parts of intrusions seem to draw on a prepared pool of exploits, choosing the best one for a given target.[71] Britain also prepares exploits for later use.[72] Given the money that is reportedly available to brokers of exploits—a contract revealed the NSA paid more than $25 million in one year to a single French company for access to zero days it discovered,[73] and leaked emails from other vendors reveal some coveted zero days going for upwards of half a million dollars[74]—it seems fair to think that the market for zero days is a lively one.[75]

Intruders can do significant work on other steps in advance and share progress between different operations to improve speed and cost efficiency. For example, security researchers discovered that a wide range of intrusions against a variety of disparate targets relied on many of the same tools. These tools helped the intruders as they performed their operations. The researchers analogized this effect to a digital "quartermaster"—someone who focuses on increasing efficiency in the supply chain so that the operators at the tip of the spear can focus on their tasks.[76] Similarly, key parts of malicious code appear to be shared between a number of cyber operations conducted by the United States and its allies. Four operations likely of United States and/or Israeli provenance all share some modules and core functionality, even though the purposes of the four are divergent.[77] The prior existence of these modules reduced the time required to prepare and deploy new operations using them, both because of reduced development time but probably also because of a reduced need to train operators on new systems. A key part of what enables effective scale in computing generally is the re-use of code and interfaces. It is no different for intruders.

Further, the infrastructure from which intruders launch their operations can be pre-positioned and re-used for operational tasks. A notable example of this is APT30, a long-running cyber espionage group that employed the same specific infrastructure and tools in many operations.[78] This infrastructure is the computers or servers from which the operators will send commands to the malicious code, receive data back, and generally coordinate the operation as it takes place in the target network. Intruders usually do not want to be easily linked to machines they actually own. They are unlikely to use a publicly known government computer, for example, and more likely to employ a computer victimized in a previous cyber operation or a presence on the web registered under plausibly deniable pretenses.[79] Obtaining such infrastructure is certainly doable, for state and non-state actors alike, but is probably best accomplished in advance of a cyber operation to save time. Documents from the Canadian signals intelligence agency indicate that it regularly launches efforts to "acquire as many new [Operational Relay Boxes] as possible in as many non 5-Eyes countries as possible" to increase plausible deniability when those computers serve as midpoint infrastructure in operations.[80] As ever, intruders want operational options before they need them.

### Conclusion: The First Pillar of the Cybersecurity Dilemma

Through these four overarching ideas and the model from which they derive, this chapter has illuminated the first pillar of the cybersecurity dilemma: states that desire the option of future cyber operations need to take action in advance to make these operations possible. This includes action that is analogous to activities covered in the traditional security dilemma discussion, such as building capabilities or training operators. Those actions might be threatening, if discovered, for the reasons that any military or intelligence build-up is sometimes threatening: under security dilemma logic, as a state makes itself more secure, it risks making other states feel less secure.

At a basic level, cyber operations amplify this dynamic, since states are able to do more kinds of preparation. Because of the human speed of cyber operations, the lack of momentum in operational end stages, the power of persistence, and the possibility of preparation, states have good reason to do more than plan and build—they have incentives to intrude and gain access.[81] Their preparations will often leave their own borders and involve intruding on the networks of others, furthering the development of targeted malicious code. There may not be time to perform these tasks once a conflict starts. All told, it is better to develop contingency capabilities and not need them than to need them and not have them.

It is possible to stop the cybersecurity dilemma discussion here, if desired. If a state discovers another state's capability-building intrusions, it faces a dilemma of interpretation. The intruding state may be planning an imminent attack, but it might also simply be building out contingency options, as almost all sophisticated states do in some form,[82] and not harboring malicious intent. The state suffering the intrusion will have to decide which of these possibilities is correct, despite having only imperfect information, and respond. If the discussion stopped with the misinterpretation of contingency capabilities, the cybersecurity dilemma would make sense. Contingency plans have long posed the risk of being misunderstood, as a variety of security dilemma cases have shown.

Yet there is no need to stop the investigation of the cybersecurity dilemma there. By itself, the first pillar is enough to reveal some of the ways in which unwanted escalation could occur in cyber operations. But these are not the only dangers. The next two chapters explore how the cybersecurity dilemma logic can go further, moving first beyond contingency planning to the more immediate task of network defense.

3

# THE DEFENDER'S VIEW

*Overview*

At some point in the mid-2000s, the NSA came up with a new code name that evoked, intentionally or not, both an empire and a dark message: BYZANTINE HADES. The code name was a replacement of sorts for a previous one, TITAN RAIN, that had made its way into media reports, including a big story in *Time* magazine.[1] The two code names described one of the biggest threats facing the American computer networks: Chinese intrusions. Behind both names were cases of stolen secrets, the exfiltration of classified information, and an eventual threat to American capabilities and competitiveness. The subject matter was vast. BYZANTINE HADES had numerous sub-groupings, each with their own code name. BYZANTINE RAPTOR, BYZANTINE ANCHOR, BYZANTINE VIKING, and BYZANTINE TRACE were just a few examples.[2] But naming was the easy part. The real challenge lay in pushing back and defending the many American computer networks of interest against the Chinese intrusions, including more than 500 major cases.

No single account will do justice to what surely was and is a massive and largely secret effort to secure American networks. But one often-overlooked document leaked by Snowden makes a revealing sub-plot public. In response to intrusions launched by a group the NSA code-named BYZANTINE CANDOR, the defenders at NSA's Threat Operations Center sought more information. They asked the network intruders in the agency's Tailored Access Operations unit, which carries out intrusions, for assistance in gathering "actionable intelligence" on the Chinese hackers.[3] The American intruders went to work, gaining access to infrastructure used by the foreign operators. Once they gained this access, they were able to observe the adversary in action from these midpoints.[4] But the NSA unit went deeper still. They were able to penetrate five computers from which the Chinese launched their operations. In effect, they had hacked the hackers, following the Chinese operators back to their virtual base and gaining "excellent sources of data" on a wide range of the adversary's activities.[5]

The data the NSA collected by penetrating BYZANTINE CANDOR's networks had concrete forward-looking defensive value. They included information on the adversary's "future targets," including "bios of senior White House officials, [Cleared Defense Contractor] employees, [United States Government] employees" and more. They also included access to the "source code and [the] new tools" that the Chinese used to conduct operations. The computers penetrated by the NSA also revealed information about the exploits in use.[6] In effect, the intelligence gained from the operation, once given to network defenders and fed into automated systems, was enough to guide and enhance the United States' defensive efforts.

This case alludes to important themes in network defense. It shows the persistence of talented adversaries, the creativity of clever defenders, the challenge of getting actionable intelligence on the threat, and the need for network architecture and defenders capable of acting on that information. But it also highlights an important point that is too often overlooked but directly relevant to the cybersecurity dilemma: not every intrusion is in service of offensive aims. There are genuinely defensive reasons for a state to launch intrusions against another state's networks.

This chapter argues that fully maximizing network security necessitates intrusion into the networks of other actors. While there are many security measures that provide a baseline level of protection sufficient for the vast majority of networks, some of the most advanced defenders, including well-resourced intelligence agencies, go further.

By breaking into the networks of their potential adversaries, and the networks of the targets of their potential adversaries, these top-tier defenders can gain valuable information. This includes information they might not be able to get in any other way or that other organizations, like corporations, might not legally be able to obtain. As such, performing network intrusions can be deeply and uniquely useful in advancing a state's cybersecurity.

This chapter consists of three parts. The first section outlines a model of network defense. Similar to how Chapter Two's model approached intrusions, this model provides an overview of the challenges facing defenders and how they meet those challenges. In particular, this section highlights the challenge of detecting malicious code. The second section of the chapter discusses the ways in which intruding into other networks can aid the defensive mission. The effect these intrusions can have on improving the detection capabilities of defenders is particularly pronounced. The chapter's conclusion links this discussion back to the overarching cybersecurity dilemma argument.

## A Network Defense Model

Network defense is a significant undertaking. Some networks can have thousands or tens of thousands of computers, large ever-changing rosters of users, and troves of valuable data stored in many different ways in many different places. This model seeks only to present the high-level operational concepts. These concepts are organized once again into a series of steps, focusing on what defenders must do when facing a network intrusion. Though the methods of intrusion and defense will continue to develop over time, these general operational concepts will persist.

Six steps form the defensive model presented here. The first, *preparation*, occurs before the intrusion has taken place. The rest, beginning with *detection*, follow the intrusion. After detection, two steps, *data collection* and *analysis*, recur throughout the remainder of the defensive

Figure 2

effort. *Containment* is next, in which the defenders seek to protect the network from the intruders who are inside and thwart any exploitation or attack efforts before they can achieve their intended outcome. Lastly, the model finishes with *decontamination*, as the defenders clean the network and try to improve their security going forward.[7]

The *preparation* of networks is the first concept in the model. This step reveals a key idea: network intrusions are by definition fought on a defender's turf. Network administrators make the decisions about what hardware and software to deploy or permit on the network. In these choices, security should often be a priority concern. With judicious decision-making in this area, defenders can reduce what is called the attack surface—the number of potential weaknesses that intruders can target.[8] Defenders should try to verify the security of the software they deploy, to disable software that is not needed by the network's users, and to remove links between unrelated parts of the network. For example, administrators failed to do this in an Ohio nuclear plant in 2003, which enabled a computer worm known as Slammer to infect the facility subsequently.[9] By constraining the number of possibilities available to intruders, the defensive side can make it harder for intruders to break in and easier to find them once they do.

This pre-intrusion preparation is a process to manage, not a problem to solve. Maintaining an appropriate network configuration is essential for keeping the attack surface small. One of the most important ongoing tasks for defenders is applying regular patches—updates issued by vendors that often fix security vulnerabilities—to the software running on the network. While it is very easy to say that administrators should install all appropriate patches right away, in practice patching can be time-consuming and resource-intensive. Before patches can be installed on large networks, administrators often need to test the updates to make sure they do not cause changes that might impact how other programs run, since the fixes can sometimes unwittingly create interference.[10] This process is still more complex in critical infrastructure networks, which often are esoteric and can only go offline for maintenance at certain intervals. For this and other reasons, vulnerabilities can persist for quite some time in large organizations. One empirical study of 50,000 organizations found that it typically took between 100 and 120 days to remediate vulnerabilities, often far too slow to prevent even poorly-targeted intrusions.[11]

Another part of keeping a network up to date is monitoring user accounts. Administrators should check user databases to make sure that once members leave the organization, their accounts are promptly disabled. This ensures that they cannot log in remotely. It also ensures that intruders cannot take over the accounts once they have made entry to the network and use them to perform additional malicious activities. This is a real risk. NSA documents indicate that intruders compromised thousands of accounts at American defense firms and government agencies. Data from internal reviews indicate that thousands of accounts have remained active after employees have left the government.[12] More effective checking of user accounts ensures that intruders have not gained access and created, modified, or used additional accounts for their own malicious purposes.[13]

The effort required to carry out these initial tasks reveals another important point: unlike proverbial guerrilla forces defending their homeland and intimately aware of all its nuances, defenders often do not have great knowledge of their own network. Only through good preparation is such knowledge possible. For example, defenders can reduce the number of possible entry and exit points to the network. With just a few large connection points for all devices, defenders can minimize the potential ways in which intruders can gain access and more easily watch the flow of traffic at those points.[14] They can deploy systems to monitor the flow of traffic into, out of, and within their network. This network awareness will be deeply important to later defensive steps, as it will enable defenders to spot deviations from the normal baseline. In this vein, the head of NSA's Tailored Access Operations team advised defenders that "If you really want to protect your network you have to know your network, including all the devices and technology in it."[15] The better prepared and better informed defenders are, the more advantages they will have once the intruders show up.

Assuming the defenders cannot block an intrusion attempt on the perimeter of the network, their goal is swift *detection* of a successful intrusion. This is sometimes a substantial and complex challenge, but one that is essential. The longer the intruders can remain undetected, the greater amount of time they have to explore the network, develop a persistent position, and achieve their objectives.[16] There are two kinds of detection: external and internal. External detection occurs when a third-party organization, such as law enforcement, informs a victim of a breach. This means that the organization missed the opportunity to detect the intruders on its own. Internal detection occurs when the victim's defensive team uncovers evidence of the intrusion. Most of the time, this is the preferred outcome, since, if done in a timely manner, it gives the organization much better chances to thwart the intruders' actions. It is thus the focus of this section. Nonetheless, the high ratio of external detection to internal detection—one major survey indicates that approximately 90 per cent of the time organizations learn of a breach through external detection—highlights how difficult internal detection can be.[17]

A popular method of internal detection is pattern-matching or signature-based detection, in which some network activity matches the sort of activity thought to be malicious.[18] Pattern-matching relies on the fact that intruders often re-use code, techniques, and infrastructure. Some intruders might have many networks to target and might be perpetually in a rush, or might have standardized procedures to ensure efficiency and consistency. Others might be careless, complacent, or poorly trained. Still others might not have many resources to invest in obfuscation; for these intruders, the complete rebuilding of infrastructure and changing of techniques on a regular basis can be prohibitively expensive. Whatever the reason, areas of overlap will develop between different intrusions. While this has benefits for intruders, it also creates an opportunity for defenders. Information from one intrusion, properly entered into defensive systems, can help thwart the next one. If defenders can regularly force intruders to alter their tools and methods, they can drive up the time and cost of intrusion operations.

Network defenders sometimes call information like this an "indicator of compromise."[19] Uncovering an indicator of a compromise within one's network is evidence of an intrusion. These indicators fall into one of three categories. Atomic indicators refer to specific data points that are suspicious. For example, if intruders re-use command and control infrastructure between operations, and if defenders know an Internet Protocol or web address of that infrastructure—an atomic indicator— the defenders could automatically scan the network to make sure no computers are connecting to that address. If some computers are making such connections, it is a sign of intrusion.

Computed indicators are another type. Every piece of computer code has what computer scientists call a hash. The hash is an alphanumeric signature generated by taking the contents of the program and running it through a mathematical algorithm. Two programs with the exact same code will always produce the same hash. Defenders can learn the hashes of malicious programs either by observing malicious activity on their own networks or from external sources. They can check the hashes of programs installed on their network's computers. When the hash of a program running on a computer matches the hash of a program known to be malicious, it is a sign that an intruder's software is present.

The last type of indicator is a behavioral indicator, and is more general than the other two. While atomic and computed indicators are discrete pieces of data, behavioral indicators focus on patterns in an intruder's activity. There are many ways to accomplish each step of a successful intrusion. Just as criminals sometimes establish a method of operation common to all their crimes, the same is true of network intruders. Behavioral indicators refer to the operational and tactical patterns common to a specific group of operators or to the presence of malicious code. While behavioral indicators are sometimes not as easy to spot or as discrete as computed or atomic ones, judicious and well-informed scanning for anomalous activity can reveal them. They can also be combined with other kinds of indicators to develop reputation-based heuristics for evaluating potentially malicious software.

Pattern-matching tools can be quite useful in establishing a strong foundation of security. There are a number of services, both commercial and freely available, that curate databases of indicators of compromise. Many public malicious code reports include an appendix of indicators,[20] many more indicators are for sale by cybersecurity companies, and organizations can make use of standardized formats to facilitate information sharing.[21] Network defenders can rely on these services as sources of intelligence to inform their automated scans and defensive tools. For example, some tools can scan incoming email attachments to look for files known to be malicious (often based on computed or behavioral indicators), while others can try to ensure that no machines attempt to connect with malicious infrastructure (often based on atomic indicators). Other tools seek to evaluate the programs running on a computer in an effort to find suspicious behavior, such as interacting with the operating system in anomalous ways; behavioral indicators can enhance these efforts. Overall, by marrying indicators of compromise with good network architecture, defenders can make things more difficult for intruders.

But there are serious limits to the utility of broad scanning. By themselves, pattern-matching and heuristics are not enough. Intruders can develop malicious code in such a way that it changes its hash regularly.[22] Zero day exploits, by definition, do not have known signatures. Careful attackers can obtain and obfuscate new infrastructure and change methods of operation. As a result, to provide further security and enable better detection, good defenders practice what is sometimes called active defense or hunting.[23] Hunters are analysts who proactively look within the network for weaknesses and for malicious code that may have exploited those weaknesses; they will likely only be effective if proper network architecture is in place first. Top United States policy-makers, including former Deputy Secretary of Defense William Lynn, have argued for the necessity of such an active approach.[24]

Network security monitoring is a key part of hunting.[25] The term was first formally defined in the early 2000s and is "the collection, analysis and escalation of indications and warnings to detect and respond to intrusions."[26] Defenders employing network security monitoring carefully look inward at their network, understanding the flow of information into, out of, and within its boundaries. They collect information on the network's traffic, ranging from data about the digital communications to copies of the communications themselves. Analysts then examine this data to find anomalies, relying in part on their knowledge of the potential adversary's likely targets and methods of operation. For example, analysts might carefully scrutinize the traffic exiting the research and development part of a company's network, the better to see if an adversary seeking trade secrets is exfiltrating large amounts of sensitive data.[27]

Another example of hunting is searching individual computers for the presence of malicious code. If investigators suspect a compromise of a machine, they can perform what is known as memory analysis. This sort of analysis focuses on Random Access Memory (RAM), which is different from the information stored on the hard drive. RAM reflects the current operations of the operating system, rather than information saved for longer-term storage.[28] Contained within RAM is information about which programs are running, what characteristics those programs have, how they are interacting with the operating system, what connections to other computers they are making, and more. Analysts search for anomalies. Possible red flags are programs asking for unusual amounts of access or pretending to be one thing at a surface level and then actually doing something quite different at a more technical level. Memory analysis can detect malicious code, including zero day exploits, missed by other defensive systems.[29] It is also one of the best tools for finding malicious code that leaves minimal trace on the hard drive.[30]

Penetration testing is an additional component of active defense. It involves employing or hiring skilled intruders to attempt to break into the network. These intruders simulate many of the techniques real intruders would use, including both social and technical approaches. Popular tools, such as Metasploit, enable them to use many of the same exploits available to potential adversaries. The penetration testers then report the results of the test, including which methods worked and which methods did not, to the rest of the network defense team. A penetration test gives defenders a clear path forward for improving security in the network, as they can close the weaknesses exploited by intruders. Additionally, the test provides analysts leads that they can use to detect intruders who may already have made entry using similar methods.[31] But penetration testing has limits; some more subtle flaws may elude penetration testers who gain access by exploiting obvious weaknesses.

Even given this panoply of methods, the challenge of detection is significant. On average, according to industry surveys, intrusions are discovered 146 days after they take place.[32] Improving detection is a key part of strengthening overall network defense. It can be easy to develop a false sense of security when intruders are not found. In those circumstances, by definition, defenders recognize no sign of an adversary's presence. But this illusion of success can be damaging, giving intruders time to burrow more deeply into the network, explore its layout, and gain further access. Therefore, a combination of well-informed automated defense methods and aggressive hunting is essential. Network defenders must always be looking outwards for the next threat, but also inwards for the last one they missed. As network security monitoring pioneer Richard Bejtlich advised, if he became head of information security for a high-profile target, "the first step I would take would be to hunt for intruders already in the network"—that is, cases where detection had previously failed.[33]

The challenges of detection would seem to confer an enormous benefit on intruders. Indeed, greater time before detection does provide an advantage—which is why states and organizations are willing to take a range of steps to increase their detection capabilities—but it is not an insurmountable one. The reason is that, as the last chapter outlined, both cyber exploitation and attack missions often take time to unfold. If intruders are able to see valuable secrets briefly but not copy them out of the network, the damage is greatly minimized. Similarly, if the intruders are able to launch malicious code, but defenders block the attack before it can have any effect, the defenders can largely claim victory.[34] Thus, assuming the detection is not much too late, what the defenders do after detection matters greatly.

After defenders detect the intruders, they must gather and examine as much information as they can. This is *data collection* and *analysis*.[35] These two steps work in tandem: data collection informs analysis and vice versa. There is a wide range of approaches that defenders can pursue when it comes to data collection. For example, there is no guarantee that the defenders will detect the intruders at their entry point, so at some point during the investigation the defenders will have to work backwards to find the entry point and method. Defenders will similarly have to collect information on which computers and accounts on their network the intruders compromised. Ideally, the defenders will swiftly obtain a copy of the malicious code as well.

Once defenders gather this data, they must work quickly to analyze it using a variety of methods.[36] The data produced by any significant intrusion will almost always be of a large enough quantity that it will take a dedicated team of responders of varied training to examine it well and inform defensive actions. Investigators will use log files to reconstruct events, such as the use of USB drives, the opening of documents, and the visiting of websites.[37] Investigators will also de-construct the actual malicious code in order to understand how it works and what it can do. These analysts will often consider how the code spreads throughout the network, how it communicates with command and control infrastructure, and other related questions. Investigators might also look for unique properties of the code, such as files it leaves on computers it has infected, which can serve as indicators of compromise for further investigation.[38] They will also try to understand the code's payload and objectives, so that defenders can better secure those targeted parts of the network.

Intruders sometimes take steps to confound the collection and analysis steps as much as they can. If the intruders are prioritizing stealth over speed, they often try to mislead the defenders. As part of this effort, they might deploy new and previously unknown code. They might erase logs or modify time-stamps so that their actions are hard to follow. They may pivot to multiple parts of the network at once, for the purposes of either furthering objectives or becoming more difficult to track. The malicious code itself may feature red herrings and smokescreens, the better to obscure the code's source, intent, or capabilities. This occurred with a piece of malicious code called Inception. That malicious software had so many disorienting attempts at obfuscation that investigators named it after the film thriller featuring Leonardo DiCaprio and a journey into multiple levels of human subconsciousness.[39] These kinds of anti-forensic efforts are not flawless. They can leave their own data traces that defenders can then find and analyze. Overall, however, defenders must verify the integrity of the data under analysis and should always be on the lookout for false flags and misdirection.

It is here, in the data collection and analysis steps, that the importance of preparation emerges once again. If the network is properly set up, gathering data is much easier. For example, if there are logs of data traffic in and out of the network, defenders will be able to look more quickly for signs of entry. If defenders know which devices are on their network and have the means to scan those devices remotely, they can immediately begin new scans based on the indicators of compromise discovered during the analysis phase. Likewise, they can configure perimeter defenses to thwart malicious code of a similar sort in the future. On the other hand, if the defenders lack visibility into their own network, then the challenge of collection and analysis gets much harder. Even the best incident responders need data with which to work.

After defenders draw conclusions from data collection and analysis, they must *contain* the threat and thwart the effects of the malicious code.[40] A wide range of defensive actions can achieve this and give the defenders time to retake the initiative. A first step in containment is to take the intelligence gained from the analysis step and update auto-mated defensive systems to prevent further propagation. Other possi-bilities include installing a previously neglected patch from a software vendor. In other cases, defenders might need to take more drastic actions, such as simply disconnecting a sensitive portion of the network until the threat can be more properly mitigated.[41] Still other responses, such as stopping physical processes like industrial control system operations, may take longer, and may require more bureaucratic input from non-technical decision-makers.

The containment process can also involve directly interfering with the operations of intruders.[42] For example, if the defenders can iden-tify the mechanism the intruders are using for command and control, they might block it or observe the commands to inform their defen-sive actions. The defenders might set up honeypots, tempting targets that will distract intruders and potentially reveal information about their method of operations.[43] In some cases, the intruders will have already made it to their target before the defenders can stop them. The defenders must then block the effects of the intruders' action. In the case of exfiltration, this means preventing the sensitive data from leaving the network. But in the case of a rapid-effect digital attack, like those that wipe critical data on targeted computers, there may be little that defenders can do. In one case of this sort defenders resorted to physically running through the building disconnecting the comput-ers to which the worm had not yet spread—obviously, a less than enviable situation.[44]

Skilled intruders can make the task of containment as difficult and as time-consuming as possible for the defense. In the case of exfiltration, the intruders will often encrypt the stolen information before copying it out to help obscure its contents and avoid detection. Intruders will sometimes use different exit routes to make real-time detection diffi-cult. As with command and control communications, these routes can sometimes be unconventional. For example, the NSA has developed a means of exfiltration that transmits the pilfered data in an obscure way to its sensors in the infrastructure of the internet.[45] In the case of kinetic attacks, the intruders could employ operations against human-machine interfaces. These interfaces provide information to network administrators and operators about how the computers and hardware are functioning. By compromising these interfaces, the intruders make it difficult for the defense to know what the status of the system is, what commands it is obeying, what alerts it has suppressed, and even if the network operators can have any influence over what will happen next.[46]

Lastly, once defenders have thwarted the intruders' efforts, they must immediately *decontaminate* their network. A persistent presence in a target network is extremely powerful. The intruders will often try to maintain as much of a secure beachhead or foothold as possible, so that in future operations they will not have to gain entry again. To do so, they will use a variety of persistence methods discussed in the last chapter. Shawn Henry, the former top official for cyber investigations at the FBI, summarized the problem succinctly: "Once they're in," Henry said of intruders, "they're in."[47]

Decontamination is therefore a major undertaking. Sometimes this can entail taking networks entirely offline for days to search and decontaminate them thoroughly, as the State Department did on several different occasions to its email system.[48] In other cases, it can mean throwing out computer hardware entirely, to ensure that the intruders cannot return from their presence beneath the operating system level, such as in the BIOS or firmware.[49] Even short of these dramatic steps, decontamination can mean deep and intense scans for malicious code and anomalous activity. This will require action by human investigators and automated computer tools. It is a lengthy process more likely measured in months than minutes. Like much else in the defensive cycle, it can be expensive to do if undertaken without proper preparation.

Decontamination is no good unless defenders stop the next operation, too. Part of decontamination therefore is adaptation. The defenders must perform a detailed after-action investigation to determine which procedures and pieces of software they need to change to meet the threat. This could require the deployment of more automated tools or better intelligence for those tools. It could mean changing network procedures, such as patching or remote connection policies, or it could mean hiring and training new people. All told, the defenders need to consider a wide variety of technical and non-technical responses that could impact a significant number of people within the organization.

As a result, the changes may require broader organizational approval. The process, once again, is likely to take a long time to complete fully, but it is essential. If an organization is worth targeting once, it is almost surely worth targeting again.

## How Network Intrusions Can Help Defenders

The last section outlined a conceptual approach to defending a network that blended automated and human-directed efforts. Such an effort is an effective baseline. Yet, for actors facing serious threats, such as the intelligence agencies of major states, this baseline will be insufficient. These entities will need or want to go further in securing systems they protect. Former Secretary of Defense Leon Panetta indicated as much in a far-ranging speech on cybersecurity. He said that the United States "won't succeed in preventing a cyber attack through improved defenses alone." He also alluded to ongoing American efforts to "detect an imminent threat of attack ... to take action against those who would attack us ... [and] to counter threats to our national interests in cyberspace."[50] In short, the development of network penetration capabilities, often carried out by a signals intelligence agency, can be part of a state's defensive effort. States can develop these capabilities in an effort to establish deterrence—a concept that, thus far, applies inexactly to cyber operations.[51] More concretely and immediately, however, these intrusion capabilities can directly aid defensive efforts by gathering specific and useful items of intelligence.

In this vein, the network defense model has set the stage for a critical part of the cybersecurity dilemma argument. Defense, even with good preparation, timely indicators of compromise, and active human-led analysis, is still a challenge, especially against capable intruders. This operational reality drives a response with strategic implications: to make full provision for the security of their own important networks, states have great incentive to penetrate the networks and operations of other states, even before they are themselves targeted. In so doing, they can gather additional information on how specifically other states might intrude into their networks, on the infrastructure used by other states, and on other states' internal organizational procedures, techniques, and targets. This can improve performance in almost every part of the defensive model, but especially in preparation, detection, and data analysis. For some states, these intrusions are a key part—perhaps even a necessary part—of the defensive mission. States can sometimes launch them with genuine defensive intent.[52]

These kinds of intrusions are illegal for private citizens and corporations in many jurisdictions, including the United States. There is good reason to forbid private actors from engaging in them, with risks of vigilantism and greater instability. As a result, at least in many jurisdictions, the defensive options available to private citizens and organizations end with activities carried out within one's own network. These restrictions do not apply to states, however, as there are few rules in an anarchic international system. Some states may choose to impose constraints on their intelligence agencies, but these limits are not imposed by an external actor. It is thus in the realm of states and state-sponsored actors that the cybersecurity dilemma, animated in part by intrusions for defensive purposes, is most present.

The most straightforward way for intrusions to be useful for a state's defensive purposes is if they directly target the networks, infrastructure, and operations of a potential adversary. These kinds of operations can be further subdivided. Some of these operations can serve as wide-ranging signals intelligence collection, casting a broad net and complementing other forms of intelligence collection. They seek to gather information on the political and military leadership or strategic priorities of the potential adversary as a whole rather than just on the potential adversary's cyber capabilities. These kinds of more general collection efforts can inform defensive preparation, shape defenders' resource allocation, and provide warning about future concerns. These operations can be of great defensive utility, but it is obvious to all involved that they will be directly threatening, since no state wants to suffer the loss of secrecy at the strategic level. They are also of value for purposes that are not defensive in nature. For that reason, they are more properly discussed in the next chapter, which outlines how intrusions into important networks can be threatening and of use in ways that go beyond defense.

Other operations may be more narrowly focused. They may collect information that is of pure defensive utility. From the perspective of those carrying out the intrusion, these operations are not directly threatening; they do not seek to damage the other state's integrity or security, and seek only to thwart its efforts at performing network intrusions. This sort of information can come in a variety of different forms. As a generalization, though, it is operational in scope and enables specific defensive countermeasures.

This defensive enhancement can take many forms. Intruding into another state to learn the location of its command and control infrastructure for cyber operations enables traffic to and from that infrastructure to be more easily blocked. Gathering information on the type of malicious code developed by an adversary enables defenders to develop tailored indicators of compromise. Determining the adversary's likely method of entry and potential targets permits a state to preposition defenses and minimize the risk. Finding a zero day vulnerability that an adversary will soon employ can give the defenders time to alert the vendor or otherwise protect its own systems. President Obama spoke broadly about these kinds of efforts, saying, "We cannot prevent … cyberthreats without some capability to penetrate digital communications, whether it's to … intercept malware that targets a stock exchange, to make sure air traffic control systems are not compromised or to ensure that hackers do not empty your bank accounts."[53] A former member of the NSA's Office of General Counsel was more specific, writing that signals intelligence efforts can "gain information of critical importance to the defensive mission—say by intercepting the plans of a malicious actor against U.S. networks in advance."[54]

Defenders can also use information gained from these intrusions to better determine whether the intruders have already made entry. The cybersecurity coordinator at the United States National Security Council, Michael Daniel, implicitly acknowledged the intruders' need for secrecy, and the defenders' incentive to counteract it. He said, "If you know much about it, [cyber is] very easy to defend against … That's why we keep a lot of those capabilities very closely guarded."[55] There is therefore often immediate operational value to the information gained through defensive-minded collection.

When it comes to the United States and its partners, there is ample evidence that this sort of collection takes place and informs defensive practices. The NSA's targeting of BYZANTINE CANDOR mentioned at the start of this chapter is one specific example. Other Snowden files shed more light, describing an interrelated and complex set of United States programs to collect intelligence and use it to improve protection of its networks. The NSA's internal documents call this "foreign intelligence in support of dynamic defense."[56] The NSA begins by gathering information on a likely threat, including information on the network from which the threat is likely to come. This involves intercepting the communications of the potential adversary—often via positions in the infrastructure of the internet—and targeting the devices processing those communications.[57] The gathered information can "tip" malicious code the NSA has placed on servers and computers around the world. Based on this tip, one of the NSA's nodes can act on the information, "inject[ing a] response onto the Internet towards [the] target."[58] There are several responses that the NSA can inject, including resetting connections, delivering malicious code, and redirecting internet traffic.[59]

Similarly, if the NSA can learn about the adversary's "tools and tradecraft" early enough, it can develop and deploy "tailored countermeasures" to blunt the intended effect. The NSA can then try to discern the intent of the adversary and use its countermeasure to mitigate the attempted intrusion.[60] The signals intelligence agency feeds information about the incoming threat to an automated system deployed on networks that the NSA protects.[61] This system has a number of capabilities, including blocking the incoming traffic outright, sending unexpected responses back to the adversary, slowing the traffic down, and "permitting the activity to appear [to the adversary] to complete without disclosing that it did not reach [or] affect the intended target."[62]

These defensive capabilities appear to be actively in use by the United States against a wide range of threats. NSA documents indicate that the agency uses the system to block twenty-eight major categories of threats as of 2011. This includes action against significant adversaries, such as China, as well as against non-state actors.[63] Documents provide a number of success stories. These include the thwarting of a BYZANTINE HADES intrusion attempt that targeted four high-ranking American military leaders, including the Chief of Naval Operations and the Chairman of the Joint Chiefs of Staff; the NSA's network defenders saw the attempt coming and successfully prevented any negative effects.[64] These files also include examples of successful defense against Anonymous and against several other code-named entities.

A separate American system, run by the Department of Homeland Security and known as EINSTEIN, attempts to serve a similar role for other networks protected by the government. Newer versions of this system, according to the blunt phrasing of former Secretary of Homeland Security Michael Chertoff, seek "like an anti-aircraft weapon, [to] shoot down an attack before it hits its target."[65] To do so, the system tries to integrate a wide variety of sources of threat intelligence and pass them to other components of network defense. A Homeland Security official confirmed in Congressional testimony that one of the sources of information used by a new version of EINSTEIN is classified threat intelligence.[66] These various NSA and Homeland Security protection systems were and are not panaceas—intruders continue to be sometimes successful—but they do demonstrate how gathering intelligence can help the defensive effort and how the United States and its partners have invested in developing such capabilities.

Some might object that this is the argument that proves too much, that only the most sophisticated states could be capable of such activities. Indeed, in many ways, the activities of the United States and its partners in cybersecurity are exceptional, and it is unwise to assume that the techniques in use by the Five Eyes are within the grasp of other states.[67] But it is also quite likely to be the case that the Five Eyes need to rely less on network penetrations to gain actionable defensive intelligence than other states. This is because the Five Eyes have tremendous passive collection capability from the core routers and switches of the internet. In large measure, this passive collection capability is due to the five nations' extensive partnership with some of the world's most important telecommunications providers that carry the internet traffic, and to their broadly established network of sensors.[68]

For example, Canada's signals intelligence agency has developed a system of more than "200 sensors deployed across the globe" that "scales to backbone internet speeds." It uses this system to "track known threats, discover unknown threats, [and provide] defence at the core of the internet."[69] While the Five Eyes' passive collection is supplemented with active and more focused collection inside the networks and infrastructure of other states, it nonetheless enables by itself the acquisition of information useful for the defensive mission. Other states without such advanced and scalable passive collection do not have such an advantage. To gather information on their adversaries, these other states likely need to intrude more actively. Nonetheless, while there are data on intrusions linked to foreign governments, in the absence of a Snowden-like leak it is impossible to divine whether defensive intentions motivate some of those intrusions.

Regardless of actor, if the intrusions launched in the service of defense were entirely narrow in scope, the cybersecurity dilemma might not be so acute. If states targeted only the specific parts of other states most likely to pose a threat, such as their cyber operations divisions, or the infrastructure they use in cyber operations, the overall threat would be somewhat contained. Although these are important targets, they are comparatively limited and relatively unsurprising; intelligence services have long targeted one another. There are two main forces pushing states to target more broadly, however, even if the states are largely defensive-minded. This broader targeting increases the acuity of the cybersecurity dilemma. The first has already been mentioned and will be discussed in more depth in the next chapter: by collecting intelligence on the broader government and strategic apparatus, the state can learn a great deal of information, including information of defensive value.

The second impetus for broader targeting is that a state can derive great value from uncovering its potential adversary's operations as they are in progress. To do this, a state can target the networks of interest to their potential adversary, even if the state itself has no significant intelligence interest in those networks. In effect, states have incentives to target neutral, or even allied, states to learn what their potential adversary is up to. States that pursue this kind of analysis most effectively will target many more networks than states that do not, all in an effort to find potential adversaries in action.

The net result is that some targets will be penetrated by multiple states. Kaspersky Lab highlights one network at an unnamed research institution that they call "The Magnet of Threats" because at least five different well-known malicious code operations have penetrated it.[70] A leaked Canadian document echoes this theme, noting that the "state-sponsored landscape is very busy."[71] It is unknowable whether all these actors had a broader intelligence interest in these kinds of targets or whether some only sought information on the others' capabilities. It is clear, though, that by virtue of being on the same network, each actor could watch the activities and capabilities of the others up close. This kind of observation, the same Canadian document states, can increase "situational awareness," help discover "new actors," and "track … known actors."[72]

Other government files confirm this trend. Documents from the Five Eyes indicate that intelligence services seek to learn about the activities of other intelligence services when they have both penetrated the same target. The Five Eyes use a tool known as WARRIORPRIDE (known more popularly to some security researchers as Regin)[73] for exploitation against a wide range of targets. Documents describe it as a "scalable, flexible, portable [Computer Network Exploitation] platform" shared amongst the Five Eyes members.[74] This tool has a wide variety of modules that suit various collection missions. A noteworthy set of modules is useful for what the Canadian documents call Counter-Computer Network Exploitation (CCNE).

These modules seek to detect other malicious code on a computer. They can determine which other actors may have manipulated the operating system and can examine network activity to see who else might be connecting.[75] Some of the modules can be quite complex, with dozens of sub-modules tailored to assist in answering narrowly focused questions. Many of these questions are similar to questions asked by defenders hunting for malicious code within their own network.[76] The software can send the results of these scans back in real time to intelligence analysts and alert analysts when it finds suspicious activity.[77]

A useful case study illustrates how this works in practice. In 2009, Canadian analysts using WARRIORPRIDE on an exploited foreign network uncovered anomalies indicating the presence of another intruder. These unusual behaviors, such as use of the command line to create password-protected folders, were out of character for normal users. Analysts wrote that it "felt like" they were investigating a foreign intelligence operation rather than a criminal enterprise seeking profit.[78] Using their tools, the analysts were able to find and extract the unknown actor's malicious code on the machine and reverse-engineer it in order to understand its techniques, including how it communicated with command and control servers.

The Canadians then targeted the unknown intruder's infrastructure to gain more information. Ultimately, analysis of the infrastructure, targets, and the malicious code indicated that the operation was likely the work of a French intelligence agency. Even as the French operation developed and became more sophisticated, the Canadian analysts were able to use the intelligence and access they had obtained from the CCNE effort to continue to follow it. Thus, a Canadian intrusion into a non-French network led to greater defense against French cyber capabilities.[79] Penetrating many targets has defensive value.

A natural question may arise in response to the preceding discussion: if a state collects this defensive intelligence via secret cyber operations, surely the advantage conferred by the information is limited by the fact that it must remain secret? To some degree this need for secrecy does indeed constrain the value of the intelligence, but not unduly so. Many states do not have a large separation between their government and their critical infrastructure. In some states, the government owns or operates critical utilities and the private sector does not participate much in developing military and intelligence capabilities or orchestrating operations. In many states, state-owned corporations manage large strategic interests outside their national security, such as energy acquisition or technology development.[80] When there is not a large gap between the private and public sector on important issues, states can more easily manage protocols for sharing intelligence in secret.

In addition, states with significant roles for the private sector in critical infrastructure have begun working on ways to increase information sharing.[81] The United States is one of these nations, with private companies operating large portions of the power grid, a broad array of defense contractors enabling its military and intelligence operations, and a thriving private financial sector. As a result of a large number of intrusions against these strategically important non-governmental entities, the United States has created information sharing agreements with private sector entities of most interest to other states. The federal government has pressured private sector companies to employ more people with security clearances to handle secret information and has established temporary clearance programs to facilitate greater sharing of intelligence.[82] The information shared is broader than just intelligence gathered from penetrating other networks. Nonetheless, these arrangements have the effect of giving the

American government greater ability to influence the defensive approaches employed to protect those corporations. It can also inform those approaches with actionable information, including information it alone can legally obtain.[83]

This aspect of network defense has received significant high-level attention. President Obama is an advocate for these joint efforts, arguing that "There's only one way to defend America from these cyber threats, and that is through government and industry working together, sharing appropriate information as true partners."[84] Similarly, the Department of Defense's Cyber Strategy calls for supporting information sharing with major private-sector actors, because doing so "can significantly improve an organization's ability to defend itself against a wide range of cyber attacks."[85] Congress passed broad information sharing legislation in late 2015, though it is too early to see how effective the law will be when implemented. In general, however, with mutual defense and data sharing mechanisms in place, the intelligence gained from network intrusions becomes still more actionable and important.

## Conclusion: The Second Pillar of the Cybersecurity Dilemma

This chapter has outlined the second pillar of the cybersecurity dilemma: sophisticated states have genuinely defensive reasons to launch intrusions into the networks of other states. Doing so can enhance network defense efforts, gather actionable information, and uncover future risks. All of this can often remain covert. In a time of perceived threat, when network defense poses persistent challenges and when many states feel vulnerable, defensive-minded intrusions can seem like an appealing and even necessary step.

In one sense, the existence of defensive-minded intrusions in cyber operations is quite a departure from the traditional logic of international relations and the security dilemma. With conventional forces, it is probably true that states could improve their defenses by stationing a military presence in the territory of a potential adversary. This military unit could see preparations for attack, ready its armaments, and thwart the invasion before it made any progress. But the unilateral stationing of troops in a foreign country is an invasion and a violation of sovereignty, even if the invading state claims that the troops were there to carry out a defensive mission. Defensive invasions with conventional forces are still invasions, and carry with them the very strong likelihood of escalation and conflict.

Defensive-minded network intrusions, on the other hand, are not invasions, but intelligence efforts. States carrying out these sorts of intrusions are gathering information on other states' capabilities and attempting to do so in a covert fashion. To some degree, intelligence collection is a long-accepted part of international politics. Simply put, all states spy, and all states know this. But there are still dangers. As Chapter One showed, when intelligence collection is particularly threatening or easily mistaken for an imminent attack, it can animate the security dilemma. The key question is whether network intrusions, even defensive-minded ones, can be similarly threatening. The next chapter addresses that matter head-on.

4

# HOW NETWORK INTRUSIONS THREATEN

*Overview*

Stuxnet demonstrated the possibility of kinetic cyber attack and eventually attracted enormous attention. NITRO ZEUS, the American contingency plan, has since caused much discussion as a possible successor. Commentators speculate on what might come next in the pantheon of destructive cyber attacks. But it is at least as revealing, though often glossed over, to consider what came first: the efforts that preceded and enabled Stuxnet's destructive power.

To have the desired kinetic effect, Stuxnet required detailed knowledge of the Iranian facilities' configuration.[1] As discussed in Chapter Two, the operation required knowledge of the specific software that controlled the centrifuges. Stuxnet took advantage of deeply obscure or unknown vulnerabilities in the software in order to gain powerful access.[2] Collecting this information took effort. The later destructive versions of Stuxnet were preceded by elaborate and specific reconnaissance operations designed to learn about the target.[3] Kaspersky Lab indicates that the NSA, as part of this preparation, penetrated five relevant Iranian contractors, collecting information about their networks and operations.[4] The same five contractors served as an unwitting conduit across the airgap when a major version of destructive code was delivered.

At the time, had Iran discovered such a snooping operation, its officials might not have been immediately fearful. After all, it was probably no secret that the United States were generally interested in information about the country's nuclear program, perhaps to determine how far the Iranian effort had progressed. Informed by examples of Stuxnet and other destructive attacks, however, Iran and other states are now surely more cognizant of the destruction that could follow such reconnaissance. With this knowledge, the reaction might be one of fear.

Fear is at the core of any security dilemma. It results from perceived threats. Much scholarship has examined the nature of threats,[5] some of it with particular reference to network intrusions.[6] A potential adversary must have the capability to cause harm in order to qualify as a threat. It must also have the opportunity to act at a time and place where the capabilities will have a negative effect. In the case of purposeful harm, intent is also required.[7] Given the intricacy of sophisticated cyber operations, however, accidents do happen.[8] A state might intrude into another state's networks for the purposes of intelligence collection or contingency planning, but inadvertently take some action that causes damage. For example, a mysterious and massive internet outage in Syria in 2012 appears to be the result not of an intentional attack, but of an NSA collection operation that targeted Syrian routers and went amiss.[9] Due to the possibilities of accidents and in lieu of knowledge about intent, states often draw inferences about the capabilities and opportunities of other states—an approach that has a historically poor track record.[10]

In this vein, this chapter argues that intruding into a network of strategic importance in another state is likely to be inherently threatening. This is the case even if the intrusion serves purely defensive purposes. Regardless of the true intent, the act of establishing a presence inside a potential adversary's network gives intruders enormous opportunities for further action and can advance the development of capabilities. When a state uncovers an intrusion into one of its important networks, it faces the dilemma of interpretation. The ways in which an intrusion can cause harm influence how states resolve this dilemma of interpretation and decide on a response. Even if an intrusion is of the defensive sort described in the last chapter, the state suffering the intrusion will nonetheless fear that it poses more serious threats.

There are four types of threats that can result from network intrusions. First, network intrusions can inform specific follow-up cyber attacks and provide a means of launching them, affecting both capability and opportunity. The enabling operations that preceded Stuxnet's destructive components show this, as do other cases. Second, network intrusions can establish a persistent beachhead from which a state can launch additional operations, even those yet unplanned. This is a clear advantage in opportunity. Third, network intrusions can obtain information that changes the general conditions under which future conflict or competition takes place, shaping future capabilities. Fourth, network intrusions can pose significant counterintelligence challenges, altering both capabilities and opportunities.

The rest of this chapter consists of sections that unpack each type of threat. Each section demonstrates three things: that performing intrusions can prepare options for the state that conducts them; that suffering an intrusion causes fear; and that, though these points have theoretical heft, there are already real world examples on which to rely. The chapter's conclusion links back to the need for states to respond, briefly examining how and why states escalate the situation when they feel threatened. The fear caused by any major intrusion into strategically important networks is the last key part of the cybersecurity dilemma. It is what can cause tension even if all states desire only peace.

### Network Intrusions Can Enable Targeted and Powerful Cyber Attacks

As the Stuxnet case shows, network intrusions can enable targeted and powerful cyber and kinetic attacks in a way that generates specific and realistic options for more immediate follow-up. States suffering a network intrusion experience fear not just because it might change the balance of some far-off conflict, but because it might herald something closer to the beginning of one. That is, states can worry that the intrusion might set up a potential adversary's offensive capability for possible use. A state's best chance to thwart the possible attack may well be to root out the intrusion right away or to respond pre-emptively. In such circumstances, fear and uncertainty persist. Even though the sample size of destructive cyber attacks is comparatively small, there is enough evidence of state behavior to observe empirically the enabling role of intelligence in attacks.

Cyber attacks fit into two categories. In the first category are those attacks that require substantial amounts of information about the target to tailor the attack effectively. Such attacks usually have a specific purpose in mind. As a generalization, these attacks rely on exploitation operations to gather intelligence that make the destructive attack possible. In a coordinated and deliberate attack operation, the exploitation and attack components can work in tandem, with the attack effort often slightly behind the exploitation effort, but benefiting from the fruits of its labor. These kinds of attacks are the focus of this section. The next section discusses attacks not requiring such detailed targeting information.

The information required by these sorts of attacks varies tremendously based on the operation. Operators might need knowledge of the target's particular detailed software configuration, intelligence that goes beyond just the operating system and other easily obtained data. Alternatively, they could require the specifics of the physical machinery controlled by the target's computers or information for target verification checks. Some attack operations, like Stuxnet, necessitate all of the above. A rule of thumb is that the more powerful the physical effect an operation seeks, the more specific knowledge and tailoring it requires.[11]

Stuxnet is not alone as an example. On 23 December 2015, the power in the Ivano-Frankivsk region of Western Ukraine went out. The cause was a cyber attack—the first time a widely-reported cyber attack has ever caused a blackout. As more than 230,000 residents lost power, the network intruders, potentially Russian in origin, continued methodically to wreak havoc. With access to the computer systems that controlled electricity distribution, they systematically manipulated circuit breakers and took power substations offline, almost sixty in all. In some of these substations, the attackers wiped critical software components so that the devices were unresponsive to operators' frantic commands to bring the system back online. The attackers also disabled the backup power supplies to some of the distribution centers, blacking out the system's operators. A simultaneous attack against the customer call centers complemented the operation, preventing customers from calling in to report issues and receive status updates. For good measure, the intruders wiped vital software from the operators' computers, causing them to crash and rendering them unable to reboot. All told, the attack was a watershed moment, publicly demonstrating what is possible with cyber operations.[12]

Like other sophisticated cyber attacks, this one took a great deal of time to prepare. The intruders performed important preliminary work for months before the attack. They gained access with spear-phishing emails to workers at three different power companies. Next, they performed reconnaissance and pivoted throughout the well-segmented Ukrainian networks. To gain additional access, they stole user credentials and eventually made their way to the systems that controlled the electricity operations. Detailed reconnaissance enabled them to understand how the networks worked and how to have the desired effects. In these unglamorous and time-consuming phases, the attackers showed their skill. The investigation's report concluded: "the strongest capability of the attackers was not in their choice of tools or in their expertise, but in their capability to perform long-term reconnaissance operations required to learn the environment and execute a highly synchronized, multistage, multisite attack."[13] The intruders' surreptitious presence, unnoticed for months, enabled the eventual damage.

Policy documents and discussion have accounted for this operational reality. The need for exploitation efforts to inform specific attacks directly is implicitly acknowledged by some states, including the United States. The National Intelligence Officer for Cyber Issues, Sean Kanuck, highlighted the overlap in tools and access used in both exploitation and attack, noting that "The ability to hold your opponent at risk [uses] the exact same set of technologies you would use to collect information on them."[14] Former NSA Director for Information Assurance Mike Jacobs, once in charge of key parts of the American cyber defense mission, spelled out the stakes of such information-gathering intrusions. He said, "If you are engaged in reconnaissance on an adversary's systems, you are laying the electronic battlefield and preparing to use it ... In my opinion, these activities constitute acts of war, or at least a prelude to future acts of war."[15]

On the offensive side, United States policy recognizes the need to develop options through preparation and reconnaissance in advance of conflict.[16] In 2012, President Obama signed a classified document,

Presidential Policy Directive 20, which established a protocol for how the United States should handle cyber operations with "significant consequences."[17] Among other things, it directed the cyber operations community to prepare a "plan that identifies potential systems, processes and infrastructure against which the United States should establish and maintain [Offensive Cyber Effect Operations] capabilities; [and] proposes circumstances under which [Offensive Cyber Effect Operations] might be used ..."[18] The directive itself acknowledges the importance of prior preparation: Offensive Cyber Effect Operations, which by the document's definition are inside or against foreign networks, "can offer unique and unconventional capabilities to advance US national objectives around the world with little or no warning to the adversary or target and with potential effects ranging from subtle to severely damaging. The development and sustainment of Offensive Cyber Effect Operations capabilities, however, may require considerable time and effort if access and tools for a specific target do not already exist."[19]

Other military and intelligence community documents bear out the important role of exploitation in advance of an attack. Officials in the Department of Defense saw a need to distinguish between intelligence collection operations, which can gather information for a variety of reasons, and specific reconnaissance operations, which enable a follow-up cyber attack. In response, they have advanced the notion of "Cyber Operations in Preparation of the Environment" (C-OPE). Department of Defense documents define these operations as:

> Non-intelligence enabling functions within cyberspace conducted to plan and prepare for potential follow-up military operations. C-OPE includes but is not limited to identifying data, system/network configurations, or physical structures ... for the purpose of determining system vulnerabilities; and actions taken to assure future access and/or control of the system, network, or data during anticipated hostilities.[20]

A 2010 memo from the Vice Chairman of the Joint Chiefs of Staff instructs military personnel to use C-OPE where they previously[21] would have referred to computer network exploitation or computer network attack operations "as an enabling function for another military operation."[22] Cyber Command's 2010 announcement message, declassified in 2016, states that planning and executing such efforts is one of its responsibilities.[23]

This definition, with mention of ensuring access and control, makes it clear that C-OPE goes beyond mere scanning and target acquisition. A separate and previously written classification guide from the NSA indicates that the intelligence community has a similar practical understanding of the tight connection between cyber espionage and cyber attack, even if the operational authorities are different.[24] The NSA document states that it is an unclassified fact that the signals intelligence agency "performs [computer network exploitation] to support U.S. Government [computer network attack] efforts."[25] Without first collecting intelligence, sophisticated attacks are near-impossible.

Other states are less open about their views of the linkage between exploitation and attack. Nevertheless, what evidence does exist indicates that they perceive things in much the same way. The Chinese *Science of Military Strategy*, a major document published once every fifteen years that provides an outline of the state's doctrine and approach, makes this clear. Some analysts of Chinese doctrine quote the *Science of Military Strategy* as extolling the virtues of network intrusions for exploitation purposes, believing that other states will not see them as a reason to escalate into conflict. Nonetheless, the Chinese authors write, "one need only press a button" to switch from exploitation to attack—presuming one has done enough preparation to build the capability.[26] Both the United States and China recognize the threat of exploitation that leads to attack. If left unchecked, the prospect of impending damage can serve to increase a state's fear of suffering intrusions into strategically important networks.

*Network Intrusions Can Provide a Beachhead for Further Operations*

The second category of cyber attacks comprises those efforts that do not require a separate substantial exploitation operation in advance of the attack. As a result, these missions are more self-contained, following the intrusion model more linearly. Previous intrusions, even genuinely defensive ones, can make these sorts of attacks more easily achievable by providing access to the target network. In so doing, they can animate the security dilemma by making any intrusion seem more threatening.

A great deal of information can make a cyber attack more precise in its effects. The reverse is also true: relying upon only basic targeting information means that attacks are likely to be less carefully calibrated and controlled. This does not mean that they are necessarily impotent, however, as some can be quite damaging. It means only that they are harder to wield carefully and with predictable effect. NSA's public guidance therefore warns of this danger and reiterates the importance of keeping intruders out in the first place:

> Once a malicious actor achieves privileged control of an organization's network, the actor has the ability to steal or destroy all the data that is on the network. While there may be some tools that can, in limited circumstances, prevent the wholesale destruction of data at that point, the better defense for both industry and government networks is to proactively prevent the actor from gaining that much control over the organization's network.[27]

An example of this sort of damaging but imprecise effect is a 2014 attack against Sands Casino, which spread erratically throughout the Sands network, destroying computers and server software as it went. In total, the attack wiped three-quarters of the computers in the company's Las Vegas facilities. The attackers, who probably did not have an appropriate testbed or a detailed understanding of Sands' global information technology operations, missed an opportunity to do still more damage. Their code erased key nodes that stopped the malicious effects from spreading to the overseas parts of the casino's network, something that greater planning and reconnaissance before the attack might have been able to avoid. It seems likely that the Sands attackers did not have the skill, resources, or time to carry out a more complex operation; the limitation probably was not time, as the attackers spent months in the Sands network.[28]

The Sands incident is not alone. Similar attacks were launched, likely by different attackers, against Aramco,[29] the world's largest oil company, in 2012; against South Korean banks in spring 2013;[30] and against Sony Pictures Entertainment in the fall of 2014. Iranian organizations suffered attacks of a somewhat similar nature, but less evidence is available on those cases.[31] In each known case, once the attackers activated the payload, the destructive effect quickly spread across thousands or tens of thousands of computers. Employees noticed that their computers simply stopped working and their screens displayed a message of triumph or threat.[32]

A pattern emerges from these cases. Lower-tier actors carried out the attacks as part of a response to a political moment: the Sands attack is attributed to Iran in response to comments made by the casino's owner, Sheldon Adelson;[33] the Shamoon attack appears to be an Iranian response to Stuxnet and to the attack on the country's oil and gas industries;[34] and the attacks on South Korean banks and on Sony are widely thought to be the work of North Korea in response to political tensions.[35] Each of the attacks also inflicted a sizable amount of damage, though the attackers might have hoped for more.[36] Each of the targets eventually recovered, though each was in some ways shaken by the episode. The lasting effects were primarily political.

But not all future attacks of this sort will be similarly limited or symbolic. Adversaries more capable than Iran and North Korea may be able to have a greater effect with the same levels of access, may obtain a greater level of access in their routine intrusions, may act in response to security concerns instead of political ones, and may have less fear of reprisal. The small sample size of this set of attacks and their more imprecise nature does not mean that future ones do not pose a threat.

These attacks follow the intrusion model in a particularly interesting way. A technique common to this class of attacks is overwriting critical code in as many computers as possible. Frequently, this critical code serves as a foundation for the rest of the computer's functioning. Once an attacker wipes it, the machine will crash. The software to achieve this is widely available and does not require particularly intricate knowledge of the target system.[37] Attackers might only need to know, for example, the version of the Windows operating system in use, not detailed configuration information. As a result, developing a payload of this sort is comparatively easy and, with enough access, activating it is also reasonably straightforward. Therefore, the early parts of the model—determining the target, making entry, pivoting and gaining privileges within the network—are what can take the most time and effort for attackers of this sort. Without obtaining such access, nothing can happen.

This is where an unrelated previous network intrusion can play an important role. The access gained by such an intrusion can be valuable, even if the intrusion is for an entirely different purpose. Attackers can piggyback off this already-existing presence, skipping the early steps of the intrusion model, and get right down to their business of deploying and activating the attack code. The operational effect is simple but important: well-placed network intrusions in a potential adversary's systems can serve as a series of beachheads for later attacks, ensuring that operators can deploy attack code with minimal interference and delay. These intrusions can reduce the time required to launch attacks and provide commanders with options in the case of conflict. Scholars have long seen the ability for a state to act quickly and without warning upon a newfound intention as a cause of fear and escalation in international politics.[38] Cyber operations are perhaps one of the best new examples of this dangerous possibility.

Network intrusions oriented towards gathering information serve as very good beachheads because they so thoroughly gain control of the targeted system. Even those operations that are not terribly sophisticated can often entirely compromise the victim's computer, capturing keystrokes, recording sounds and video (via the computer's camera), and monitoring general activity. Intruders often gain administrative access at the operating system level and load additional software, much of which is also widely available, to perform the collection. For a sophisticated collection operation, the level of access may be even greater still. For example, the previously mentioned Five Eyes malicious code known as Regin, which does not appear to have been collecting intelligence in preparation for any specific attack, had remarkably deep access to the systems it victimized.[39]

An excellent illustration of the fact that espionage and attack require, in many cases, similar levels of access is that many of the wiper attackers also stole sensitive information. When intruders targeted the Saudi oil company Aramco, for example, they also published internal data from within the company's networks as part of a message claiming credit. The message, which coincided with the pre-planned strike date in the code, included lists of the company's network infrastructure, passwords to email accounts, and credentials for accessing the network remotely.[40] The much-publicized Sony intrusion, likely carried out by North Korea, followed a similar model. In the aftermath of destroying the data on many of the company's computers and servers, the intruders began leaking corporate secrets online, including embarrassing emails, passwords, employee information, and movie scripts.[41] The attackers of

Sands Casino also posted a video of themselves scrolling through more than a terabyte of data taken from the corporate network.[42]

The net effect of this strong linkage between exploitation and attack is to complicate both the dilemma of interpretation and the dilemma of response. A state that detects an intrusion into one of its important networks, even an intrusion that does not appear to gather information to enable an attack,[43] will face a number of hard challenges. The state will have to decide what the intent was in launching the intrusion and if that intent might change over time. It will have to determine if the intruders have made entry before and whether those entry points might still be able to serve as beachheads for later attack. If so, a response that removes one beachhead might not mitigate the overall threat, but may escalate tensions with the intruding state if done in public view. Decision-makers must make all of these determinations in a context fraught with uncertainty and fear, making the cybersecurity dilemma more real.

### Network Intrusions Can Change the Conditions of Conflict and Competition

Intrusions into important networks can also pose a more general threat. Like all forms of intelligence collection, the acquisition of strategic intelligence via network intrusion can shape how future conflict and competition take place. This sort of collection is of enormous value to virtually every state and can be tremendously broad in scope. While the collection of such information can serve narrow defensive aims, it will often go beyond that. Simply put, when it comes to strategic intelligence, the state collecting the information is better off, while the state suffering the loss of secrets is worse off. Network intrusions can aid this effort in at least three ways.

First, information gained from network intrusions can be enormously valuable in establishing joint military operations[44] with cyber effects. Many states have announced plans for adding cyber units to their military and intelligence arsenals, but few have discussed the challenges of doing so. In addition to the major issues in doctrine, organization, training, and technology development, specific integration issues persist.[45] In order to be well integrated and useful for joint operations, capabilities must meet a few difficult criteria. Commanders seeking to use a capability must have a reasonably solid idea of the target, must know that the capability will work against that target, must have some idea of the effects, and must know that its use is legally and ethically permissible.

An anecdote illustrates the point. In 1999, at a closed-door symposium of high-level American military officials working on information warfare, the senior Air Force officer in Europe, General John Jumper, addressed barriers to the use of cyber capabilities. He said:

> I picture myself around [a] targeting table where you have the fighter pilot, the bomber pilot, the special operations people, and the information warriors. As you go down the target list, each one takes a turn raising his or her hand saying, 'I can take that target.' [But the info warrior] says, 'I can take the target, but first I have to go back to Washington and get [presidential approval].'[46]

Additional administrative hurdles make capabilities less appealing.[47] Although Jumper was speaking in the context of authorization, legal, and oversight issues, one can also imagine the same discussion focused on the methods used. The tools of bombers, fighters, and special operators are obvious to all around the table. But the network intruders will go through the long process described in the intrusion model and, in many cases, see no obviously visible sign that they have destroyed the target. Indeed, the target to them will frequently be different in kind, as they will often affect the software, rather than the physical presence, of the adversary. Their methods, authorities, and capabilities—at least until integration and routinization take place— are much more opaque to the others.[48] This is true even if they are sometimes better for the job. For example, during a key point in the Gulf War, the United States risked greater collateral damage when it opted to bomb an Iraqi telecommunications tower rather than use then-newfangled cyber capabilities.[49]

Network intrusions in advance of conflict can collect information that can alleviate some of this uncertainty. At scale, these intrusions can therefore make it easier to integrate cyber attack options more generally into joint operations and to move such capabilities into more mainstream military focus. By so doing, they can provide more workable options to commanders, increase the capabilities of military forces, and advance overall prospects for success in conflict. This is another reason why states have incentives to prepare operations, or parts thereof, in advance.

Thorough digital reconnaissance, often aided by network intrusions, is key. By understanding what possible targets are out there, intruders in effect take care of the first part of any future operation: target acquisition. Widespread collection of information on hardware and software configuration reduces the time before operators can launch an attack against those targets. Sometimes operators can obtain this information by scanning, but at other times they must launch intrusions. Feeding all of the collected information back into a centralized location—building, in effect, a map of potential targets for cyber operations—is an enormous challenge, but one that can help tip the scales of future conflict if done successfully.

Another important point follows: widespread reconnaissance of various forms can enable the development of capabilities most likely to be of use. With a detailed understanding of a wide range of potential targets, states can find, acquire, and develop exploits most likely to work against the hardware and software used by those targets. They can do the same for the tools they will use after obtaining access. Once states develop these exploits and tools, they can test their capabilities in simulated environments, informed by the intelligence gathered from network intrusions and general collection. Such tests can give them greater certainty about what the effects of the cyber capabilities might be. Over time, this confidence, and the successful demonstration of operations, can reduce the need for hyper-specific legal oversight, increase reliability, and improve joint efforts.[50]

The United States carries out reconnaissance efforts of this sort. The Defense Advanced Research Project Agency (DARPA) within the Department of Defense has begun something titled Foundational Cyberwarfare, but far more commonly referred to as Plan X. Plan X is a largely secret effort, but because of the contracts associated with the project (worth at least $110 million), some information is public. The project is explicitly not a cyber weapons development program,[51] but it is "complementary" to such programs[52] and enables exactly the sort of integration and routinization discussed above.[53] Among other things, Plan X aims to build a continuously updated map of targets for commanders. In so doing, it will enable the swift launch of cyber operations against these targets. Former acting DARPA Director Ken Gabriel described the map as "a rapid, high-order look of what the Internet looks like—of what the cyberspace looks like at any one point in time."[54] The military does not overtly state that the data sources for this map include network intrusions. Without specifying a source, officials have made clear that the project aims for particular information on potential targets.

This granular information can enable attack operations within Plan X. The *Washington Post* interviewed General Michael Hayden, former Director of the NSA, and reported on his vision for "a map with red dots representing enemy computers and blue dots representing American ones. When the enemy upgrades his operating system, the red dots would blink yellow, meaning the target is out of reach until cyber operators can determine what the new operating system is" and, presumably, what vulnerabilities it has.[55] Early prototypes shown to reporters reveal something close to Hayden's idea.[56] When the system identifies a potential target and collects enough information about configuration and potential weaknesses, the target appears in red. In the prototype Plan X interface, the operator of the system can select the potential target and see the available cyber capabilities best suited for use against that target. The operator can then select one of the available capabilities and fire it against the target, launching the cyber attack.[57]

Although Plan X is not an exploit development program, the effort aims to study the potential usage and effects of cyber capabilities and to increase the confidence around that sort of analysis. It includes ambitious research that seeks to make execution of mission plans in cyber operations as easy and automated as "the auto-pilot function in modern aircraft."[58] It also tries to develop "formal methods to provably quantify the potential battle damage from each synthesized mission plan."[59] In other words, the information from reconnaissance is of great use when coupled with information on operational capabilities—including cyber capabilities developed outside of Plan X—and how those capabilities perform under certain conditions.

DARPA Director Arati Prabhakar summarized the intended overall effect of Plan X succinctly and in such a way that, if realized, leaves no doubt as to its value for joint operations in future conflict. The effort, he said, seeks:

> [to] allow cyber offense to move from the world we're in today—where
> it's a fine, handcrafted capability that requires exquisite authorities to do

anything ... to a future where cyber is a capability like other weapons ... A military operator can design and deploy a cyber effect, know what it's going to accomplish ... and take an appropriate level of action.[60]

But fully achieving this shift almost certainly requires a great deal of information on foreign networks, including information often best gained from network intrusions. And lest there be any confusion about whether the plan might be threatening to potential adversaries, the documentation which DARPA has made public is clear about the effort's end goal: to "dominate the cyber battlespace."[61]

The intelligence community in the United States also does this sort of reconnaissance and preparation, though still further from public view. Within the NSA, there is a separate effort underway to map as much of the internet as possible. Known as TREASUREMAP, NSA documents describe it as a "massive Internet mapping, exploration, and analysis engine," one that seeks to provide users with a "near-real time, interactive map of the global internet."[62] The documents note how such a map is of great value both for defensive missions, but also for performing reconnaissance into foreign networks and "computer attack [and] exploit planning."[63] The system takes information from a number of sources into account, including data from unauthorized network intrusions into routers and computers around the world.[64]

In addition to enabling joint operations, breaking into foreign networks can also change the general conditions of future conflict by providing insight into the potential adversary's intentions, capabilities, and decision-making processes. In this regard, network intrusions can serve a role long filled by other forms of signals intelligence. In the post-Snowden world, there is much to discuss in this area, but a few examples will suffice for demonstrating that such activities are possible—and at great scale—via cyber operations.

Network intrusions can provide insight into the strategy of other states. The United States conducted intelligence operations via cyber capabilities that targeted 122 world leaders, including major allies like Germany and Mexico, according to NSA documents. Though American officials did not confirm the count or scale of such collection, they have implicitly acknowledged and reportedly somewhat curtailed such activities.[65] These operations targeting political leadership could involve electronic close access. For example, in the case of Mexican president Peña Nieto, the NSA collected and analyzed the cell phone communications of Nieto and "nine of his close associates," including almost 85,000 text messages. The agency also penetrated the devices of Nieto's predecessor, Felipe Calderón. NSA documents highlight the method and the access obtained: operators "successfully exploited a key mail server in the Mexican Presidencia domain within the Mexican Presidential network to gain first-ever access to President Felipe Calderón's public email account."[66] Other states almost certainly attempt or perform similar types of intrusions; the apparent intrusion by Russian intelligence into the networks of the Democratic National Committee in 2016 is but one example.[67]

The value of intrusions is not limited to understanding foreign political leadership, however. The United States also targets the military communications of other states, something else in which it is surely not alone. For example, as part of general and ongoing collection, the United States targeted the networks often used by Chinese military officers.[68] In other cases, such as immediately prior to NATO operations in Libya, collection fulfills specific pressing military needs.[69] Although journalists have withheld many of the details of American activities because they involve ongoing operations against potentially adversarial states, enough has entered the public domain that one can be reasonably confident that such intrusions are occurring. The high-level American documents that journalists have published describe intrusions targeting "priority" targets of China, Russia, and Iran—none of which should come as a surprise, given geopolitical circumstances.[70]

In addition to intercepting political and military communications, intrusions can shed light on potential adversaries' capabilities. Such information can find weaknesses that a state can exploit at the right moment. The United States Defense Science Board, a committee of national security experts, highlights the danger. Among the more than two dozen "compromised" technologies mentioned in the report are the Joint Strike Fighter, other advanced aircraft, anti-air defenses, and naval capabilities.[71] The public summary concludes: "The cyber threat is serious and ... the United States cannot be confident that our critical Information Technology (IT) systems will work under attack from a sophisticated and well-resourced opponent utilizing cyber capabilities in combination with all their military and intelligence capabilities ..."

The report specifically cites network intrusions against American targets as a basis for this conclusion.[72] Other sources confirm this assessment. A 2016 report from the Pentagon's chief weapons tester warned that "cyber opposing forces frequently attained a position to deliver cyber effects that could degrade operational missions, often significantly,"[73] while a separate set of leaked documents appear to confirm the American intelligence community's belief that actors in China obtained "many terabytes" of data on key weapons programs.[74]

The danger is that intruders who obtain such information in advance of conflict aim not only to discover vulnerabilities in vital military systems, but also to aid developing parallel capabilities. For example, there are similarities between recently developed Chinese military aircraft and American aircraft whose plans were copied via network intrusion.[75] One American military pilot compared the new Chinese jets to their American counterparts by saying, "I think they'll eventually be on par with our fifth gen jets [the class of the Joint Strike Fighter]— as they should be, because industrial espionage is alive and well."[76] States can also use intrusions to keep an eye on the technological developments of other states, even when the intent is not necessarily to copy their developments. The NSA's tracking of "high priority Israeli military targets," including drone aircraft and advanced missile systems, is an example of this.[77]

The third way in which network intrusions can affect the general conditions of interstate competition is in a non-military fashion. While the security dilemma is largely focused on conflict, the discussion can extend to economic and political competition as well. Because of such concerns, a network intrusion may be threatening for reasons that do not relate to war. This is particularly important when considering intrusions between allies or neutral states. Even if such states are unlikely to do battle with one another in the foreseeable future, network intrusions can nonetheless cause fear and animate a security dilemma of sorts. This is increasingly true in a post-2008 financial crash context, in which economic security is an increasingly important part of national security and all states compete in a globalized economic marketplace. In the Obama Administration, the intelligence community produces a daily "Economic Intelligence" briefing.[78] Such knowledge is tightly controlled, even amongst close allies. British documents note that "Economic well-being reporting cannot be shared with any foreign partner"—a prohibition which is comparatively rare for the United Kingdom, given its incredibly close intelligence relationship with the United States.[79]

There is great debate about the value of network intrusions on economic competitiveness.[80] Though important and interesting, this debate is largely beyond the scope of this text. The perception, right or wrong, that network intrusions can provide gains in economic competitiveness is what can escalate something akin to the security dilemma. Within the United States, this perception is fueled by the indictment of Chinese People's Liberation Army officers for conducting industrial espionage against American entities,[81] regular media discussion of intellectual property theft,[82] and a large number of intrusion reports.[83] Outside the United States, a similar perception thrives. The Snowden documents provide evidence that the NSA, for a variety of potential reasons, targeted economic entities such as private corporations, to international consternation.[84] But this is not a new trend. Even before the Snowden debates, allies accused the United States of harmful economic espionage. American officials deny that their espionage against economic targets is for competitive advantage, instead arguing that it is defensive in nature and seeks to guard against the deleterious effects of foreign corruption on American business.[85] All of these activities are not about war, but parallel the security dilemma nonetheless.

Overall, network intrusions can provide information and access valuable in conflict, in peacetime, and, potentially, in economic competition. For policy-makers who know they will have ready cyber operations capabilities and insight into the leadership and capabilities of other states, the risks of conflict, escalation, and competition surely appear more manageable. For policy-makers who know or fear that their networks have been penetrated—even, or especially, if they do not know the degree—the risks surely appear greater. The ways in which a network intrusion can change the future power dynamic, with options and capabilities for one side and fear for another, shows how threatening they can be.

### Network Intrusions Can Pose Major Counterintelligence Challenges

A final way in which network intrusions can threaten states is by enabling counterintelligence operations. Counterintelligence, the art of understanding and thwarting other actors' espionage attempts, pre-dates cyber operations. It has long been essential to gathering and using intelligence. Nor is it a new idea that counterintelligence could involve penetrating other organizations. Well before the era of cyber opera-tions, the American spymaster Allen Dulles argued for offensive coun-terintelligence that proactively targeted potentially adversarial intelli-gence services.[86]

In cyber operations, effective counterintelligence can threaten a foreign intelligence service by gathering information on how the intel-ligence service works and what it knows. As the last chapter showed, this can have immediate defensive value. Effective counterintelligence can go beyond near-term defenses, however, providing a means for the intruding state to increase understanding, manipulation, and weaken-ing of its counterpart's services. This can be a threatening prospect to the intelligence organization suffering the intrusion.

An obvious counterintelligence threat is an intrusion into the central networks of an intelligence service. In such cases, the counterintelli-gence gains for the intruders are easily apparent and exceed that which is useful for narrow defensive purposes. If the intruding state pene-trates far enough, it can learn about the internal workings, operations, capabilities, and communications of its counterpart. Department of Defense documents directly acknowledge this sort of collection. A 2009 strategy, later declassified, outlines how counterintelligence teams will "penetrate our adversaries' intelligence operations to assess their tradecraft, source networks, and leadership structures, while validating the reliability of our own sources and methods."[87] After Snowden, there is little doubt about the amount of information con-tained on these networks. For this reason, therefore, the security of intelligence agencies' computer systems is of paramount importance.

The targeting of foreign intelligence agencies is therefore a sensitive topic. Journalists, even those with access to classified documents, rarely discuss the particulars of these operations. Although states are likely to try to penetrate each other's intelligence services with at least as much regularity in the digital age as before it, there is only some evidence of these attempts. One related example, which came to light because it did not involve directly targeting an intelligence agency, gives a few hints. The United States targeted Huawei, a Chinese government-owned telecommunications company that the United States had long suspected of ties to the Chinese espionage apparatus. In part, NSA documents indicate, the United States operation sought to uncover the nature, if any, of these connections. If the link was as tight as some suspected, the intrusion could reveal valuable information. One NSA document from the operation quotes an analyst as saying, "If we can determine the company's plans and intentions, we hope that this will lead us back to the plans and intentions of the [People's Republic of China]."[88] The documents do not say what the intruders learned.

Another report shows how entities with any possible connection to intelligence activities become targets. Once the NSA began building a new Utah data center, the agency's largest, signs of attempted network intrusion against Utah government networks dramatically increased. State officials estimate that the new level of "attacks" increased ten-thousand-fold after the NSA began construction. This was the case even though the NSA networks are entirely separate from those of the Utah government. Nevertheless, other American states without NSA data centers did not experience the same jump in targeting. Utah Public Safety Commissioner Kevin Squires told a legislative committee that he thought the reason for the spike in activity was the arrival of the signals intelligence agency. "I really do believe it was all the attention drawn to the NSA facility ... That's a big deal," he said.[89]

A second counterintelligence threat is that a network intrusion could reveal what an intelligence agency knows about a particular subject and the capabilities it employs to gather that information. While the core networks of intelligence agencies are (in theory, at least) carefully defended, other parts of an intelligence agency's infrastructure might not be. For purposes of obfuscation, operators often rent infrastructure from third-party hosting providers or otherwise place it outside their core network. An adversary could penetrate these servers and learn operational details. Chapter Three showed how information on an adversary's operational capabilities can inform defensive measures, but the counterintelligence risk goes deeper than that. Compromise of an intelligence agency's infrastructure can reveal the results of secret operations to an intruder. This fulfills two central goals of counterintelligence: to know *what* the other side knows about important matters, and to know *how* the other side knows it.

The NSA refers to this sort of collection, which piggybacks on another state's existing operations, as "fourth-party collection."[90] Documents contain a few examples.[91] In one file, an intelligence community employee recounts how the Five Eyes targeted South Korea's signals intelligence operations. In the course of doing so, they learned of South Korean espionage operations against North Korea, also a state of great interest to the Five Eyes. They compromised the exfiltration points of those operations through which the South Koreans brought back the data. A separate NSA document describes this sort of operation as fourth-party "active acquisition."[92] In so doing, the NSA analysts understood the sources of South Korean intelligence as well as the content—a clear counterintelligence victory.[93]

This example leads into a third way in which network intrusions can pose a counterintelligence threat: suffering a network intrusion could bolster the intruding state's operational opportunities. The intruders can do more than just collect the information gathered by the fourth-party state's compromised operation, as appeared to happen in the South Korean case. Indeed, the intruders can use their fourth-party's position as a jumping-off point for further access of their own. Alternatively, or in addition, the intruders can examine the exploits and tools used by the fourth-party state and adapt them for their own use, potentially in other operations.

Once again, NSA documents confirm that these ideas have resonance within the intelligence community. The documents include a multi-layered "decision-tree" that clarifies the various options available under fourth-party collection. The document discusses "Victim Stealing/Sharing," which "exploits weaknesses in foreign [computer network exploitation] implants and [Command and Control] systems to gain access to victims and either take control of the foreign implant or replace it with our own."[94] This is not a disruption or attack operation, but one designed to get better access to a target. The document describing the South Korean/North Korean case indicates that the Five Eyes eventually developed their own position, as part of an effort to avoid unduly "rely[ing] on an untrusted actor [South Korea] to do your work for you."[95]

The NSA's fourth-party decision tree document also highlights that the agency has at least considered the concept of adapting another intelligence service's exploits, as opposed to just its access, for their own operations—a concept not unique to the agency.[96] The briefing notes the ways in which this can advance the NSA's capabilities and accelerate its operational process: "*Re-purposing* utilizes captured foreign [Computer Network Exploitation] components (implants, exploits, etc.) to shorten the development of our own [Computer Network Exploitation] tools."[97] What happens after the agency repurposes the exploits is not clear from the documents made public, however. One possibility is that a network intrusion resulting in repurposing enables a state's own tools to be used against it, which is rightly worrying. More destabilizing still might be the prospect of using repurposed exploits to carry out false flag attacks, for which a state might be wrongly implicated. A final prospect is that the repurposed exploit could be used against the same target, since it is effective; NSA documents suggest that the agency did this in one case, but provide few details.[98]

Before concluding the discussion on counterintelligence, it is worth returning to the works of Michael Herman, the practitioner-turned-academic who applied the security dilemma to intelligence operations. Herman, writing about counterintelligence generally, noted the strong sense of paranoia that arose in the discipline. This paranoia, he explained, was ultimately deeply damaging,[99] delaying operations and arousing suspicion in such a way that could eventually contribute to the security dilemma. Intrusions into certain sensitive networks might well evoke the same degree of paranoia. While counterintelligence officers have always worried about double agents in their midst, now they have much greater cause to fear the corruption of their agency's technology as well.[100]

## Conclusion: The Third Pillar of the Cybersecurity Dilemma

This chapter has made the case for the cybersecurity dilemma's third and final pillar: states will interpret most or all intrusions into strategically important networks as threatening, for at least one of the above reasons. If they cannot determine the intent of an intrusion or if there is ambiguity in the dilemma of interpretation, they will have a tendency to err, sometimes significantly so, on the side of caution. All else being equal, they will assume the worst.

Practically, how does this tendency to feel threatened affect the response? It certainly varies by circumstance. Weaker states will have limited means of countering stronger states. One recourse for these states is discreet diplomatic discussions with the intruding state, but these can be difficult if there is plausible deniability or if the states do not trust one another. Another approach is to lodge protests in international institutions, making the case public. But this can sometimes be of limited value in an anarchic self-help system, especially if there are not clear norms of behavior. A final option is to pursue asymmetric means of response in retaliation—escalation in the only way a weak state can.

Medium-tier states, especially when confronting other medium-tier states, might pursue more symmetric responses. These states can launch intrusions of their own, try to develop new capabilities, or call on allies for assistance. Once they have observed the intruders' operational techniques, they will likely try to root out the intruders from their networks as best they can. In short, they will try to reassert their control over the situation as much as possible. They might seek to assure their own freedom of action, developing offensive options while denying the same to their potential adversary. From the perspective of the potential adversary, particularly one that launched its intrusion with purely defensive intent, this approach could possibly seem escalatory and threatening.

Strong states have still more options. Most significantly, they might perceive a serious threat, yet feel somewhat reassured by their deterrence capabilities and the resilience of their networks. In other words, a state that truly believes in its capacity to deter other actors or absorb the effects of an intrusive network breach can worry less about the network intrusions described in this chapter. This strong state can assume the worst—that another state has gained the ability to do harm to its important networks—and be somewhat confident that the other state will nonetheless be partially constrained in its behavior. The strong state suffering an intrusion may still seek to root out the intruders and to deny the potential adversary's capability, but it will likely not feel the same need for escalation.

Nevertheless, a state's belief in its capacity for deterrence and resilience has limits. Most obviously, if a state is trying to deter the act of intrusion, rather than of attack or other operational effect, the need for a credible response can be a cause for escalation. Even if the state tries to deter an attack with a promise of a second strike, important constraints remain. Deterrence might be less effective if the adversary is a non-state actor, if the adversary does not have much of value to hold at risk for retaliation, or if the adversary is not rational. Further, a strong state's vulnerability may be so great that, even if the state is somewhat confident in the resilience of its systems, intrusions into truly important networks will still cause consternation. Deterrence and resilience often offer only partial ways out of the problem.

As a result, strong states suffering intrusions also sometimes fear what might happen next. Two cases from the United States that are now in the public domain illustrate this point. In 1998, at a time of rising tensions between the United States and Iraq, American network defenders detected intruders in the military's logistics and communications networks—a case known as Solar Sunrise. American officials were deeply concerned that these intruders could hamper the military's ability to fight in a crisis. General John Campbell, then in charge of information operations for the Joint Staff, described the fear of what the intruders could do to the military's key computers: "If you take one part of that machine, and disable it, you['ve] got a real problem trying to make a deployment take place."[101] Eventually, after frantic investigation and remediation, the United States identified the intruders. They turned out to be not Iraqi operators, but three teenagers, two American and one Israeli. Yet even this amateur intrusion had set off alarm bells throughout America's senior leadership because of what it appeared to portend. A sophisticated intrusion by another state would likely be of still greater concern.

The second example shows just what this greater level of concern might look like. In 1996, intruders of Russian government origin penetrated a large number of American military, academic, and government networks. In 1998, American investigators discovered this effort and code-named it Moonlight Maze. Very senior policy-makers again feared the worst. They launched a massive international investigation, spanning multiple agencies and involving military, law enforcement, and counterintelligence personnel. As part of the response, the United States government launched intrusions against Russian computers, seeking to gather information.[102] The investigation showed that the intruders had gathered a wide range of sensitive data. This led Richard Clarke, then one of the government's most senior officials handling cybersecurity matters, to spell out the stakes in cybersecurity dilemma-esque language, warning that these intrusions constituted "cyberwar reconnaissance."[103] Then-Deputy Secretary of Defense John Hamre interpreted the intrusions still more forcefully, bluntly telling a classified meeting of the House and Senate Intelligence Committees in 1999 that "We're in the middle of a cyberwar."[104] Fortunately for the United States, no follow-up attack ever came.

It is not known to what degree these cases represent the high-water mark of fear and anxiety in response to a network intrusion. On the one hand, they are older cases. It is likely that the United States and other nations have since become more used to network intrusions and have developed more level-headed and bureaucratic methods of handling them. These methods could serve to calm the fears of policy-makers, minimizing the cybersecurity dilemma. On the other hand, the 2015 case cited in this book's Introduction reveals that, even for minor incidents, defenders seek to act swiftly and strongly in order to avert the possibility of trouble.

Additionally, in some important ways the risks, perceived and real, have dramatically increased. Although Solar Sunrise and Moonlight Maze were significant, neither operation targeted classified American systems.[105] Since those incidents, states have stored more and more valuable information, classified and not, on computer networks. Computer systems are central to many parts of society, which creates the possibility of significant vulnerability, even for states with their own capabilities. The capacity for destructive attack is widely appreciated after Stuxnet, while the possibility of devastating strategic attacks looks more credible in light of the NITRO ZEUS effort against Iran. Popular media hype might amplify the perceived dangers further for some policy-makers. These higher stakes lead to greater urgency and fear, not less.

With high enough stakes,[106] escalation makes sense. In an anarchic system, these reactions of fear are natural, expected, and maybe even wise. But they also drive the cybersecurity dilemma forward and make its dangers real. Policy-makers need a method of reassurance, something to act as a brake on the cycle of growing tension. The next chapter will return to international relations scholarship in search of the factors that encourage restraint.

5

# THE FAILURE OF TRADITIONAL MITIGATIONS

*Overview*

President Theodore Roosevelt possessed a remarkable perspective on the interplay between military developments and international affairs. Long before his political career, he wrote a seminal work on the naval combat of the War of 1812. During the Spanish–American War, he earned praise for his bravery. While in the White House, he understood the importance of projecting strength, sending the American Navy's Great White Fleet on a global journey. But Roosevelt also recognized the value of avoiding and ending conflict. He eventually won the Nobel Peace Prize for his efforts to end the Russo-Japanese War.

In 1904, as Roosevelt surveyed the geopolitical scene, he noticed something peculiar and dangerous. The German Chancellor, he observed, "sincerely believes that the English are planning to attack him and smash his fleet, and perhaps join with France in a war to the death against him." Yet Roosevelt knew that the British had no such intentions. Instead, he understood that they were "themselves in a condition of panic terror lest the Kaiser secretly intend to form an alliance against them with France or Russia, or both, to destroy their fleet and blot out the British Empire from the map." The concept of the security dilemma had not yet been formally articulated, but Roosevelt called the matter "as funny a case as I have ever seen of mutual distrust and fear bringing two peoples to the edge of war."[1]

Roosevelt had the luxury of being a third party. Almost as if he were a scholar, he could observe both states from a distance. He could see what neither side could recognize. But he was of course a practitioner at the time, not an academic. Even with the power of the presidency, however, there was not a lot he could actually do to resolve the matter, to make each state feel secure without causing insecurity in the other. The obvious practical difficulties in mitigating the security dilemma even pre-date scholars fleshing out the idea.

In the time since Roosevelt, and alongside the articulation of the security dilemma, scholars and policy-makers have addressed the challenges of mitigation. These mitigators accept the notion that anarchy is a powerful force and that states' need for security is deeply felt. As a result, states will develop military capabilities and collect intelligence, perhaps always to the greatest degree they think they can get away with. Nonetheless, the mitigators argue, states can minimize the security dilemma in some important respects. They can keep its force enough at bay for the system to function with a sufficient degree of stability.

Research has demonstrated that, as a matter of history and practice, the security dilemma is not constant: states are more or less wary of other states, depending on time, place, and circumstance. The inconsistency in the security dilemma in history has enabled the identification of variables, such as the offense–defense balance and offense–defense differentiation, which either amplify or lessen it. It also makes possible identification of ways in which cooperation can emerge, even if in necessarily limited measure. By shaping these variables to the degree that they can, states can reassure each other that their activities are benign in intent. This possibility is the foundation of mitigator logic and the focus of this chapter.

Mitigator logic has been the subject of much debate, with generally favorable assessments. Indeed, states have taken action in accordance with the proposed mitigations, both before and after the variables' formal scholarly articulation. The mitigators' work has proven to have real world applicability in overcoming the security dilemma. Successfully shaping the variables of the security dilemma has created more stability in the international system.

Mitigations of the cybersecurity dilemma are less evident, however, particularly when it comes to activity that is short of cyberwarfare.[2] A key aim of this chapter is not just to present examples of mitigator logic, but also to apply those examples to network intrusions. This application draws on the intrusion and defense models and on the threatening nature of network intrusions just outlined. With this foundation, the chapter argues that the variables introduced by mitigators indicate that the cybersecurity dilemma poses risks. The mitigations that have worked elsewhere to shape those variables do not translate well. The particulars of the practice of cybersecurity and the multiple ways in which network intrusions can threaten states limit the relevance of traditional mitigations in a digital context.

Drawing on perhaps the two most famous works of classic mitigator logic, by Robert Jervis and Charles Glaser, this chapter examines the variables of the security dilemma. It outlines the two key variables that each author proposes. Next, it examines the mitigations that result, the ways in which states can take actions designed to change the variables and thus minimize the dangers of the system. Each section evaluates one variable and its related mitigations for their applicability and utility in the context of cybersecurity. The conclusion takes a broader view, reaffirming that the cybersecurity dilemma remains a challenge to mitigate.

## Offense–Defense Balance

The first variable is whether decision-makers perceive the overall security environment to be better suited to the offensive side or the defensive side.[3] Mitigators contend that the worst form of the security dilemma arises when the only means of security are through aggressiveness or expansion.[4] When the offense has the advantage, it is easier to penetrate enemy territory than it is to stand firm and defend one's own. Under such conditions, in order to be confident that adversaries are not planning or capable of a damaging first strike, a state must actively seek to disrupt its potential adversaries' plans and capabilities. Since the defense is at a disadvantage, states do not have the luxury of waiting for more information. By acting aggressively, a state can weaken its potential adversaries' positions, putting them on the defensive and minimizing their ability to retaliate meaningfully.

The converse is also true. If the defense has the advantage, then a state that seeks only to protect itself and not to expand can obtain security without threatening others. If the defense has very strong advantages, aggression may well be prohibitively difficult.[5] An environment dominated by defensive capabilities is one in which states with no massive advantage in overall power are reluctant to be the first to try to penetrate the domain of another. The incentives point instead towards prudent defensive preparation. States will stay within their own perimeters, focus on keeping their adversaries out, and be secure in the safety that their defensive capabilities provide. The result is a more stable system, even if it is still anarchic, with fewer changes in the status quo and more incentive for cooperation.[6]

With offense–defense balance it is perception, not reality, that is most important. A two-part example best illustrates this point. In advance of World War I, the common view among decision-makers was that the offense enjoyed the advantage.[7] Conditioned by German Chancellor Otto von Bismarck's rapid and decisive ground victories in earlier decades, states built tight and entangling alliances, increased military spending, viewed future conflict as quick and cheap to prosecute offensively, and favored pre-emption.[8] But, revealingly, these preparations for aggression extended only to the armies of the time. With no similar precedent for decisive offensive advantage on water, the European navies believed that defense had an advantage. They therefore relied on their submarines, mines, and naval fortifications to support a much less aggressive posture.[9] The high seas, less caught up in the offensive hype, remained more stable.

The World War I example demonstrates that offense–defense balance is something that varies by situation, even within the same conflict. The example also shows that the offense–defense balance is often subject to great misperceptions. Once the war began, the bloodshed and stalemate made it evident that the offense did not have the advantage on land, after all. While military commanders expected decisive victories, the prolonged and deadlocked trench warfare demonstrated the deadly consequences of getting the offense–defense balance wrong.

Two factors determine whether in fact the offense or the defense enjoys the advantage in a given circumstance. These factors can help answer the questions of resources and capabilities, and thus hold enormous influence over states' actions. The first, geography, is straightforward. The more impediments to the offense's movements—in the

form of muddy terrain, steep mountains, narrow straits, and the like—
the better the situation is for the defense. Such geographical features
slow the offense's pace, provide more time for the defense to prepare,
and often offer more opportunity for the defense to inflict damage on
the exposed offensive forces. For this reason, among others, state borders over time reshape to match terrain.[10] Geographic features often
provide natural points of stable equilibrium.[11]

The variable of geography can aid mitigation. States trying to preserve the status quo can attempt to manage the security dilemma by
using the curiosities of the Earth's surface to strengthen the credibility
of political agreements. An excellent example is the Washington Naval
Treaty, an intricate system devised by five victorious World War I countries. The agreement utilized the distances between important points
in the Pacific Ocean as part of a political and military effort to reduce
the possibility of escalation and attack by any party.[12] Even if no such
natural features exist, states can try to develop artificial geographical
barriers of their own. A noteworthy example of this is the different
gauge size employed on Russian railroads, which had the effect of
greatly slowing movement across the border. Like the Washington
Naval Treaty, the different train gauges constrained all sides' ability to
attack. In addition to making it more difficult for invaders to encroach
on Russian territory, it made it more difficult for the Russians to
expand outwards. In order to address the security dilemma, such mitigations must provide reassurance to every state involved. If such measures inhibit just one side, they are merely unilateral defenses.[13]

Technology is the second consideration for determining offense–
defense balance. The weapons in play and the susceptibility of those
weapons to damage are deeply important. When a state's offensive
capabilities are vulnerable to attack, the state must use the capabilities
before they are destroyed or otherwise rendered irrelevant. Here the
advantage belongs to the offense, since if a state can strike first and
destroy the vulnerable weapons of its adversary, the state can achieve a
decisive edge. On the contrary, when a state's own penetrating capabilities are hardened and well-protected, the capabilities can withstand
a first strike and still enable retaliation. In this circumstance, the
defense enjoys an advantage because the state preserves its options
even in the face of such a strike. Crucially, it is difficult to determine in

advance whether it is the offense or the defense that enjoys the techno-logical advantage in a coming conflict. Again, perception has only sometimes matched up with reality, leading to costly miscalculations and mistakes.[14]

In cybersecurity, the intruders appear to have an edge. This is par-tially because geography, a factor that so often favors the defenders, is minimally present in cyber operations, at least as it relates to the cybersecurity dilemma.[15] The sort of natural barriers that normally aid defensive missions in physical space do not have exact parallels.[16] Furthermore, almost all states virtually border one another, to the extent that the concept of borders applies in a digital space. Not only are there no natural fortifications in cyberspace, but there are no inter-mediate states and also no natural places of equilibrium.[17] Geographical proximity in physical space is the greatest predictor of conflict over time,[18] in part because of competing local interests, but also in part because it is easier to penetrate the territory of close neighbors. When all states are in virtual proximity to one another, there are fewer such constraints. The intruders, uninhibited by difficult geography, therefore enjoy greater freedom of action.

The natural follow-up question is whether states could artificially add barriers, in the way that the Russians artificially adopted a different railroad standard. The answer unambiguously is yes. Almost any given state (save for perhaps those that share significant telecommunications infrastructure with another state) could add technical barriers to match its national borders, such as blocking certain kinds of internet traffic. But doing so would not mitigate the cybersecurity dilemma. To be effective in providing stability, the geographic feature or barrier has to be self-limiting in some way, as the Russian technique was.[19] The sorts of technical barriers and interfaces common to cybersecurity practice, such as firewalls, deep packet inspection systems,[20] and routing proto-cols, do not serve the role of artificial geography. In the context of the cybersecurity dilemma, they are simply defensive technologies.

While geography is less relevant to the cybersecurity dilemma, technology is more so. Digital technologies, unlike land or sea, are a human creation. It is technology, and indeed the flaws in technology, that makes network intrusions possible in the first place. As detailed by the foregoing discussion of operational practice, such intrusions often rely on vulnerabilities in an adversary's software. These vulnerabilities fall into two categories: zero day vulnerabilities that are previously undiscovered, and other vulnerabilities that have been found and fixed in an updated version of the software.[21] The kind of vulnerability and the way the intruders exploit it has great bearing on whether they will be successful. This discussion assumes that the zero day vulnerability is found in software used by both a state and its potential adversaries; Chapter Eight describes other scenarios in more detail.

As discussed in Chapter Two, zero day exploits provide an advantage because the defenders cannot prepare as much for them. But the advantage gained by collecting zero day exploits is often short-lived and vulnerable. The knowledge of zero days provides little defensive value, provided the state also wants to retain the possibility of using the exploits for intrusions. At most, a state could use that knowledge to ensure that the most important computers over which it has direct or perhaps indirect control are not exploited by the zero day. If the state spreads news of the zero day too widely, however, other states will learn of the vulnerability's existence and defend their networks accordingly. Once the details of the vulnerability have been widely disseminated, much of the unique intrusion value of the zero day—and thus the offensive advantage that goes along with it—is lost. In addition, a state that learns of a zero day but does not use it runs the risk that another state will also find it and exploit it, or that the relevant software vendor will discover it and patch it. Once again, if any of these events occur, the state has squandered the potential offensive opportunity. Thus, all else being equal, states with zero days have an incentive to press their advantage in intrusion while they have it—a spur to action that negatively affects stability.[22]

This discussion may seem to warn of an offense-dominated world in which network intruders are unstoppable and where states act with impunity to collect their adversaries' most valuable information. There is an enormous countervailing factor that constrains the overall role of zero days in network intrusions, however: they are rare and therefore often expensive, in time or resources, to obtain. While the most sophisticated operations, like Stuxnet, have employed up to five zero days—each for a different purpose—these are remarkable outliers.[23] In 2015, for example, there were only fifty-four zero day vulnerabilities used in publicly studied attacks.[24] Thus, while zero days do confer a significant advantage on intruders who have and use them, and while they are more common in operations by some sophisticated actors, they are rare enough that they cannot confer a general benefit on intruding forces writ large.

As discussed, most network breaches rely instead on known vulnerabilities or on the gullibility of users.[25] In the case of known vulnerabilities, the relevant software vendor may have issued a patch, but the target may have failed to apply it. The difficulty in applying patches quickly to complex computer systems means that they often remain vulnerable, even when proper defenses have been designed and deployed elsewhere. Indeed, recently patched zero days can provide information on what vulnerabilities might still be present in unpatched systems. Intruders target zero day vulnerabilities five times as frequently once they become widely known;[26] one study showed that would-be intruders attempted to exploit the top five zero day vulnerabilities of 2013 almost 200,000 times in the thirty days immediately following their public disclosure.[27] Nor is there a shortage of targets running dated software. Many computer systems, even those in high-priority networks, run old operating systems that are more likely to be vulnerable.[28] All told, zero days are not always necessary for intrusion.

Examining the perception of offense–defense balance in cyber operations more generally, other notable sources agree with this offense-dominant perspective. In 2010, then-Deputy Secretary of Defense William Lynn wrote in a much-publicized academic journal article that "In cyberspace, the offense has the upper hand."[29] He contended that this is because of the structure of the internet, which largely does not take maximizing defense as a primary goal. Lynn wrote:

> The Internet was designed to be collaborative and rapidly expandable and to have low barriers to technological innovation; security and identity management were lower priorities. In this view, structural reasons dictate that the U.S. government's ability to defend its networks always lags behind its adversaries' ability to exploit U.S. networks' weaknesses. Adept programmers will find vulnerabilities and overcome security measures put in place to prevent intrusions.[30]

That is, for as long as the security model remains in effect—and there are no signs it is radically shifting—Lynn argues that the intruders will retain an edge.

This perception of offense-dominance seems particularly pronounced among policy-makers.[31] Lynn has developed this view at the most length, but even President Obama has echoed the theme, saying that "Offense is moving faster than defense … [The Internet] was not designed with the expectation that there'd end up being 3 or 4 or 5 billion people doing commercial transactions … they thought this would be an academic network to share papers and formulae."[32] Other advocates for the potency and power of the offense in cyber operations generally include Richard Clarke,[33] the former head of cybersecurity and counterterrorism in the United States, and Joel Brenner,[34] the former United States National Counterintelligence Executive and former Inspector General at the NSA. Both go so far as to paint the threat of cyberwar as real, including vivid portraits of what a cyber attack might look like.[35] Michael Hayden, the former Director of the NSA, uses mitigator-esque language in outlining the offensive advantages: "The inherent geography of this domain … plays to the offense. There's almost nothing inherent in the domain that plays to the defense."[36] Similarly, Chris Inglis, the former Deputy Director of the NSA, remarked that if cyber operations were scored like soccer, each side would net hundreds of goals per half—that is, offense would dominate.[37]

Nor is this offense-dominant view limited to the United States. Some Chinese military writers have also advanced the notion that offensive cyber capabilities can be of great value in conflict, provided states use them quickly and decisively. According to other Chinese thinkers, these offensive capabilities can also contribute to strategic operations, including those with psychological and economic effects.[38] One analyst's summary of the Chinese view sounds quite like the offense-dominant views that armies held in 1914: "Chinese doctrine stresses that striking first and striking hard against the most important networked targets is essential, because victory at the beginning of the war will determine its end."[39]

Even the proponents of defensive capability acknowledge many of the intruders' advantages. Some operational approaches arguing that the defense could someday enjoy the better position proceed from the foundational idea that currently the advantage belongs to the intruders.[40] These advantages of flexibility and initiative enjoyed by the offense are themes also expressed by Richard Bejtlich, a network defense pioneer. Bejtlich observed that intruders can often focus more fully on their tasks while "[d]efenders usually have a lot on their plate besides incident handling."[41] For high-skill intruders, this focus can lead to better familiarity with the code to be exploited. Intruders, he concluded, "may know more about target software and applications than some of the developers who write them, never mind the administrators who deploy them."[42] Bruce Schneier, one of the most quoted sources on cybersecurity, agreed, saying, "We know, on the internet today, that attackers have the advantage ... A sufficiently funded, skilled, motivated adversary will get in."[43] Capable defenders can, with good preparation, information, and creativity, make things harder for intruders, but defenders still face significant challenges.[44]

A minority of scholars argues that cyber operations are defense-dominant. In this group, most offer dissents that are of limited applicability to the cybersecurity dilemma argument. These writers have focused more on the question of whether large-scale cyber attack is possible, rather than on the threats of intrusions more generally.[45] Skeptics deploy terms like "Phantom Menace," "Cyber-Scare," and "Cyber Doom" to highlight the degree to which the threat has been inflated.[46] Their focus on catastrophic cyber attack, however, means that many of the foregoing claims about intruders' advantages in the context of the cybersecurity dilemma emerge unscathed.[47] While some make arguments about the limited economic value of the intelligence collected via network intrusions, they do not offer a case that such intrusions are particularly hard to do, or that the defense operates from an advantageous position in seeking to thwart such collection.[48] All told, it seems fair to conclude that many influential individuals agree that intruders have advantages in current practice and perhaps also long-standing advantages intrinsic to the fundamentals of network technology. Such perceptions of offense-dominance amplify the risks of the cybersecurity dilemma.

## Offense–Defense Differentiation

Even if the offense has the advantage, all hope for mitigation is not lost. A second mitigator variable, the differentiation of offensive and defensive capabilities, also holds significant sway in determining the potency of the security dilemma.[49] Indeed, this differentiation has the capacity to render questions about offense-dominance beside the point. If states cannot use for offense what they use for defense, then the animating tenets of the security dilemma are irrelevant. In such circumstances, a state will be able to secure itself with defensive technologies without unintentionally threatening others.[50] States may still fear the aggression of another, but they will have greater and earlier knowledge of their potential adversary's intent, since the potential adversary will have to make a willful choice in advance to develop obviously offensive capabilities. States that develop only defensive technologies will stand out, enabling cooperation among like-minded security-seeking states.[51]

Indeed, such collaboration among status quo powers could reach the logical—though in practice unlikely—conclusion: arms control of all offensive weapons. President Franklin Roosevelt proposed as much in 1933 at the Geneva Disarmament Conference, suggesting that "If all nations will agree wholly to eliminate from possession and use the weapons which make possible a successful attack, defenses will immediately become impregnable, and the frontiers and independence of every nation will become secure."[52] By mastering offense–defense differentiation, states can mitigate—or even perhaps solve—the security dilemma.

There is a paucity of international agreements that attempt to approach this ideal, even in limited and controlled circumstances, however.[53] Mitigators offer several explanations. The first is that states are not willing to assure the security of other states. The second and more developed explanation is that it is hard to distinguish between offensive and defensive weapons and that even states seeking stability could see some degree of utility in offensive weapons. Such states might fear that the offense–defense balance is greatly tilted towards the offense (in which case equivalent defensive procurement could be prohibitively expensive), they might want offensive capabilities as insurance, or they might need offensive weapons to aid an attacked ally.[54]

As far as offense–defense differentiation in cyber operations is concerned, there is first the question of whether or not purely defensive mechanisms exist. The answer is unmistakably yes. Entire suites of security products function solely within the province of a given computer network or on a given computer. These include firewalls, antivirus scanners, user account management software, software patches, authentication mechanisms, and much more. They have little utility outside of one's own virtual territory and provide no mechanisms for breaching another computer network. They are the essential fortifications of the digital world. It is almost always good practice to deploy them and to keep them up to date.

The next category of tools is only somewhat more complex to analyze. A sizable number of forensic mechanisms for gathering information are of great utility when deployed on a friendly network. When combined with the defenses described above, these pieces of software partially enable what Chapter Three calls active defense or hunting. The goal is to set up a secure network perimeter, then look assiduously within that border for anomalous network and computer activity. These forensic tools make that search easier and more effective. They have some offensive utility, insofar as intruders could use some of them within an adversary's networks to look for valuable information or to move laterally. Most tools in this category do not exploit vulnerabilities and cannot enable intrusions into other networks on their own, with the exception of penetration testing tools.

Yet, as previously noted, even actively looking within their own networks for intrusions is often not enough for states. In order to enhance its own security, a state can conduct intelligence operations in potential adversary networks and in the networks of neutral third parties. In such cases, it will often exploit vulnerabilities to gain entry. According to one definition, the code to do this or to gather information from networks might seem demonstrably offensive, insofar as it involves intruding without authorization into the computer systems of others. But, under another definition, the code might seem defensive, in that it is sometimes in furtherance of a defensive mission.[55] Without reference to particular capabilities, President Obama acknowledged this ambiguity. He said, "This is more like basketball than football, in the sense that there's no clear line between offense and defense. Things are going back and forth all the time." In security dilemma-esque language, he added, "when you develop sufficient defenses, the same sophistication you need for defenses means that, potentially, you can engage in offense."[56]

At first glance, this haziness is not a problem. A weapon-based paradigm accepts that some capabilities might be offensive or defensive, depending on how an actor uses them. Analogously, to determine whether an intrusion is offensive or defensive, the intruders' actions after gaining access matter most. If they start to attack, or even prepare to do damage, the intrusion is more clearly offensive. If they look for valuable economic information or some kinds of counterintelligence secrets, the intrusion might seem offensive in a different way. If the intruders just gather narrow tactical intelligence to feed into their own intrusion detection systems in pursuit of better defenses, a mitigator would probably not consider the intrusion offensive.

It is here that the mitigators' paradigm breaks down when applied to the cybersecurity dilemma. That paradigm relies on the widely shared notion that offensive technologies are threatening and defensive ones are much less so. As the previous chapter shows, however, while some intrusions are not offensive, they are still nonetheless threatening, for a variety of reasons. Even if a state has managed to conclude that a particular intrusion is solely defensive in nature—something that it is unlikely to do authoritatively—the presence of a potential adversary in the network still poses a threat for the future. Indeed, the intrusion is threatening in a variety of ways that the traditional defensive technologies envisioned by mitigators, such as mines and fortifications, simply are not. The nature of an intrusion can change with a state's intention. As a result, even if states could increase offense–defense differentiation, it would not provide lasting reassurance in interpreting intrusions. Once offensive capabilities and threatening capabilities are no longer synonymous, much of the value of mitigations seeking to sharpen offense–defense differentiation fades away.

## Greed

A third mitigator variable is greed. The relationship between greedy states—that is, those that seek to disrupt the status quo in a way that benefits them, even if they are already secure—and the security dilemma is widely debated in international relations. According to mitigator logic, "In a world of pure security seekers, the security dilemma helps solve a basic puzzle—that even when states have compatible, benign goals, there is competition and conflict."[57] If the states involved, or some meaningful fraction of them, are greedy, perhaps there is not the need for the security dilemma logic after all. In such circumstances, the conflict is likely just a result of the greedy states' actions.[58] For mitigators, the intentions of a state are deeply important.

States can use at least three possible methods to signal their non-threatening intentions to others. One approach is to try to come to arms control agreements with the other states. Such agreements, particularly those that limit offensive weapons, signal a willingness to constrain the possibility of offensive action. The signaling value of signing arms control agreements may have benefits that extend beyond the practical restraints that such agreements impose.[59] Such signaling could indicate a peace-seeking approach, since a greedy state is more likely to pursue offensive missions and capabilities and avoid limits on their development.[60]

Another possibility is to adopt a policy oriented entirely towards defense, opting for a defensive doctrine even as adversaries assume more offensive postures. When the offense has the advantage, and when it is therefore more cost-efficient to develop offensive capabilities, this build-up of defenses can be an expensive proposition. In such circumstances, the state will have to spend more on defense to balance out its counterparts' offensive spending. Nonetheless, there can be strong signaling value in undertaking this added expense. The state is showing that it is so committed to stability and security that it is willing to devote additional resources to protecting its security in a non-threatening way.[61]

A final approach is counterintuitive. The state may adopt a posture of unilateral restraint. To do this, the state will, as a means of signaling, intentionally limit its military might to levels insufficient for defense and deterrence.[62] This might be particularly useful on the tactical level, in an attempt to prompt a similar sort of restraint from the adversary. It might lead to a virtuous cycle of growing de-escalation.[63] The net effect is that the state communicates a commitment to improving relations and not showing greed. There is an obvious risk, which dissuades many states from trying this approach: a potential adversary may well sense weakness and attempt to take advantage. That can make confrontation more, not less, likely.[64]

Overall, the greater the greediness of states, the less value these signaling policies have. Indeed, the greater the number of greedy states, the less useful the security dilemma construct becomes. When greed is rampant, states are pursuing competition and conflict not out of fear and insecurity inadvertently caused by another state, but out of a desire to attain a greater position. In such circumstances, pursuing any of the preceding three policy prescriptions is quite risky. Greedy states may perceive other states seeking arms control or practicing unilateral restraint as lacking resolve. While adopting unilateral defense may provide some security, it reduces a state's ability to deter its potential adversaries, since the state lacks offensive weapons with which to counterattack.[65]

Applying this logic to the cybersecurity dilemma, it is difficult to establish how many greedy states exist. For example, supporters of the United States intelligence collection programs contend that those efforts, though at times vast, focus on responding to threats. These include terrorism, political instability, and economic risk. These supporters would note as well that, while the United States has targeted foreign companies with network intrusions, there are no examples of it using the acquired information to benefit specific American corporations—a sign of restraint not practiced by many other states.[66] On the other hand, critics allege that the United States is excessive in its operations,[67] that it gathers and stores much more data than is necessary,[68] and targets innocent third parties in the pursuit of its intelligence.[69] To those holding these views, the United States is greedy and excessive, rather than oriented towards stability.

As interesting as this debate might be, it seems largely beside the point. The proposed signaling mitigations do not translate well to cybersecurity, even if the system is not characterized by greed. Under the best of circumstances, in which every state seeks only its own security, most of the greed-related mitigations do not have the same value in cyber operations. Arms control is a widely discussed subject in cybersecurity, but it is difficult to imagine a verifiable arms control regime.[70] If it is not possible to verify that other states are following the agreements, and if there are lower barriers to entry in developing capabilities, arms control accords are not very reassuring, although there may be still some signaling value if a state is willing to engage in negotiations.

Unilateral lowering of defensive capability is of limited signaling value in cybersecurity. The baseline of cybersecurity defensive practice is already too low and many intrusions are enabled by obvious security oversights on the part of defenders. As a result, it is difficult for states to know if others' weaker defenses are part of a signaling mechanism. States could promise not to perform some kinds of activities, such as intruding in other networks for defensive purposes. This may be a confidence-building measure, but it may also be hard to verify without intrusions of one's own. Again, the challenge of verification—proving a negative—is significant. Further, any meaningful lowering of cyber-security defenses risks vulnerability to attack. Unlike in traditional security dilemma formulations, in cyber operations the attack might come from non-state actors as well as from other states. These non-state actors render security dilemma calculations, and signaling in general, more complex.[71]

In cybersecurity, a state may pursue a policy of unilaterally strong defense. But this too is of mostly limited effectiveness as a method of signaling. On the one hand, deploying additional defensive technologies, such as firewalls and intrusion detection systems, makes a state less vulnerable to attack without threatening others. Hiring skilled security practitioners can serve a similar function, though other states may fear that those practitioners could turn their skills to intrusion without much public notice. But the forms of advanced defense that will require reconnaissance and penetration of foreign networks are once again problematic, because it is difficult to distinguish these defensive-minded penetrations from other kinds of more malicious intrusions. When such differentiation is a challenge, unilateral defense loses its effectiveness. All three of the mitigators' previously proposed signaling mitigations regarding greed are therefore of limited value in cybersecurity, even under the best of circumstances.

### Unit-Level Analysis

Unit-level analysis is a final mitigator variable worth exploring. Within the context of international relations literature, the basic unit is frequently the state. Scholars focusing on the structure of the international system often do not delve too deeply into the particulars of a given state. They instead examine its position, particularly regarding power, relative to other states.[72] Some international relations theories, however, do look at the unit level, particularly those theories that consider the importance of internal economic and political systems. Introducing a similar level of analysis to the cybersecurity dilemma concept might provide insights and a mechanism for mitigation; it has previously proven useful in past analysis of the conventional security dilemma.[73]

Resolving uncertainty is at the core of this proposed mitigation. If a state can know with certainty that its potential adversary seeks only to provide for its own security, not to harm others, then the security dilemma is much less of a problem. When structural variables such as offense–defense balance and offense–defense differentiation are not sufficient to mitigate the dilemma, and when signaling mechanisms are also not sufficient to demonstrate intentions, knowledge of the other state may help to fill the gap.[74] If a state could obtain information about a potential adversary indicating a willingness to avoid conflict, this might reduce uncertainty.[75]

One example of this kind of analysis is most prominent: Democratic Peace Theory observes that democracies are much less likely to go to war with each other. If a democracy's decision-makers believe that this theory holds true, they should be less concerned about the development or deployment of military capabilities by a fellow democracy.[76] In addition, the decision-making process of a democracy is often more public, perhaps especially around decisions to go to war, and may further clarify intentions.[77] States that are more democratic, open, and transparent in their decision-making might therefore be able to mitigate the security dilemma better, at least with each other.

Yet taking this kind of analysis too far can in fact amplify the risk of unwanted escalation. For example, unit-level analysis can give a democratic state too much self-confidence. It may assume that other states see it as it sees itself. The democracy might think that others can interpret the machinations of its political, military, and intelligence apparatuses in an accurate way, understanding its true intentions more fully as a result. The democracy may believe that other states know that it seeks only security. It may therefore feel free to pursue policies that it would otherwise avoid due to fears of animating the security dilemma. In fact, the other states may fear the democracy just as they would fear an authoritarian state, or they may not understand it. This kind of misunderstanding was sometimes visible during the Cold War, in which United States policy-makers did not always appreciate the Soviet fear of American aggression.[78]

Unit-level mitigations also seem unlikely to overcome the cyber-security dilemma. Democratic Peace Theory applies to democracies and conflict, but there is little evidence that it also holds true for intelligence collection or for network intrusions. Indeed, the United States has developed some of the most advanced cyber capabilities in partnership with its four major democratic signals intelligence partners. Upon publication, these actions have prompted sometimes sharp protest from many other states, including democratic allies not included in the Five Eyes.[79] As a result, it seems incorrect to say that status as a democracy provides much reassurance to other states when it comes to cybersecurity.[80] If anything, some Five Eyes activity may be an example of overreach, in which the group failed to appreciate how other states might receive its actions once they became public.

Unlike the decision to go to war, which in the United States and other democracies is often subject to announcement by the head of government and approval by the legislature, the authorization of network intrusions is usually much more secret. Often, these operations are highly classified.[81] This is frequently with good reason, as the intrusions often serve to gather covert intelligence or prepare for a future conflict, and can be threatening to others if uncovered. While these operations are not without some legislative, executive, or judicial oversight, such oversight is often conducted out of public view.

In the United States, for example, the Intelligence Committees in Congress frequently hold closed sessions, many of the relevant presidential Executive Orders (such as Presidential Policy Directive 20, discussed in the last chapter) are highly classified, and the court that oversees some of the activity meets in secret. When cases reach open court, the government often invokes a state secrets privilege to protect sources and methods. To some degree, journalists will amend their reports in consultation with the government to protect ongoing or possible future operations, somewhat limiting the transparency that comes from even large intelligence leaks.[82] Such secrecy can be quite effective. As one very significant Kaspersky Lab study of American operations shows, sometimes intrusion capabilities can be in active use for more than a decade before reaching the light of day.[83] But that public disclosure came about not through unit-level processes, but by the diligent work of security researchers. All told, there is thus far less encouraging evidence of mitigations to the cybersecurity dilemma made possible by unit-level analysis.

## Conclusion: Reaffirmation, Not Mitigation

This chapter has presented previously successful mitigations to the security dilemma. In light of the above analysis, it can be tempting to dismiss the work of well-known mitigators as irrelevant to the cybersecurity dilemma or as old ideas without modern salience. This would be a mistake. Offense–defense balance and offense–defense differentiation are variables still worthy of consideration when it comes to network intrusions. They indicate that the cybersecurity dilemma is severe. Many practitioners perceive cyber operations to be offense-dominant, and it is hard to tell defensive intrusions from offensive ones. It is the traditional mitigations, such as the use of natural and artificial geography, which do not translate well. Few such workable equivalents, with the appropriate self-limiting effects, have been widely deployed in network security—although Chapter Eight offers some new possibilities.

The same is true of greed and unit-level analysis. These latter two variables similarly confirm the dangers of the cybersecurity dilemma. This chapter did not resolve whether or not states are greedy in their network intrusions. The perception of greed and the confounding problem of non-state actors seem strong enough to make many of the signaling mitigations too risky. For unit-level analysis, not only is the potential mitigation of Democratic Peace Theory and similar ideas less relevant to intelligence operations, but it also appears that the Five Eyes group may have at times miscalculated.

Based on the preceding discussion, the overall conclusion is easily apparent. The variables advanced by security dilemma theorists, while helpful in yielding mitigations in other contexts, in cybersecurity only reaffirm the problem. But before the hunt can continue for solutions, it is worth considering the ways in which the cybersecurity dilemma might be more complex than the traditional security dilemma. Chapter Six handles that task.

6

# INFORMATION DISTRIBUTION
# AND THE STATUS QUO

*Overview*

Five anecdotes have opened the previous five chapters: the U-2 mission gone wrong during the Cuban Missile Crisis; the NITRO ZEUS contingency plan for a broad cyber attack against Iran; the American efforts to gain intelligence on the Chinese hackers in BYZANTINE CANDOR; the foregoing network intrusions that enabled Stuxnet; and the dilemma in which President Roosevelt found himself, unable to convince the British and the Germans that they need not fear one another. These mini-narratives have shown how the security dilemma has emerged in various forms.

The importance of gathering and conveying credible information appears in all of these cases. The U-2 incident, NITRO ZEUS, BYZANTINE CANDOR, and the preparations for Stuxnet were all efforts to acquire intelligence to enable offensive options or to enhance a state's security. The British and the Germans each failed to convey credible reassurance to the other. The role of information is at the core of international politics, driving competition and impacting security.

A second theme emerges: the importance of a status quo. The accidental U-2 invasion nearly caused conflict because it violated mutually held understandings about state sovereignty that had long limited aggressive behavior. Stuxnet rose to prominence because it represented a new paradigm for cyber attacks; NITRO ZEUS could possibly have extended that even further. The NSA's operation against BYZANTINE CANDOR covertly attempted to thwart ongoing Chinese intelligence collection, reasserting a status quo on American terms. Roosevelt's dilemma mattered because he saw how Europe's ordinary way of doing business risked a slide towards war.

In the canonical security dilemma discussion, these two themes are often implicit. The original concept usually assumes that states have access to quality information about capabilities but not intentions of other states. When one state makes a decision to develop or deploy a capability, the other states learn of it with enough time to interpret it and, if they choose, make a countervailing decision. Similarly, the model assumes that a status quo—some baseline of expected state behavior—exists. This status quo is the broader context in which policy-makers must make decisions. It includes the conditions and dominant understandings when states confront the security dilemma. Deviations from this status quo, through the development or deployment of new capabilities, cause the dilemma of interpretation and risk escalation.

This chapter argues that these assumptions about information distribution and the status quo need greater nuance when it comes to cybersecurity. When these ideas are more fully examined, it emerges that the cybersecurity dilemma is in some respects more complex to mitigate than the security dilemma. Information distribution and the status quo are not constants in cybersecurity, but are better viewed as variables. As with the variables outlined in the last chapter, they can often increase the cybersecurity dilemma's dangers, but may also sometimes provide opportunities for mitigation.

To make this argument, this chapter works in a fashion somewhat divergent from the previous one. Rather than revolving around texts that explicate mitigator possibilities, it instead focuses on what is left mostly unsaid. The first section considers information distribution. It outlines why simplifying postulates that worked well in previous contexts do not have the same value in cybersecurity. The inequality in information distribution in part increases the severity of the cybersecurity dilemma. The second section focuses on the status quo. Drawing on history, it shows how new technologies can complicate interpretation and cause instability. Once a new disruptive technology emerges, states need time to devise understandings of mutually acceptable behavior. The second half of this section examines the nascent status quo in cyber operations.

The chapter's conclusion contends that, in the process of moving from the security dilemma to the cybersecurity dilemma, practitioners and scholars must replace these assumptions with more nuanced considerations. Removing the suppositions regarding information distribution and the status quo reflects the additional difficulty that states have in navigating the cybersecurity dilemma. With fewer constants and more ambiguity, mitigation becomes harder still.

*Information Distribution*

In general, the utility of information has at least two components: timeliness and quality. In intelligence and military affairs, the timeliness of information is critical. If a state learns of a potential adversary's arms build-up after it is too late to do anything about it, that information is demonstrably less valuable than if a state obtains it years in advance. But the quality of the information is similarly vital. If information is wrong, vague, or incomplete, then it has little or even negative operational and strategic value. The challenge for intelligence officials is providing warning to policy-makers early enough to be useful and late enough to be credible and specific—a daunting problem.[1]

In past articulations of the security dilemma, however, this difficulty is mostly ignored in favor of a simpler model in which information about capabilities is overt and decisions are transparent. The security dilemma logic makes three assumptions regarding information about capabilities: states learn of the procurement or deployment decisions of other states not long after those decisions are made; the time from decision to effect is lengthy; and the characteristics of the developed or deployed capabilities are visible to other states.[2]

Although weapons are of course not always fully transparent, there was good reason historically to rely on these assumptions and use a simpler model. States in relatively close proximity are more likely to have knowledge of one another. Physical weapons can often take a great deal of time to develop and deploy. Strategic surprise attacks are comparatively rare. Indeed many strategic surprise attacks, such as the attack on Pearl Harbor, utilize overt and acknowledged capabilities; the surprise in a surprise attack is more often in the attack's technique or timing than its means or ends.[3]

Furthermore, security dilemmas of any sort require some degree of transparency. The concept would not apply if states could develop or deploy capabilities in an entirely covert fashion. If states knew that they had no good means of obtaining quality information on the decisions and behavior of others, they could not be reasonably threatened by the information they did uncover, as they would know it was unreliable. States in a position of such ignorance would still face potential risks, as other states may still seek their destruction, but the details of those risks would be largely unknowable. With no credible knowledge, states do not know what to fear. This leads to a fear of its own, but a different and less specific kind than the sort described in the security dilemma. Put simply, without at least some information, there is no dilemma of interpretation and thus no security dilemma.

Similarly, security dilemmas of all types require that capabilities be at least somewhat slow to develop and deploy relative to the speed with which states obtain information.[4] If states could easily build and use capabilities, they could rapidly obtain their own capabilities when it was clear that an attack was imminent. But if capabilities take longer to acquire, it means that a state must interpret the actions of others and decide on a response far enough in advance, and therefore with much less information, to assure that it has sufficient time to build its own arsenal. Thus, the timeliness of information relative to the speed at which capabilities develop and deploy is an essential factor. If there is no prospect for timely information, there is once again no dilemma of interpretation and thus no security dilemma.

Comparatively slow-developing and transparent capabilities also make offense–defense differentiation a powerful mitigating factor. If a state can determine early on that its potential adversary's technologies are defensive, the state draws reassurance from the fact that it will take a fair amount of time for the adversary to build new and different offensive capabilities. If states could quickly develop and deploy offensive capabilities or quickly convert defensive capabilities to offensive ones, offense–defense differentiation would be vastly less comforting. Likewise, if a state determines that a potential adversary is starting to build offensive capabilities, the length of the development process gives the state a window in which to ready its own countermeasures. The processes through which states develop and deploy capabilities, plus the information that states learn about other states' processes, are thus at the center of both the traditional security dilemma and its mitigations.

A spectrum of information utility could be imagined, with no credible or timely information on the left end of the spectrum and plentiful credible and timely information on the right end.[5] The dilemma of interpretation is most severe in the middle region of the spectrum. In this region, the information is reasonably credible, such that it could plausibly form the basis of action. Nevertheless, in this part of the spectrum states have limits on what they know regarding others' capabilities and very severe limits on their knowledge of others' intentions. Likewise, this information is timely enough to be useful, but does not provide enough time for states to gather more decisive information.

In the construct of the traditional security dilemma, states are substantially to the right of this dangerous central zone of the spectrum. While they have no knowledge of the intentions of other states, the security dilemma concept usually assumes that they have complete and timely knowledge of the decisions and capabilities of other states. The possibility of surprise attack with covert capabilities is therefore completely ruled out. The only risk facing states is that they will draw the wrong conclusions about others' intentions when given information about their decisions and developments. Regarding capabilities, the problem is one of potential misinterpretation, not missing information.

But the circumstances of the cybersecurity dilemma tend to position states more firmly in the dangerous middle of the spectrum.[6] When it comes to the development and use of cyber capabilities, states in general have baseline information that is less specific, less complete, and less timely. An example of information that is not operationally valuable comes from the rhetoric that states have employed about their cyber forces. Many states have made no secret of their sizable investments in cyber operations capabilities. The United States has announced the creation of its military's Cyber Command and its intention to hire and train thousands of people to staff it.[7] The United Kingdom, China, Iran, and many others have all alluded to their own investments.[8] But no state wants to disclose too much specific information, especially about intrusion capabilities. In the absence of more credible details, states have a hard time sorting out genuine threats worth addressing from posturing that is safely ignored.

Sometimes, reasonably specific information about state capabilities does enter the public domain. The Snowden revelations are an obvious example of this. At times, the information contained within the published documents was specific, revealing strong tradecraft and particular techniques that had previously only been the work of theory. For example, certain documents disclosed what appears to be a significant American effort to weaken cryptographic standards and bypass encryption implementations.[9] The documents indicate that the United States spends hundreds of millions of dollars annually targeting encryption procedures and methods. Despite a few reasonably narrow exceptions, however, the published files did not identify specific algorithms or procedures that the NSA had compromised.[10] The documents sowed concern but did not enable other states to improve their own particular means of encryption in response.

Cybersecurity companies can also put specific operational information into the public domain. These private sector analyses of malicious code further reveal capabilities, sometimes in great detail and in a way that aids defenders. But—through no fault of the companies—occasionally these reports can do more to spark fears than they do to provide lasting reassurance. As discussed, in 2015 Kaspersky Lab disclosed that the NSA has the capacity to target the firmware of hard drives.[11] In effect, penetrating the firmware of a device would give the intruders a persistent presence on a victim's computer that is extremely difficult to detect and remove. Virtually all tools at the operating system level are unable to spot malicious code buried underneath.[12] The Kaspersky conclusion, which appears credible and well-researched, therefore animates concern about undetectable intruders. Its net effect is to arouse greater suspicion—making it harder for a state or organization to disprove the presence of an adversary in its networks—but as yet there is no corresponding means of addressing those concerns.

While the Snowden leaks may have increased fear of a known actor, the NSA, other information can create new fears entirely. In 2014, for example, Kaspersky Lab unveiled Careto, or "The Mask," a cyber espionage operation that affected computers in thirty-one countries.[13]

Although the researchers did not attribute the campaign to a specific actor, one of the most surprising features of the malicious code was the presence of significant Spanish language artifacts. At a time when most of the public discussion revolved around suspected American, Russian, and Chinese activities, it may have taken many states by surprise that Spanish-speaking actors were also conducting operations. The Kaspersky report, which included a fair amount of specific detail on indicators of compromise, seems to have revealed a group's previously covert capabilities and hinted at the possibility of future threats from a new actor.

The indicators of compromise that Kaspersky revealed about Careto were quite useful in detecting ongoing intrusions. But they were likely less relevant for future ones. Assuming that the actor changes its infrastructure and techniques, the report does little of significant lasting value to help defenders detect a forthcoming piece of malicious code from the Spanish-speaking organization. It thus gives enough information to raise future fears about an intrusion from a new threat and to raise the costs of operation for that actor, but does not provide enough information to provide long-term reassurance.

This same dynamic holds more generally for most private sector analyses on malicious groups. These reports often include large amounts of specific detail of significant value in detecting ongoing operations, including long lists of indicators of compromise. Even a very partial list of notable documents of this sort, at least some of which concern groups that are likely state-sponsored, is sizable: APT1,[14] APT30,[15] Putter Panda,[16] Cloud Atlas,[17] Elderwood,[18] and Equation[19] are just a few examples. However, assuming the group in question changes its techniques, exploits, and infrastructure—which the best actors do, though the response to scrutiny does vary by group[20]—those indicators of compromise will be of diminishing value. The knowledge that the potential adversary exists and has some measure of operational capabilities will persist, as will the fear of those capabilities. The ability to anticipate and blunt the capabilities based on the published information, however, fades with time after the report's publication.

Detection therefore remains a significant and ongoing challenge, even for states with well-developed capabilities. To recapitulate briefly, the average time from intrusion to detection is more than a hundred days. In a large percentage of cases the detection is not uncovered by the penetrated organization, but rather by a third party. Intruders can make entry to large networks in a myriad of ways, including using social engineering, spotting technical oversights, and relying on physical devices. Zero day exploits render many signature-based efforts insufficient and mean that detection is harder still. Anticipating that an adversary might intrude is straightforward enough; finding a specific intrusion from a sophisticated adversary is vastly more challenging without detailed intelligence.

All this has a two-part effect. On one hand, states recognize the risks and threats. They see the public domain information about cyber operations and they understand, to varying degrees, the attempts against their own networks. States know that the threats they face are more than theoretical possibilities, but instead concrete and real. On the other hand, well-informed states acknowledge the difficulty in detection and the limitations of their own baseline defensive efforts, even efforts that involve actively hunting for malicious code. These states understand, at least internally, the constraints on what they can know and the difficulty of assuring themselves that their networks are free of intruders. As a result, in some ways they are knowledgeable enough to be fearful, but overall not so knowledgeable or capable that they can fully subdue the fear.

The pace at which states can develop cyber capabilities is also relevant. Some observers have argued there is a lower barrier to entry in cyber operations—a subject largely beyond the scope of this work.[21] As a generalization, effective cyber capabilities are sometimes time-consuming to develop. They are also, as the intrusion model showed, somewhat time-consuming to deploy unless states perform key steps in advance. This is likely especially in the case when a state builds capabilities internally, trains its own operators, and does not leverage already-existing tools. Even when there is a significant headstart, building capabilities at scale can be a substantial and somewhat lengthy effort. For example, the United States established Cyber Command in 2009 but expects that it will take almost a decade to staff fully.[22]

On the other hand, capabilities are not so slow-developing that states should get complacent in their security if other states seem to lag. NSA analyses indicate, for example, that Iran built up its cyber operations forces faster than many had previously anticipated.[23] Private sector reports confirm this assessment.[24] Iran caught up in part through financial investment, but also by careful observation of operations conducted against it. While there is no evidence that the country is nearly as advanced as the United States or China in its capabilities, it has carried out some reasonably effective operations. These include destructive attacks against Aramco and Sands Casino—efforts that would likely have been out of Iranian reach just a few years prior.

In short, the speed of capability development—which directly affects the timeliness of information—is also firmly in the dangerous middle zone of the spectrum. States do not develop cyber capabilities so quickly that they can afford to let others gain a significant headstart in their development or use. A failure to keep pace is manifestly undesirable for a state that aspires to have credible operational options. Yet capabilities are not developed so slowly that states can be confident that, just because a potential adversary has not made significant progress or investment, it will remain impotent for the foreseeable future. States therefore have an incentive to make regular attempts to determine the operational sophistication and signatures of other states, especially because those capabilities are otherwise largely hidden from view.

These points about the challenges of specificity, completeness, and timeliness in information distribution lead to a crucial distinction: in the security dilemma model, all states get access to the same information about other states, but in the cybersecurity dilemma construct, the quality and availability of the information vary by state. Some states will have access to more credible and timelier information than others. Information distribution depends in part on states' intelligence apparatuses, their investments, and their actions. A state's increased access to valuable information—in effect, moving itself rightwards on the information utility spectrum while leaving others in the dangerous middle—can become a competitive advantage over other states with less information.

This advantage can be something akin to the application of the security dilemma to intelligence. A state with greater access to credible and timely information will identify potential threats earlier, deploy countermeasures more effectively, and have more confidence in its own security. A state with less useful information will remain prone to surprise attack, have less conviction in its ability to perceive threats, and be more fearful. Under any security dilemma logic, the more fearful a state is of external threats, the more likely it is that it will be involved in damaging conflict even if it genuinely does not seek war.

Thus the second pillar of the cybersecurity dilemma, derived from the network defense model, once again warrants emphasis: a key way for states to acquire more operational and more timely information about their potential adversaries' cyber capabilities is through network intrusions into the important networks of those potential adversaries. Well-targeted intrusions can uncover other states' capabilities, gather information that can inform countermeasures, and provide early warning of future operations by potential foes. Even narrowly targeted intrusions into the right networks can obtain specific information of future value. More intrusive and more widespread penetrations into communication networks that serve a potential adversary's decision-makers and strategic planners can shed still further light, hinting at intentions as well as capabilities. All told, by actively using their intrusion capabilities to shape information distribution well in advance of conflict, states can minimize their fear and increase their security.

And yet, the third pillar of the cybersecurity dilemma also emerges once more: the intrusions through which states can gain more information are often in and of themselves inherently threatening, even if they are for defensive purposes. Strategic-level intrusions that shed light on a state's intentions and overarching priorities are directly threatening to that state. But narrowly targeted intrusions that serve only defensive aims are also threatening. Any state suffering an intrusion to an important network will possibly fear that it is a potential precursor to powerful targeted attack, a beachhead for future (potentially as yet unplanned) operations, and a cause for significant counterintelligence concern. The result is apparent: once information becomes a variable instead of a constant, states need to compete for better access to it. But, in the cybersecurity dilemma, their means of doing this—the way in which they alleviate their own fears—only makes the system-wide danger more acute.

*An Uncertain Status Quo*

The security dilemma is about what happens before conflict. Implicit in the discussion is a baseline that is at least somewhat stable until one state or another begets the dilemma by deviating—or appearing to deviate—from it. This baseline is the status quo, or the existing state of affairs. A status quo, by definition, serves to divide all possible activities into one of two categories: those that are acceptable and adhere to the status quo, and those that are unacceptable and do not. Which activities fall into which category depends first on the particulars of each status quo. What is natural and accepted for one status quo might be destabilizing in another. For example, a long-standing status quo permits the United States to have many armed agents on the Mexican border. The creation of a similarly large and equipped presence on the United States' boundary with Canada would be a departure from the status quo.

The clarity and definition of a status quo also varies tremendously by case. Sometimes, often in more highly contested situations or with more sensitive topics, states define the status quo meticulously. Bilateral or multilateral negotiations often agree on means of verification for all involved parties to ensure compliance. Frequently, however, the status quo is more implicit, emerging over time as a natural equilibrium. Sometimes this type of status quo is quite stable, drawing on a reservoir of trust between the involved states and requiring no formal agreement. At other times, this type of status quo can be piecemeal and tense, even if it is successful. A prominent example of this latter kind is the Concert of Europe, an informal arrangement among the leading nineteenth-century European powers to meet regularly to establish acceptable behavior and resolve disputes.[25] A security relationship between any two states is likely to be a combination of status quos of various types on various issues.

Status quos do not imply inertness. On the contrary, actions can be part of the status quo. For example, regular troop exercises and mobilizations of a certain size may adhere to a status quo, as might certain kinds of weapons tests or weapon development. It is not the activities themselves that matter most, but other states' interpretation of those activities. Once a state takes an action that might represent a potential deviation from the status quo, and once other states learn about that action, the other states need to decide how they will view it. This, once more, is the dilemma of interpretation. If these other states perceive the action as a threat to their security, they can choose to respond forcefully, contesting the action and seeking to restore the old status quo. Alternatively, the other states might view the original action as benign. By not responding to it, or by signaling reassurance, they implicitly or explicitly acquiesce to a new status quo.

Sorting out which category a particular action falls into—obviously non-threatening, defensive but potentially misinterpreted, and offensive—is often a challenge. But it is less of a challenge when the status quo involves technologies that are already understood well by all the involved states. As mentioned in the last chapter, the Washington Naval Treaty is a prime example of the security dilemma and its mitigations in action. The treaty also serves as an example of established technologies contributing to a stable and explicit status quo. The agreement attempted to ensure a stable equilibrium for the future by utilizing geography and the common understanding of the powers and limitations of the then-current naval technologies.[26] The treaty was undone in part by the eventual development of new forces, in particular aircraft carriers, which could travel and project power farther and in new ways. When all parties understood the capabilities, policy-makers were able to construct a status quo to account for them. But as disruptive capabilities emerged, the status quo broke down and the security dilemma returned in greater force. Similarly, when states deploy well-understood technologies in new ways, the status quo can also fracture.[27]

Nuclear weapons are another instance of a new technology upending a status quo, with varying reactions. While large numbers of ground or naval troops had fought previous wars, the potential for strategic attack and strategic vulnerability characterized the post-World War II era. States differed on how to approach these new concepts. President Eisenhower suggested the Open Skies Treaty in 1955. Under the proposed treaty, each state declared its strategic bases and then permitted other states to fly over its borders to enable verification. For their part, the Soviets had a different vision—in part probably informed by the fact that they already understood the United States' strategic capabilities—and rejected the idea.[28] Not until decades later, when nuclear fears had moderated somewhat and a common understanding was easier to achieve, did the two sides sign the treaty.

Alongside the formal and slow-burning Open Skies process, the scholarship of the early decades of the Cold War shows how an implicit status quo can develop, still somewhat slowly, around a new technology.

Concerned about the possibilities of nuclear war—even a nuclear war desired by neither side—scholars sought to clarify what a stable and achievable status quo might look like. They used theory to help outline, in view of policy-makers on both sides, potential roles for nuclear weapons. They also explored limits on the weapons' strategic effectiveness. Some of this work, by Thomas Schelling, was so useful in advancing common understanding and fostering stability that it earned the Nobel Prize.[29] Schelling also received the "Award for Behavioral Research Relevant to the Prevention of Nuclear War"—a clear link between his articulations of strategic possibilities and the successful development of a peaceful nuclear status quo.[30]

There is a key exception to this trend of slow adaptation, however. Sometimes a new technology emerges and before too long all the involved parties share the same beliefs about how the technology will or should be used. This can lead to a reasonably quick incorporation into the status quo. For example, during the Cold War, the anti-ballistic missile was a weapon that was demonstrably defensive. This would ordinarily look as if it would increase stability, but the status quo of nuclear deterrence functioned differently. A defensive technology that could thwart a retaliatory strike unsettled policy-makers, as it could make a strategic first strike more palatable. Both the United States and the Soviet Union were simultaneously working on anti-ballistic missiles in the late 1960s, and American leaders first proposed the idea of banning the missiles in 1967. Soviet decision-makers initially rejected it. Yet as the technology developed further and the possibilities and dangers became clearer, the two sides concluded that they should ban the deployment of anti-ballistic missiles. They signed the treaty in 1972 and preserved it past the demise of the Soviet Union.[31]

Cybersecurity has nothing approaching such a consensus. The beginnings of a status quo, best expressed by four principles of agreements at the United Nations, are only just emerging.[32] These agreements represent the result of years of international engagement and are the strongest foundation for future international consensus. Even so, international negotiators are still working on some very fundamental questions about the intersection of statecraft and cyber operations. The agreements represent signs of early progress, but none offers any immediate hope of a status quo that overcomes the cybersecurity dilemma.

The first principle is the most general: international law applies to cyberspace. In a major report issued in 2013, a group of twenty United Nations member states, including the United States, China, and Russia, agreed on this norm.[33] While seemingly bland, this idea contains several important implications. When international law applies to cyberspace, traditional notions of the rights and responsibilities of states also carry over. One analysis of the agreement spelled out some of these obligations, noting that "In cyberspace, states have to comply with the prohibition on the use of force, the requirement to respect territorial sovereignty and independence, and the principle of settling disputes by peaceful means in the same way as in the physical world."[34] When confronted with an armed attack, states also have the right to self-defense. This includes the use of force, provided they exercise it in accordance with the principles of international humanitarian law.

On the one hand, it was an important first step that the group achieved consensus.[35] Although a range of states have made proposals in various different international bodies dating back to the 1990s, few have gained traction.[36] Some agreements that did win approval, such as the Council of Europe's Convention on Cybercrime, lacked the support of key powerful states like China and Russia. Overcoming barriers to reach consensus, even if only on a general principle, is potentially the strongest indication yet that a mutually agreeable and stable shared status quo in cybersecurity is someday possible.

States have much to do to operationalize the agreement, however. The text does not provide precise definitions for key terms, such as armed attack, and leaves many additional areas to flesh out. To remedy this, a group of international law specialists produced guidance called the Tallinn Manual, which seeks to offer further detail and recommendations on how states can follow their obligations under international law in cyberspace.[37] The Tallinn Manual is also nonetheless limited in scope and power. Most significantly, it is non-binding and focuses mostly on destructive cyber attacks. For that reason, it has diminished applicability to the cybersecurity dilemma, which mostly concerns the interpretation of intrusions before they reach the level of destructive attack. The next version of the manual will attempt to address a fuller spectrum of intrusions and to provide additional clarity on issues of sovereignty, state responsibility, and due diligence. If this coming work can meaningfully build on the generally agreed-upon principle and apply it in practice to a broader range of activities, it could form an important pillar in a future status quo. Yet that is still nothing more than a possibility.

The second area of international agreement is that states should not use cyber attacks to wreak intentional damage on the critical infrastructure of other states in peacetime. This proposal, accepted in 2015, sought to tamp down the potential development of the most deadly cyber capabilities, about which there is little public evidence and discussion. It also seeks to minimize the extent to which cyber conflict can cause a loss of life, especially among the civilian population. In that respect, it attempts a partial implementation of important principles of international law. Signed in 2015, it is thus a noteworthy follow-up to the 2013 agreement.

If fully accepted in practice, such a proposal might help to provide overall mitigation to the cybersecurity dilemma. As the next chapter will spell out in detail, the cybersecurity dilemma is only potent as long as states fear what other states can do to them after intruding into important networks. If international agreement on the limitations of the potency of cyber capabilities were to happen convincingly, the consensus could reduce the dangers posed by the cybersecurity dilemma. States would feel less pressure to respond forcefully, in effect, because they would think that the intruders were less likely to do damage. Credible international agreements can aid interpretation of intentions.

While signs of growing international agreement on this principle are positive, there are nonetheless many reasons for skepticism. The agreement has major limitations on its practical applicability. Most obviously, while there is some overlap between networks of critical infrastructure and the networks of strategic importance to which the cybersecurity dilemma pertains, this overlap is only partial. Some strategically important networks will not be defined as critical infrastructure under an international definition, but will nonetheless be of great significance to particular states.[38] The proposal does little to prevent the cybersecurity dilemma on these networks.

Furthermore, the document refers to causing intentional damage, not intruding into critical infrastructure networks. In other words, the agreement does not explicitly forbid an intrusion, only the destructive attack that might follow that intrusion. As previously outlined, the linkage between exploitation and attack is very strong and the transition from the former to the latter can sometimes be quick. At a minimum, the time for payload activation can be short once operators have done their preparatory work. The strong linkage between exploitation and attack once again complicates mitigation.

For example, intrusions prepared possible American cyber attacks against Iranian infrastructure as part of the NITRO ZEUS contingency plan. The agreement does not forbid these kinds of operations—but this would likely have been of small comfort to the Iranians, should they have detected the American presence.[39] A state that detects an intrusion into critical infrastructure but takes comfort in the intruder's acceptance of this United Nations principle is giving itself very little time to blunt an attack should the intruder renege. More likely, a strong state suffering an intrusion will take more comfort in its ability to respond in kind if attacked than it will in international law. Yet preparing that retaliatory option, if using cyber capabilities, can be destabilizing in the manner suggested by the cybersecurity dilemma.

The third area of agreement, also signed in 2015, is that a state should not use its computer emergency readiness teams (CERTs)—groups of individuals who normally address serious network breaches—to bolster its own intrusion capabilities. Similarly, states should not interfere with the work of other states' CERTs as they respond to intrusions. The logic of this prohibition makes some intuitive sense. By establishing CERTs as purely defensive entities, states can somewhat shift the overall advantage to the defense and potentially limit the damage wrought by intrusions. This has precedent. States have, for a variety of reasons, agreed to grant special status to medical units in traditional conflict. But these parallels are inexact. CERTs thwart intruders' activity more directly than medics do for conventional forces. Intruders can also target a CERT's internal communications to see if the CERT has uncovered their intrusion into a state's other networks. Credible consensus on the CERT principle would yield the potential for more concrete future action, but there is a long way to go.

Within the context of the cybersecurity dilemma, this concept could help. To the extent that the proposal can meaningfully bolster the defense's response to an intrusion and distinguish CERTs from offensive forces, it will provide some mitigation. This is in accordance with the two variables of offense–defense balance and offense–defense differentiation. The problem is that there are few mechanisms for states to verify that other states have practiced such isolation and differentiation with their CERTs. Short of launching network intrusions of one's own, it is difficult to determine conclusively from afar whether another state is developing intrusion capabilities. Without credible means of demonstrating commitment to tilting the offense–defense balance and increasing offense–defense differentiation, states may simply not believe that others have implemented this principle in a meaningful way or would abide by it in times of crisis. The challenges in applying mitigations will not be overcome simply by fiat, even fiat backed by international agreements.

A final part of the United Nations' 2015 document stipulates that states should assist other states' investigations launched from a state's territory. If states were to reach actionable multilateral agreement on this issue,[40] it would mark important progress in international engagement. Such cooperation could build trust and improve working relationships. Fully realized, it would enable better and more coordinated action against cyber criminals operating without the support of a state. It would have positive effects for all those seeking to operate securely, although it would negatively hurt states that benefit from the income brought in by these criminals. Such cooperation could reduce plausible deniability by making attribution easier. This would enable better deterrence and response, potentially making states somewhat more reluctant to launch intrusions.

While these are all good outcomes in and of themselves, each is of limited applicability to the cybersecurity dilemma. Criminal actors generally operate below the threshold considered by the dilemma. They usually focus not on a state's strategically important networks, but on extorting or stealing from ordinary individuals with poor defenses. As important as fighting cyber crime is, it is a largely separate discussion. Nor is it evident that somewhat increased attribution will mitigate the cybersecurity dilemma. For reasons discussed in the next chapter, it seems that strong states can perform attribution fairly well if the stakes are high enough. Even if states do truly answer one another's requests for assistance, those requests would come after a state has detected an intrusion. Within the context of the cybersecurity dilemma, it is detection of sophisticated intrusions into important networks that is of primary concern, not attribution. Thus the idea of increased international cooperation on incidents has value, but is most relevant to the cybersecurity dilemma as a sign of increasing trust, not concrete mitigation. In this respect it is similar to the other principles of agreement.

*Conclusion: New Variables, New Opportunities*

This chapter has suggested two new potential variables in assessing the severity of the security dilemma: information distribution and the status quo. Though scholars have not usually treated them as such, these variables may be of use in analysis of conventional security dilemma cases. They appear worthy of further study, drawing on additional cases from the historical record. Based on the analysis presented here, it seems fair to conclude that they are indeed variables, not constants. States make decisions with imperfect information not just about other states' intentions, but also sometimes about other states' capabilities. The status quo varies by time, place, and circumstance; new technologies in particular affect its stability.

For the more immediate purpose of examining the cybersecurity dilemma, these variables suggest a dilemma in cyber operations that is severe. For information distribution, states are in the dangerous middle of the spectrum. They have enough knowledge to be fearful, but not enough to address those fears without intruding into the networks of other states. For the status quo, the international agreements are too embryonic to affect the cybersecurity dilemma. If there is common understanding about any cybersecurity dilemma concept, it is not those discussed in international agreements, but the structural point mentioned in the last chapter: cyber capabilities are offense-dominant. This kind of consensus has historically yielded dangerous results.

All of this paints a bleak picture. Nonetheless, it may be possible for states to shape their capabilities in an effort to mitigate the cybersecurity dilemma, just as states shaped offense–defense balance and offense–defense differentiation to mitigate the traditional security dilemma. While information distribution and the status quo are variables that provide reason to worry in cybersecurity, they may also contain opportunities for states seeking stability. Chapter Eight will take up that cause.

## 7

## LIMITATIONS, OBJECTIONS, AND THE FUTURE
## OF THE CYBERSECURITY DILEMMA

*Overview*

At this point in the discussion of the cybersecurity dilemma, it is worth pausing to take stock. The preceding six chapters have advanced a number of claims. They have argued that states have incentives to prepare key parts of offensive cyber operations early, before there is a pressing need, so that access or capabilities will be ready and effective when called upon. This involves intruding into possible future targets to develop options. In addition, narrowly targeted intrusions into the important networks of other states are valuable for defensive purposes. Yet when a state suffers an intrusion, the potential damage of a hostile operation and the difficulty in distinguishing between the offensive and defensive intrusions cause fear. A state seeking merely to provide for its own security often unintentionally impinges upon the security of others. This happens in ways that the traditional security dilemma mitigations cannot easily overcome. As the last chapter argued, the situation is even worse than in the traditional security dilemma. It appears to be an unfortunate state of affairs.

It might not be so bad, however. This chapter takes up three discrete possible objections to the claims made in the previous chapters. Each objection posits a flaw in a part of the cybersecurity dilemma logic and offers a reason to think that the cybersecurity dilemma is not as serious as it might initially seem. The objections chosen for discussion here constitute serious potential counterarguments not discussed in the preceding chapters. If any of the three objections has lasting merit, it will reveal limits on the potency of the cybersecurity dilemma.

The first objection is that attribution of an intrusion is impossible or very difficult. If this is correct, it means that even if states discover an intrusion in one of their important networks, they cannot easily know the identity of the intruder. They will thus not know whom specifically they should fear. The second objection is that no network intrusion reaches the level of an existential threat. Further, regardless of the risks posed by the intrusion, states could always escalate to kinetic operations if truly threatened. The third and final objection is that cyber capabilities are unevenly distributed. They belong mostly to states that have long held military power. States that are not as powerful have made their peace with the potential for attack from these strong states long ago. Thus the new threat posed by cyber operations does little to change the broader geopolitical calculus.

Each chapter section handles one objection. Each outlines the objection's logic in more detail, including the ways in which it might imperil the cybersecurity dilemma argument. The sections then explore possible weaknesses in the objections' claims. Each section closes with a brief trend analysis, considering whether the objection will grow more or less relevant over time. It may be the case, for example, that objections that seem irrelevant now will become more important. On the contrary, objections that seem to hold more weight now may in time become less salient.

The chapter's conclusion considers what this discussion means for the cybersecurity dilemma more generally. It argues that the cybersecurity dilemma will grow more potent in the near and medium term. In so doing, the conclusion gives a better context to the book's argument, considering the ways in which it is relevant and will continue to be significant. All told, while this chapter introduces important nuance and limitations on the core cybersecurity dilemma claims, it also reaffirms the most important forward-looking tenets.

*Objection: Attribution is Impossible*

Attributing network intrusions is the process of figuring out which actor is responsible for the digital break-in. Investigators orchestrate the process of attribution after they detect an intrusion. Undetected actions are largely also unattributed ones, and the attribution problem relates to the portion of intrusions that network defenders detect and subsequently investigate. For this reason, attribution has thus far been only implicit in the cybersecurity dilemma discussion. Elsewhere, however, it is a topic of much debate and has been for quite some time.[1] A wide range of voices make strong claims about attribution: that it is a fundamental problem in cybersecurity,[2] that it is exceedingly difficult to do without a technical or political redesign of computer networks,[3] that it is either solvable generally or not at all,[4] and that gathering credible evidence with which to perform attribution is the main obstacle.[5]

If attribution is impossible or even very challenging, there are potentially profound implications for the cybersecurity dilemma discussion. In order for the cybersecurity dilemma to be relevant, states have to know whom to fear. If a state detects a network intrusion but cannot identify the actor responsible, it may fear harm, but is unlikely to be able to isolate the threat to one actor. As a result, the objection contends, the state is unlikely to be able to respond in a way that escalates tensions. This diminishes the risk of further escalation from other states. In this case, while the general fear may be real, the cybersecurity dilemma would appear to fizzle out. The attribution objection might be stated succinctly as: *Because attribution is very difficult, states detecting a network intrusion are unable to determine who is responsible and whom to fear. A potentially destabilizing response against another state, as predicted by the cybersecurity dilemma, is therefore less likely.*

A rejoinder to this objection immediately appears: states with general fears are still potentially destabilizing actors. Even if the state cannot determine who specifically carried out a particular intrusion, the state will almost certainly be able to identify several possible culprits. To generate this shortlist, the state need not only rely on technical indicators. It may instead base its conclusions on geopolitical factors, the apparent objectives of the intrusion, and the exhibited capabilities of other states.[6] This weakens the objection's claim that when a state's fear is more diffuse across many actors, it is less likely to prompt a response.

A state's decision-makers are unlikely to content themselves with fear. Even if the fear is more general and less defined, the state has incentives to seek some resolution and clarification. As part of broad intelligence gathering or as part of a narrowly focused attempt to answer the attribution question, a state can seek to launch its own intrusions into the important networks of its potential adversaries. If confident attribution is not possible, the state may launch intrusions against several likely candidates. In so doing, it could spark potential responses and further animate the cybersecurity dilemma—perhaps even more than would have been the case had the state felt a threat from just one actor.

Although there are likely many more examples hidden from public view, a well-publicized case of attribution provides a useful brief case study. The intrusion against Sony Pictures Entertainment caused enormous public debate regarding who carried out the operation. Some participants in this debate were on reasonably solid analytical ground, looking to past attacks that used a similar methodology and exhibited similar forensic indicators at a technical level.[7] Others were on less firm footing. This included those who attempted language analysis from the attackers' limited public statements and drew overly broad conclusions.[8] In a high-profile fashion, the intrusion demonstrated some of the questions, challenges, and possibilities in the attribution process.[9]

The Sony incident also showed how network intrusions can substantially aid attribution efforts. The United States government confidently came to the conclusion that North Korean actors orchestrated the attack. The American government was initially tight-lipped on details and sought to preserve its intelligence sources and methods. However, as the intelligence community came under intensifying criticism for not providing more facts,[10] it declassified additional information and judgments, without specifying fully how it obtained its data.[11] As many had suspected, it eventually emerged that the United States had access into the North Korean networks. This access aided the attribution process.[12] The reporter who broke the story for the *New York Times*, David Sanger, indicated that he thought a presence in an adversary's system was "the only way" to get definitive attribution, though forensic evidence can still play a major role.[13]

In addition, there are good reasons to think that, based on current trends, the attribution objection will become less relevant over time. Three major factors determine whether an attribution attempt is likely to be successful: the time invested by the attributors, the resources and talent working on the investigation, and the sophistication of the intruders.[14] Examining trends involving the last two factors indicates that the attribution objection may rest on a weak foundation.[15]

With the growth of the cybersecurity industry, more actors do attribution than ever before. These organizations bring additional talent and resources to bear. As a result, they have uncovered even very sophisticated actions by state signals intelligence agencies. In so doing, they have put enough information about operations into the public domain to enable attribution. As this industry grows, firms will more regularly make states, including states without advanced detection and attribution capabilities, aware of potentially threatening intrusions by private sector actors. Even if they do not publicly identify the actor, the companies often give strong clues. With major reports on the Equation Group, APT1, and many others, the private sector's role in attribution or key parts of attribution is already readily apparent. The United States Department of Defense Cyber Strategy explicitly acknowledges as much.[16]

Similarly, states are likely to increase their own attribution capabilities in the future. As states develop a better understanding of the dangers of network intrusions, they will almost certainly invest in defensive capabilities as well as offensive ones. If states build better-designed networks and employ better-trained security personnel or firms, their ability to gather information useful for attribution will grow. While the private sector is likely to have a significant role in protecting clients for the foreseeable future, states will also often independently uncover and attribute intrusions of interest to them. All told, the more public and private sector resources and talent working on attribution, the less significant is the attribution objection to the cybersecurity dilemma.

Then there is the matter of intruder sophistication. Increased intruder sophistication can perhaps overcome increased resources dedicated to attribution. There are two reasons to think that this argument is incorrect. First, many states do not have a headstart in developing cyber operations capabilities. These states' operations are not likely to be incredibly sophisticated, at least not in the near or medium term. Even states that appear to have made reasonably quick progress in developing capabilities, such as Iran, do not appear to have built capabilities that are hard to attribute when used. While it is difficult to prove a negative, states that are investing and catching up in intrusion capabilities seem more concerned with carrying out operations than doing so stealthily.[17] These lesser states still benefit from the challenges in detection, but there is no public indication that, once sophisticated states uncover the intrusion, they have difficulty performing attribution. Defensive-minded network intrusions play a role here, too. States that regularly penetrate their potential adversaries' cyber units will have additional information on which to rely. The less sophisticated the intruder and the more sophisticated the attributor, the easier attribution is.

Second, it may indeed be the case that sophisticated states will become more difficult to attribute in their own operations. For example, it might get harder for the United States to determine whether China or Russia carried out a given intrusion if Chinese and Russian deception capabilities become more sophisticated faster than American attributive capabilities can keep up. This is speculative, especially given the increased resources of private actors dedicated to attribution, but nonetheless plausible. Regardless, even if this scenario does occur, it is unlikely to produce the sort of general paralyzing fear described in the attribution objection. It is more likely that, if the United States has difficulty separating Chinese intrusions from Russian ones, the United States will seek to gather additional information to guide its thinking more accurately. Yet again, this will likely mean breaking into Chinese and Russian networks—but those intrusions make the cybersecurity dilemma more salient, not less.

Regardless of which trend line attribution follows, the attribution objection does not significantly derail the cybersecurity dilemma argument. The spectrum of information distribution discussed in the last chapter is once again relevant. Currently, most states are in the dangerous middle zone. They are sometimes able to perform attribution on the intrusions they uncover, but to achieve more certainty in both detection and attribution, they might need to carry out potentially destabilizing network intrusions. Given the additional resources that states are investing, they may get better at attribution and need fewer intrusions for attribution purposes. Yet they will have an increased sense of which other states to fear. This may prompt intrusions oriented towards better understanding those states' capabilities and detecting their intrusions. If attribution gets substantially harder, which seems comparatively less likely, it will likely be a problem between sophisticated actors. In that case, sophisticated actors—the states most likely to fear one another—will have yet another reason to breach each other's networks. If attribution stays in the middle ground, the cybersecurity dilemma claims are largely unaffected, given the role that intrusions already play in attribution.

### Objection: The Cyber Threat is Not Existential

A re-examination of Chapter One and the canonical security dilemma literature may yield a second objection. This response, which can be called the existential threat objection, could read as follows: *The security dilemma is most present in matters of perceived existential threat.*[18] *The cybersecurity dilemma discusses threats that fall well short of this standard, since cyber capabilities are simply not as powerful. As a result, states can reasonably bear the risk of suffering a serious cyber attack because they will be able to retaliate with kinetic weapons.*

Each sentence in this objection merits consideration and response. First, the security dilemma is strongest in the cases where the threat is most severe, since states fear most the risk that they cannot bear. The possibility of a surprise existential attack therefore rightly tops the list. But states do guard assiduously against other risks as well. The extension of the security dilemma to intelligence demonstrates this point. The risk posed by the Cold War's close access programs was often indirect and not existential, yet nonetheless it was quite real and threatening for states on both sides. Each state feared what the other might learn through such penetrations, the access the other might acquire, and the strategic consequences that would result. So while this part of the objection does have some merit—yes, the stakes of any security dilemma increase as the threat becomes more serious—it does not by itself undermine the core or the relevance of the cybersecurity dilemma argument.

Second, there is debate over the existential nature of the threat that cyber operations pose. As discussed, many contend that cyberwarfare is a serious and potentially existential threat. The reported case of planned American attacks on Iran beyond Stuxnet indicates that some states can do more damage than they have actually done.[19] But although this view is not uncommon, it is speculative, and the cybersecurity dilemma argument does not need to rest on such a weak foundation. Instead, there is good reason to think that cybersecurity, even if not truly an existential risk, is of vital importance. This is true regardless of whether cyber attacks are as strategically destructive as some predict.

The amount of money and policy-maker time which states invest in cyber operations provides an inductive reason to think that cybersecurity is deeply important.[20] The fact that states continue to increase these investments despite overall budget pressure is indicative of the importance they place on cyber operations. The amount of high-level attention given to the subject by policy-makers, up to and including the American president, is similarly noteworthy. The money and attention shed light on the importance of both offensive and defensive cyber missions. On offense, states recognize the potential gains made possible by cyber operations; on defense, states fear suffering the corresponding losses. While there may be some degree of needless hype driving the actions of states, as a first approximation the increased attention and investment indicates that the concern is real.[21] So long as states value the security of their networks, the cybersecurity dilemma is relevant.

Even without existential stakes, cyber operations can affect national priorities. For the United States and Israel, Stuxnet arguably accomplished what virtually no other operation could have: delaying the Iranian nuclear program and fostering doubt in the minds of Iranian scientists and policy-makers.[22] For Iran, the effect was reversed. The American–Israeli computer worm, while remaining undetected, hindered an important national effort and caused internal discord. Strong states have fears too. The United States Director of National Intelligence has named cybersecurity risks the biggest threat facing the nation every year since 2013.[23] Other examples of cyber capabilities serving national priorities abound: the role that Chinese intrusions might have in advancing Chinese economic priorities,[24] the role that Russian cyber operations have in Ukraine,[25] even the role that Ethiopian intrusions might have in cracking down on dissent.[26] Network intrusions are serious business.

In closing, the objection suggests that states will always be able to respond to a cyber attack with a kinetic one. In the case of states with massive militaries, like the United States, this is demonstrably the case. It is hard to imagine a cyber attack that would cripple the entirety of the United States military. But just because a kinetic response remains possible does not mean that cyber operations pose no threat. Indeed, for some types of operations, an escalation to kinetic force would achieve little. For example, states often use network intrusions to try to increase economic competitiveness, yet such espionage can hardly be rebutted with kinetic strikes. While the United States has declared a doctrine of equivalence—meaning that it reserves the right to employ kinetic attacks to respond to cyber attacks[27]—it is hard to imagine that kinetic capabilities will always be sufficient.

For example, suppose an adversary launches a devastating cyber attack on the systems of the New York Stock Exchange. The attack affects the integrity of important computers and causes serious transient economic damage but does not kill anyone. In such circumstances, it seems unlikely that the United States would be able to craft a proportionate and effective kinetic response. Equivalence does not help, as a bombing of the perpetrator's stock exchange is probably not appropriate or ethical. There is no accepted precedent for killing civilians in response to near-term economic harm.[28] Given the lack of nuanced kinetic options, it is instead much better for a powerful state to threaten kinetic retaliation but to try to prevent an attack in the first place. This means taking the threat very seriously, even if the threat does not inhibit the potential for a forceful military response and does not pose an existential challenge.

The question of deterrence is bound up in this discussion about kinetic response.[29] Deterrence is hardly monolithic, especially when considering the range of actors that can carry out network intrusions. Some means of deterrence might rely on conventional kinetic activities, some might utilize economic tools, and some might depend on cyber operations.[30] Different actors require different types of deterrence. Just because a state has achieved deterrence of one actor or of one type of action does not mean that it has achieved deterrence of another.

Additionally, for activities below some threshold of seriousness, deterrence is simply not credible. Incidents in this category are ones over which the deterring state is not willing to risk escalation. The Iranian denial of service attacks against American banks appear to be an example. The attacks earned verbal condemnation and eventually an indictment, but warranted no kind of public military response.[31] Without credible deterrence, defense is the only option against certain threats. In cybersecurity, this means better network security. States can indeed take advance action in service of that goal—such as breaking into foreign networks to improve detection capabilities—so long as they believe that others will not detect their actions. The net effect is clear: in cases when deterrence, either cyber or kinetic, is insufficient, states must assure their own security. But to enhance their defenses, many states are likely to perform network intrusions that once again risk animating the cybersecurity dilemma if detected.

A brief analysis of trendlines also undermines the future relevance of the existential threat objection. The potential damage of cyber capabilities is either staying the same or increasing, making the threat more significant, even if not existential. Software and hardware continue to gain relevance in a wide variety of sectors. The growth of the so-called Internet of Things, the networking of great numbers of physical devices, best exemplifies this trend. The interconnection of many devices, from thermostats to cars, creates persistent and often unaddressed security concerns.[32] Malicious computer code is most damaging when intruders insert it into a system that is of great virtual or physical importance.[33] As more and more systems have a greater digital core, the potential vulnerabilities increase.

Security researchers provided a vivid example of this in 2015. They discovered vulnerabilities that enabled them to manipulate 1.4 million cars remotely, and memorably demonstrated this feat by using computer code to kill the transmission on a car going at 70 mph on a highway.[34] This is the latest in a long series of warnings. As early as 1980, technologists cautioned that hardware and software develop far faster than security for hardware and software.[35] It is quite likely that this trend will make network intrusions more threatening still. In contrast, it seems deeply unlikely that better security will soon render network intrusions obsolete.

Perhaps for this reason, kinetic and cyber capabilities are converging, encouraged in part by the Department of Defense projects outlined previously. Reports indicate that the United States integrated cyber effects—though not necessarily effects brought about by advanced malicious code—with special and conventional military operations in the Iraq War.[36] Other reports indicate that military planners considered cyber operations as part of the United States' opening salvos in the Libya conflict.[37] Similarly, analysts of Chinese military activities note their push towards broader "informatization." This involves the integration and manipulation of information in warfighting efforts, a concept that inexactly parallels and extends beyond cyber operations.[38]

As integration continues, it may change the notion of escalation. Militaries might before long view cyber operations as an ordinary part of joint capabilities. In that case, to speak of escalation from cyber to kinetic force might sound as meaningless as speaking of escalation from sea forces to air ones. With greater integration, the manner in which states perceive military and intelligence possibilities and threats will likely shift in unanticipated ways, but the cybersecurity dilemma concerns will hardly lose relevance. Indeed, at some point in the future cyber operations might be so joined that the cybersecurity dilemma will be so mainstream as to be called just the security dilemma.

## Objection: Cyber Capabilities are Unevenly Distributed

The third objection acknowledges most of the cybersecurity dilemma argument. According to this objection, while some intrusions are of great value for defensive purposes and can also be threatening, the overall conclusion that the cybersecurity dilemma can be destabilizing is simply irrelevant. This is because cyber capabilities are unevenly distributed. States without advanced capabilities will always fear states with them, regardless of any particular intrusion. States with advanced capabilities will also be better able to absorb the blow of a surprise attack from a weak state and still respond. Stated more formally, the uneven distribution objection might read: *A security dilemma is most acute when new evidence increases the apparent plausibility of merely possible threats. In cybersecurity, because of the uneven distribution of capabilities, threats are either obviously plausible (as occurs when weak states fear comparatively stronger ones) or barely possible (as occurs when strong states fear weak ones). Therefore, regardless of a state's capabilities, the dilemma of interpretation arising from a detected intrusion does not appreciably change a state's overall fears.*

To some degree, this objection appears to make initial sense. States with no cyber capabilities are likely to recognize that they are at a disadvantage relative to states that do have great capabilities. Regardless of whether they detect an intrusion, they are likely to feel threatened, since they know their own weakness and can assume that others might have a general idea of it. Similarly, strong states will in general have less reason to launch defensive-minded intrusions into manifestly weak states, as they have less to gain. They will likely be able to use baseline defenses to secure their networks against the weak state's capabilities.

A very significant exception is if the strong state is looking for malicious code from other states that have also intruded into the same important network of the weak state. This is a third-party Counter-Computer Network Exploitation effort. In general, however, the case of an intrusion into a weak state's network is less likely to be narrowly defensive-minded and presents much less ambiguity. While the threat to the weak state from strong states is still real, without a dilemma of interpretation the cybersecurity dilemma logic makes little difference when it comes to very strong and very weak states.

That this objection is true to some degree, however, does not render it terribly potent. A similar objection can be made about the security dilemma more generally: states with manifestly weak kinetic forces will always fear the kinetic forces of strong states, in the absence of deeply credible reassurances. Yet, despite this, the security dilemma logic remains a central and valued part of much international relations scholarship and practice. This is largely because conflict is most interesting and geopolitically destabilizing when it does not involve a very strong state against a very weak one, but instead when it involves two states of more equal clout. Given this idea, one can stipulate that both the security dilemma and the cybersecurity dilemma are of comparatively less value in understanding relationships and conflict between very strong and very weak states without much weakening either concept's value.

Such a stipulation does nothing to impinge the cybersecurity dilemma's relevance to operations conducted by strong states, such as the

United States, Russia, and China, against other strong states. These operations hold major geopolitical significance because of the potency of the states involved. The stipulation further does nothing to lessen the cybersecurity dilemma's relevance to operations by strong states against medium-tier ones, like Stuxnet, or vice versa, like the North Korean attack on Sony. This category of operations is quite important, as virtually all of the destructive cases of cyber attacks occur between a strong state and a medium-tier one or between two medium-tier states. The stipulation does somewhat diminish the relevance of strong state efforts against weak ones—an example of this might be operations by the Five Eyes against the cell phone networks in the developing world[39]—but this is comparatively less important. Thus, the objection has limited strength.

A second key limitation to this objection is that vulnerability works somewhat differently in cybersecurity than in traditional operations. Assuming the presence of dual-use weaponry in traditional military operations, strong states are less vulnerable to attack than weak ones. The strong states have greater forces and therefore by definition have greater defenses. The exception is asymmetric attacks, in which a weaker actor can exploit the greater strength or presence of a strong state, turning this strength into vulnerability. Many acts of terrorism fall into this category, as do a large number of insurgent tactics. If weaker actors are capable of doing this, they can seize the attention of the strong state, sometimes causing tremendous fear.[40]

Cybersecurity, some argue, is asymmetric in this way. Cyber operations provide a means with which weaker states and even non-state actors can level the playing field and cause damage to more powerful states. Typically, proponents of this view note the tremendous reliance that states like the United States have on computer networks for their economic and military strength. They theorize that these networks, which are often poorly secured, are potential Achilles heels.[41] There is not the space here to debate this point. Crucially, however, whether this view is in fact correct has limited relevance for the cybersecurity dilemma discussion. Instead, it is the perception of the strong states on the potential asymmetry that matters most. If strong states fear, even unreasonably so, an asymmetric threat from weak states, they might feel a need to launch defensive-minded intrusions against those states.

If the weak states detect this intrusion, they are likely to feel threatened by the strong state. This would amplify any fears they have stemming from their own weakness and might prompt them to launch asymmetric operations of their own—a result largely akin to that theorized by the cybersecurity dilemma logic. All told, the persistence of vulnerabilities despite a state's overall strength and the possibility of asymmetric attack via cyber operation indicate that the cybersecurity dilemma better overcomes the uneven distribution objection than the security dilemma does.

A brief analysis of trendlines indicates that this objection will likely decline in relevance. States are increasing their investments in cybersecurity. This is obviously true of strong states, like the United States, China, and Russia. Among those states, the commitment to cyber operations shows no signs of waning, meaning that the cybersecurity dilemma will likely be relevant regardless of what else happens. Medium-tier states, like Iran, are also investing in their capabilities; and so too are weaker states, like Ethiopia. To what degree these states newer to cyber operations can catch up remains to be seen.

If strong states continue to retain or expand their advantages over lesser ones, they can exploit the headstart they have. But there is still the question of asymmetric vulnerabilities. The strong states are likely to depend more, not less, on computer networks as they continue to grow. This greater dependence expands the already large attack surface. It provides additional points of entry for intruders, even comparatively weak intruders. In contrast to the uneven distribution objection, the strong states are likely to worry more about their vulnerability to weak states. In order for this not to be the case, the strong states would have to reduce their dependence on computer networks or improve their defenses faster than other states improve their intrusion capabilities. Further, they must improve their defenses without resorting to launching intrusions. While such an improvement of baseline defenses is an admirable policy goal, it seems unlikely that such improvements will occur with any kind of alacrity.

If the comparatively weaker states catch up, exploiting economies of scale as they develop capabilities or using leapfrogging technical advances to improve their operations more quickly, the uneven distribution objection manifestly declines in relevance. With fewer weaker states and more medium-tier states, the distribution of capabilities becomes more equal. In such circumstances, even strong states have greater reason to doubt their capacity to absorb an intrusion, greater reason for fear, and greater reason to launch defensive-minded intrusions. Potential asymmetry in vulnerability may exacerbate this still further, but it is largely beside the point. The bottom line is clear: the more level the playing field, the less important the uneven distribution objection.

## Conclusion: The Present and Future of the Cybersecurity Dilemma

This chapter has put forth objections and counterarguments to the cybersecurity dilemma. Taken together, the ideas presented here do establish some limits on this book's argument. Attribution sometimes remains a challenge, and states' struggles with it can confound their decision-making in unpredictable ways. Given this, the dilemma of response might occasionally be more complicated than the cyber-security dilemma suggests. Thus far, cyber capabilities are less potent than kinetic ones, and states may fear intrusions less than they fear other threats. The stakes might therefore sometimes be less dire than the cybersecurity dilemma could initially suggest, especially if states develop resiliency in their networks. Some states are indeed demon-strably weaker than others when it comes to cyber capabilities. In these cases, additional fears might be less relevant than is the case when incidents involve strong or equally-matched states. In light of these objections, the cybersecurity dilemma is hardly unlimited in its scope. To suggest otherwise is to misread the available evidence.

But the core of the cybersecurity dilemma argument emerges mostly unscathed. Given the trends discussed in this chapter, it seems more likely that the dilemma will continue to become more relevant, not less. If states can make some headway on attribution, the credible fears that result will increase the cybersecurity dilemma's relevance. If cyber operations attain greater potency or become more integrated into joint forces, the cybersecurity dilemma will also become more concerning and more mainstream. Lastly, if weaker states narrow the gap in cyber capabilities or if stronger states nonetheless remain vulnerable to asym-metric attack, more states will have reason to worry about the cyber-security dilemma.

All told, the conclusion to these objections is apparent: there are real limitations on the cybersecurity dilemma logic, but these limitations do not constrain the overall argument unduly. The ways in which the constraints are significant, however, outline the ways in which the cybersecurity dilemma might become more acute and more salient with time, if the limitations fade. In short, although the cybersecurity dilemma appears quite applicable, careful consideration of its boundaries foreshadows its still-growing importance. The important question, addressed in the next and final chapter, is what to do about it.

8

# MITIGATING THE CYBERSECURITY DILEMMA

*Overview*

This chapter turns towards the search for new approaches to managing the cybersecurity dilemma. Pursuit of even a partial answer is important, given the dilemma's risks, the failure of traditional mitigations, and the prospects for still greater worries in the future. A silver bullet remains elusive, but this chapter lays out steps that deserve consideration in the short and medium term to build trust on matters of cybersecurity.

The intersection of cybersecurity and national policy is rife with solutions and solutionism. This is the mistaken belief that one or two strategic or technological big-ticket innovations will dramatically improve a state's prospects and solve the crises of the day. Chastened by the lack of cure-alls and by the way in which the shine quickly rubs off cybersecurity proposals, this chapter proceeds from the notion that there is no single answer to the cybersecurity dilemma.

This chapter therefore argues that the cybersecurity dilemma is only overcome through a multi-pronged effort that increases short-term stability, starts to build trust, and begins to minimize the risks of misinterpretation. The ideas that follow are not policy prescriptions per se, but rather possible parts of this multi-pronged approach. They are not focused on the situation of any particular state and do not contain strong advocacy for a given course of action, though potential benefits are high-lighted. Wherever possible, this chapter very briefly draws out historical parallels. It demonstrates that old concepts have some applicability and highlights ways in which those parallels translate to cybersecurity.

The chapter's argument consists of four parts. The first section re-examines the importance of baseline defenses. Here, the discussion proceeds with a view not just to what baseline defenses can provide in terms of immediate security, but also to how they can simplify the cybersecurity dilemma more broadly. The second section considers the prospects of building trust with a potential adversary through com-bined efforts. When strong states solidify their bilateral relationships, they advance security and stability. The third section proposes ways in which states can take unilateral action to show a particular potential adversary or the wider international community that they seek stabil-ity. These signals, many of which require near-term action but gain credibility when borne out over time, are critical to establishing pros-pects for a long-term status quo. The fourth section outlines the ways in which states can establish and communicate a posture for dealing with the intrusions that do occur, while the chapter's conclusion once more links back to the broader cybersecurity dilemma construct.

## *The Value of Baseline Defenses*

No cybersecurity approach is credible unless it begins with a discussion of the vital role of baseline defenses. While much of the media atten-tion often focuses on the intrigue of sabotage or stealthy intrusion, the seemingly unglamorous world of defense is at the heart of the issue. In the absence of a solid defensive foundation, computer systems do not scale up without major risks. Similarly, without this foundation real progress on the cybersecurity dilemma is impossible.

The network defense model separated defensive measures into three broad categories: defenses that rely on signatures and heuristics in automated software scans for malicious code, defenses that involve human analysts actively hunting for breaches, and network intrusions that acquire threat intelligence on potential adversaries' capabilities and intentions. While there is no doubt about the value of the intelli-gence sometimes gathered by the intrusions in this last category, the proper deployment of the first two categories of defense can go a long way towards providing security and starting to build trust. These efforts are baseline defenses.

Baseline defenses provide immediate near-term security value against a large number of threats.[1] Most would-be intrusions are not terribly sophisticated. With very rare exception, most intruders do not use zero day exploits that would elude up-to-date signature-based tools. Sometimes, because of social engineering or other tricks, they use no exploits at all and instead just dupe users into directly executing the malicious code.[2] Similarly, intruders often do not employ advanced means of stealthy infiltration or lateral movement within networks and do little to cover their tracks once inside. As a result, properly configured defenses can prevent or rapidly detect many successful intrusions, including intrusions of significant importance. At a minimum, better defenses require the intruders to exert significantly more effort.

The 2015 intrusion at the United States Office of Personnel Management (OPM) provides one vivid example. The breach, and another like it, resulted in the loss of incredibly revealing confidential data on between 9 and 14 million current and former government employees—a counterintelligence gold mine for the intruders.[3] Yet the intrusion effort was hardly sophisticated. To the contrary, a string of colossal failures in management and implementation enabled the break-in. These failures included a lack of two-factor verification to check the authentication of users, a lack of encryption on even deeply sensitive databases, poor visibility into network activity, and widespread use of legacy systems that simply did not have security as a design priority.

These shortcomings were obvious. The office's inspector general revealed as much in report after report, going back years before the intrusion. The office had no information security staff until 2013.[4] Indeed, unaddressed concerns had become so severe by 2014 that the inspector general suggested that OPM should consider cutting off all access to certain critical systems until the office could implement better protection.[5] OPM leaders promised to do better, keeping the systems online while claiming that improving cybersecurity defenses was a priority. There was even great evidence that the office's databases were of enormous value to intruders and were likely targets. Intruders had previously made entry and remained undetected for long periods of time. These previous intruders failed to collect as much valuable data as the 2015 intruders did only because OPM's systems were so outdated that the earlier intruders were unfamiliar with how they worked—a defensive success that should not exactly have inspired great confidence.[6]

Nor is there much reason to think that OPM is an outlier within the United States government.[7] In 2014 and 2015 alone, the State Department, Pentagon, and White House suffered serious breaches from foreign intruders. It is not hard to see why. Federal data indicate that fixes for vulnerabilities often take on average well more than a month to apply, that the time between vulnerability scans is best measured in weeks,[8] and that many systems central to government operations are significantly out of date and lack basic security measures. Inspectors general at several agencies and the Government Accountability Office have done much to identify these shortcomings and propose specific ways of addressing them, but serious problems persist.

Beyond implementing pattern-matching and heuristic tools, an additional step is also immediately necessary if a state wants to improve its defensive position: it must root out intruders already in its networks. Fortunately, the second category of baseline defenses, human-directed hunting, is adept at this task. As part of decontaminating important networks, however, states must make efforts to increase the quality and number of these hunters and to empower them with the tools needed to do their job well. This involves hiring and training analysts who have a strongly developed sense of what network or computer activity is normal and which deviations indicate potential compromise. The resulting clean-up effort, which is likely to include greatly expanded network security monitoring and computer-based forensic investigations, is hard, expensive, and thankless work, but it is vital.

Human-directed hunting can catch intruders using new tools and exploits without relying on pilfered threat intelligence. Aggressive monitoring of a state's own important networks coupled with well-funded and well-trained teams of analysts are vital for rooting out intruders who have already made entry and for catching those who try to do so in the future. Virtually all less capable intruders could be detected in this way. These detection efforts will often succeed before the intruders can achieve their objectives or develop a persistent presence. Keeping out more intruders via automated defensive tools makes these analysts' jobs easier. In turn, more capable and better equipped analysts provide additional security. They reduce the need for breaches into foreign networks to gather specific threat intelligence, although some states might not eliminate the intelligence operations entirely.

Proper implementation of baseline defenses will therefore do much to assure a state's cybersecurity without posing any possible risk to the security of other nations. With the woeful standards of current practice, each state is likely to have—already within reach—improvements that it can make to reassure itself and minimize its perceived threats. These changes are not cheap, given the number of legacy systems that need replacement. Nor are they easy, given the number of individuals that states must hire and train. They will certainly not solve the cybersecurity dilemma entirely. Yet the improvement of baseline defense is a necessary, though not sufficient, condition on which the rest of a multi-pronged approach depends.

In addition, the improvement of baseline defenses has some value that goes beyond just thwarting individual attacks. For states, better defenses can do much to reduce the complexity of decision-making when it comes to cybersecurity. One of the primary ways in which the cybersecurity dilemma could get worse, as the last chapter noted, is if more states develop cyber operations capabilities. If the bar for a successful cyber operation is low enough, even non-state actors can be nuisances. For example, in 2015 and 2016, an intruder gained access to the personal email accounts of the Director of the Central Intelligence Agency and the Director of National Intelligence, as well as other networks. When authorities arrested one of the intruders, they found that he was a fifteen-year-old in Britain.[9] As with the previously mentioned Solar Sunrise case, in which nascent American attribution efforts mistakenly assumed that cyber operations conducted by three teenagers were from the Iraqi government, lesser states and non-state actors can complicate and amplify the cybersecurity dilemma.

The OPM breach once again provides an example of wrong-headed thinking in this regard. Under Congressional questioning, the head of OPM defended the office's failure to stop the major intrusion by claiming that the office faced upwards of ten million "attacks" per month.

The implication was that, under such a massive threat, it was inevitable that some intrusion efforts would succeed. This is an absurd figure in that it conflates broad-based scanning with credible intrusion threats. More relevant to this point, however, is that the significant meaning that the OPM director attached to this large number reveals the quantity of red herrings faced by the office's defensive systems and the attention paid to those distractions by the staff. It exposes the inability of the organization, including senior management, to separate the actually threatening intrusion from all the other noise of mostly meaningless scanning. Of the ten million "attacks" cited by the OPM director, only a small percentage would have made it through properly configured automated defenses. Fewer still, if any, could have evaded the scrutiny of well-trained analysts.[10]

Better defenses can therefore make the cybersecurity dilemma more manageable. States with a headstart over some others, like the United States, have the opportunity to exploit that advantage by fortifying their networks in advance of other actors developing better intrusion capabilities. In effect, raising the bar on defense makes it harder for others to pose a threat. It lessens the number of potentially worrying states, decreases the number of concerning intrusions, and reduces the overall complexity of decision-making. It is only the smallest subset of the observed activity—the most credible attempts launched by the most credible potential adversaries—that should have to attract high-level policy-maker attention. Simply put, the cybersecurity dilemma is best avoided entirely, wherever possible.

Practitioners and scholars often compare cyber capabilities to nuclear weapons, and it is worth drawing out this comparison in more detail on the effects of defenses.[11] During the nuclear arms race, at some point both the United States and Soviet Union possessed enough warheads to destroy the world many times over. By that point, the strategic threat had shifted. Both sides had enormous amounts of established destructive power, even possessing enough power to withstand a devastating first strike from the other and still retaliate. Threats to stability thus took a different form. It was defenses, and in particular defenses that could enable a state to strike first and block the other side's retaliation, that were destabilizing, since they made a massive surprise attack more palatable. In this circumstance, certain types of offensive-minded spending were less destabilizing than defensive-minded spending, as mentioned in Chapter Five. It is for this reason that the United States and Soviet Union agreed to the Anti-Ballistic Missile Treaty. This is also why the Strategic Defense Initiative (or Star Wars) pursued by the Reagan Administration caused such consternation among the Soviets.

The situation with regard to cyber capabilities is just the opposite. There is a good chance that many new and more devastating offensive capabilities remain for operators to discover or invent. At a minimum, there are certainly more zero day vulnerabilities in existence than states have found and exploited. A state's pursuit of such new offensive capabilities could rightfully be interpreted as threatening by other states. By contrast, cybersecurity baseline defenses are universally recognized as non-threatening and part of professional best practice,[12] not just to keep out other state-level adversaries but also to keep out non-state actors and amateur intruders. Unlike in the nuclear arena, other states are likely to see obvious non-intrusive defenses as such and not react with fear.

## Advancing Bilateral Trust

Any security dilemma, including the cybersecurity dilemma, is at its most acute when the states involved are the most powerful. Many middle-tier states benefit from security guarantees provided by other states. They can thus take some risks in interpreting the intentions of potentially hostile actors, since their stronger allies will come to their aid if they judge incorrectly and suffer attack. Powerful states have no such luxury. They are themselves the guarantors of security and they lack still stronger allies to whom they can turn for assistance in times of trouble. Therefore, they must be especially cognizant of the dangers posed by other mighty states. It is thus in the relationships among the strongest states that the security dilemma can become quite severe.

The outsize importance of the top-tier states provides an opportunity for partial mitigation. To the extent that the most powerful states can form meaningful relationships of trust, they can increase stability.[13] This is not easy. The earlier discussion of intelligence and the security dilemma provided examples of the ways in which the United States and

Soviet Union each greatly unnerved the other, sometimes unintentionally and sometimes less so. Close access intelligence collection, expressions of inherent suspicion about the other, and seemingly clashing ideological worldviews induced mutual fear. But the Cold War stayed largely cold, in part because of some of the bilateral trust-building mechanisms that the two states developed in response to dangerous crises. A few examples hold particular relevance for the cybersecurity dilemma.

One innovation that the United States and Soviet Union devised was the hotline linking the American government and the Communist Party leadership. An early advocate of this idea was Thomas Schelling, the academic and strategist. He and others cited the benefits in international stability of fostering prompt communication between strong states. The idea gained greater traction after the Cuban Missile Crisis in 1962, in which formal diplomatic communications from one side to the other took many hours to deliver. In the midst of those tense days, the delay in communications posed such an issue that the parties employed ad hoc and unofficial means, including asking television correspondents covering the events to pass messages.[14]

The two sides signed an agreement to establish a hotline in 1963. Throughout the remainder of the Cold War, the link proved valuable on many occasions. During the 1967 Arab–Israeli conflict, the United States and the Soviet Union used it to communicate information about their own military movements to the other as they stayed mostly on the sidelines of the war. This reduced the risk of misinterpretation and minimized the chances of inadvertent escalation. Not long after, both sides used the hotline in a similar way during the Indo-Pakistani War in 1971, the Yom Kippur War of 1973, the Soviet invasion of Afghanistan, and on several occasions during the Reagan Administration.[15] Most cases demonstrated the value of swift communication between the strategic leaders of strong states, as Schelling and others had predicted.[16] For this reason, even though the Soviet Union has faded, the hotline remains in place.

Similar to the hotline, in the 1980s the two sides established what is sometimes referred to as the "warm line" and is more properly known as the Nuclear Risk Reduction Center. While the hotline is mostly for strategic crises, this center deals with somewhat lower-level operational concerns. Staffed by State Department officials on the United States' side, they provide round-the-clock channels for sharing important non-crisis information. This gives staff at the operational level a mechanism through which to clarify treaty points and to provide notification of missile tests.[17] Coming more than twenty years after the development of the hotline and during a time of significantly friendlier relations between the two nations, this information sharing center was both a symbol of greater trust as well as a means of safeguarding and perpetuating that trust.

Other significant areas of trust building occurred when the states recognized the value to both sides of some limits on their forces. These often took the shape of formalized arms control agreements. One notable effort, the Anti-Ballistic Missile Treaty, has already been discussed in this chapter, while Chapter Six covered another, the Open Skies Treaty. Other significant agreements include the two Strategic Arms Limitation Talks, which limited the number and force of the two superpowers' largest nuclear weapons, and the Intermediate Nuclear Forces agreement, which will be discussed in the next section.

Of the many significant insights relevant to these bilateral agreements, several merit mention here. The first key point is that these were negotiated agreements, worked out over years by teams of experts and diplomats, with this bargaining sometimes punctuated by high-level summits between national leaders. Both sides made these efforts a priority in an attempt to thwart future crises.[18] Negotiations have a better chance of success if there is already a foundation of trust. This includes working relationships and communication mechanisms between the parties. The value in building strong bilateral relationships is not just in the present, as a means of overcoming current problems, but also for the future. Actions taken now to build trust can pay off when new threats arise down the road.

Verification of compliance comprised a vital part of these negotiations. Verification mechanisms in theory build trust in the strength of an agreement; successful verification in practice enhances trust in the other party. While some arms control treaties functioned without verification clauses, many included them. Verification, especially of secret technical developments or of other covert activities, can be quite invasive. For many states in many circumstances, a default desire is to have free rein into another state's affairs to make sure it is living up to the agreement. States are naturally wary about giving such access into their own systems to others, especially to potential adversaries. Success in verification means reaching an acceptable middle ground.

States made significant mutual concessions to enable the verification of some arms control agreements. Some of these concessions seem quite surprising in the computer age. For example, the Strategic Arms Limitation Talks II negotiators recognized the vital importance of mutual verification but also the technical difficulty in carrying it out. They negotiated a variety of mechanisms that helped facilitate the process. These mechanisms spelled out what each state had to do to enable the other party to verify its compliance. One requirement jars the modern reader: during some kinds of weapons testing, states were forbidden from encrypting their systems' telemetry, vital data on the weapons' operational status and capabilities. Sending this information without encryption enabled the other side to intercept it and verify compliance.[19]

This anachronistic view of encryption is just the beginning of how cyber operations diverge from nuclear ones. Fundamentally, incidents unfold differently. Short-fuse crises, in which policy-makers had to make decisions of ultimate importance in minutes, characterized the Cold War. Cyber operations, with less destructive capabilities, do not seem as urgent for strategic decision-makers. Network intrusions also far outnumber nuclear crises. As a result, a hotline model for defusing cyber incidents in the moment is, at best, only part of a solution. Instead, to minimize the risk of tension and to aid the other side in their dilemma of interpretation, states will have to clarify their positions, limits, and capabilities proactively before the crisis occurs.

The United States has taken some strategic steps in this regard. With Russia, it has agreed to a similar hotline to defuse potential crises related to cyber operations, though it is not clear if the states have ever used this hotline for anything other than a test.[20] With China, the United States agreed in late 2015 to set up a hotline, although the agreement is too recent to be of much use in analysis.[21] In addition, credible reports indicate that high-ranking American military delegations, including one in 2014 with then-Secretary of Defense Chuck Hagel, have flown to Beijing to provide a briefing on some of the United States' cyber capabilities and doctrines.[22] President Obama raised cybersecurity issues in one-on-one meetings with the Chinese leader Xi Jinping on several occasions, with mixed success.[23] While it is unthinkable that the United States showed its full hand in these meetings, such efforts are nonetheless a good start at establishing candid talks, although Defense Secretary Hagel said after his visit that the Chinese did not reciprocate.[24]

The United States and China have also held operational-level discussions. The two states, recognizing the need for greater engagement on issues in cybersecurity, established joint working groups. These groups, staffed in part by specialists, sought to provide an ongoing channel of communication. It is unknown if these groups would have succeeded, although the two sides did not try the concept for long; in the light of the American indictment of five PLA officers, the Chinese broke off their participation.[25] The late 2015 summit between Obama and Xi rekindled the concept of the groups but their reformation and impact remain to be seen.[26]

Other barriers make international engagement and agreements challenging in cybersecurity, even if there is a reservoir of trust. The enormous ambiguity about the definition of specific operational terms poses a challenge. Many pieces of security software present dual-use difficulties in offense–defense differentiation. Further, a security researcher may develop exploit code to prove the concept of a zero day vulnerability so that it can be fixed. Similarly, a state may use intrusion tools to test its own networks for weaknesses, a normal part of the process of configuring defenses. These difficulties tripped up proposed export control mechanisms in 2015 within the context of the Wassenaar Arrangement, an effort to constrain dangerous exports.[27] In the context of arms control with potential adversaries, where states are more likely to fear cheating by one another, these definitional troubles present even greater hurdles.

The increased possibility for cheating in such an agreement makes verification still more important. But challenges in verification are in fact another major hurdle to cyber arms control agreements. Unlike during the Cold War, when the United States and Soviet Union had the best interception capabilities, many actors in cybersecurity, including non-state actors from third-party countries, are capable of intercepting some unprotected communications. Encryption is therefore essential. Additionally, cyber capabilities are far easier to hide than nuclear missiles. To verify that a state is not developing a forbidden class of cyber capabilities, another state has to examine all of its networks and digital equipment. No modern government will ever permit such access to a potential adversary. Even partnerships between exceptionally close allies, such as the United States and the United Kingdom, do not run so deep.

Non-state actors complicate verification, too. For example, American policy-makers might think that they are negotiating a deal with the Chinese leadership that will constrain both sides' cyber operations and increase stability. But the leadership might not have complete control over every skilled hacker in the government and certainly not in the whole country. The potential for individual action introduces plausible deniability for states that want to cheat on agreements. This is why the 2015 United States–China and United Nations agreements included provisions for mutual assistance on investigations into breaches. But this is another area in which substantial and timely cooperation between potential adversaries has yet to be seen in practice. Even for states that do have more trust for one another, the possibility of unaffiliated patriotic hackers or activists complicates their ability to follow through fully on agreements.

This does not mean that cooperative action is impossible on cybersecurity matters. Strong states may face shared external threats and will devise means of jointly addressing those threats. This sort of activity is perhaps more analogous to the cooperation that eventually emerged between the United States and Soviet Union in space flight. Each state had its own program, born of a desire to win the space race. In time each recognized some value in collaborating with the other, even as each continued to develop its own civilian and military rocket capabilities. Both sides saw symbolic value in working together to overcome the shared challenges posed by the laws of physics at the edge of the human frontier. Such partnership continues in the twenty-first century, even in the face of renewed tensions between the United States and Russia.

Devising parallel efforts in cybersecurity is possible. Two areas, the handling of zero days and the strengthening of encryption, will be discussed below as candidates for unilateral action; they could easily be the source of bilateral cooperation as well. Additionally, strong states could implement arrangements for sharing threat intelligence or for providing mutual assistance in cybersecurity investigations to counter the possibility of rogue state or non-state action. In so doing, they can strengthen one another against the challenge posed by non-state actors and third parties. Each strong state will continue to develop its own capabilities, but such cooperation could be an intermediate step in relationship building. It would require some foundation of trust to implement, but would not impose enormous risks or cost on the states.

### Contributions to System-wide Security

The first section in this chapter discussed baseline defenses, inward-focused unilateral efforts that simplify the cybersecurity dilemma. The second section discussed how states can strengthen their bilateral relationships with one another. There is a third possible category of efforts: unilateral actions undertaken by a state that directly increase the security of all actors and, in the process, increase that state's trustworthiness and standing. There is potential promise for these sorts of actions as a means of indicating a willingness to overcome the cybersecurity dilemma.

An old Hollywood saying advises screenwriters that if a line of dialogue or bit of action does not serve two purposes, they should cut it out. This advice hints at a truism present in many fields: while the face value of words and deeds may be important, quite frequently what matters most is the aim they quietly serve. Economists refer to this implicit meaning as signaling value. They argue that, in areas of uncertainty, such signals can help provide clarity. One famous example contends that, in the job market, the value of a college degree derives not from the amount of knowledge a candidate has acquired in school, but from the signals it sends about a candidate's perseverance, work ethic, and tendency towards learning. All of these are of greater importance to employers in many cases than the actual knowledge imparted in the classroom.

The signaling value of the college degree comes from its expense, in both money and time. A college dropout might claim to have a great work ethic and affinity for knowledge, but his or her rhetoric is undercut, fairly or not, by a seeming unwillingness to bear the burdens of actually attending college. Not all signals have equal value—costly signals that involve the actor paying some substantial price often mean the most to others.[28]

The value of costly signals is widely acknowledged in international politics. In times of crisis, states show resolve and determination in an effort to get other states to back down. In such cases, the mobilization of military forces—at significant expense and disruption to society—signals to potential adversaries a state's seriousness about defending its position. In more peaceful circumstances, a security-seeking state might seek to reassure its potential adversaries, to demonstrate that it is not greedy but instead seeks a stable status quo. To do this, a state can send a costly signal that indicates its desire for cooperation and harmony; many proposed mitigations to the security dilemma fall into this category of action. If the cost of the signal is sufficiently meaningful, other states are likely to see it as a sign of trustworthiness and consider taking reciprocal action. At a minimum, a state seen as trustworthy is more likely to get the benefit of the doubt when other states interpret its actions.[29]

Costly signals can only lead towards stability if the recipient recognizes them as such. In 1955, Soviet Premier Nikita Khrushchev unilaterally withdrew military forces from Austria in what appears to have been an attempt at a costly signal. Khrushchev said as much, rhetorically asking, "Is there any stronger proof necessary to show that the Soviet Union does not want to seize Europe ... Who would evacuate troops if he wanted to attack?"[30] But then-Secretary of State John Foster Dulles, with his "bad-faith" model of Soviet policies, treated the move with suspicion and relations remained frosty.[31] In part, this example shows the importance of individuals in trust-building. National leaders must be able to look past biases to recognize costly signals as well as have the willingness to send them in the first place.[32]

The end of the Cold War also provides a few examples of more successful costly signals and growing trust between states. The Soviet leader, Mikhail Gorbachev, recognized by the mid-1980s that the United States did not trust his government. He concluded that the only way to reduce the risk of conflict was by convincing the United States that he wanted peace and would be a reliable partner. As a result, he made significant concessions in the 1987 Intermediate Nuclear Forces agreement, consenting to especially intrusive on-site inspections and agreeing to destroy many more missiles than the United States did. Similarly, he announced the Soviet withdrawal from Afghanistan. With this decision, he gained enormous credibility among American conservatives who thought it was deeply unlikely that the Soviet Union would ever forsake its Afghanistan interests. In 1988, he made a bold speech at the United Nations announcing unilateral troop reductions in Eastern Europe, long a region of great worry for both the Soviet Union and NATO.[33]

Gorbachev calculated deliberately. He knew the effect he was trying to have and the enormous American skepticism he had to overcome. He told the Soviet Politburo that, prior to his actions, critics could dismiss his push for engagement by saying there was "plenty of talk, plenty of nice words, but not a single tank is withdrawn, not a single cannon." He further told the Politburo that his bold moves, however, had "left a huge impression ... [and] created an entirely different background for the perception of our policies and the Soviet Union as a whole."[34] Without action, Gorbachev's speeches would have meant little to suspicious American commentators and policy-makers. In light of the costly signals and interpersonal engagement at diplomatic summits, however, even some hard-line critics recognized the possibility for cooperation between the two superpowers. No less a Soviet skeptic than Ronald Reagan walked back one of his most famous quotes. After Gorbachev's actions, Reagan was asked if he still thought the Soviet Union was an "evil empire," as he had memorably claimed in 1983. "No," the American president replied, "I was talking about another time, another era."[35]

In cybersecurity, just as in nuclear security, states can send costly signals. One potential area of interest is in the handling of zero days, the rare previously unknown software vulnerabilities that sometimes enable sophisticated intrusions. A state's policy on this issue reveals information.[36] Just as Gorbachev faced fierce resistance from some elements of the Soviet security forces over his decisions[37]—these forces claimed that he was sacrificing too much security to send his costly signal—one method of handling zero days will involve making security sacrifices unpalatable to some. These critics will prefer a different approach that may preserve a state's short-term security but might, if discovered, worry other states about its aims and intentions. How states resolve these competing priorities, and what costs they are willing to bear in doing so, sends signals to other states.

Previous chapters outlined the choices available to the discoverer of a zero day: it can be exploited operationally, it can be sold to another party who will exploit it, or it can be reported to the vendor for remediation. For states, the first and last options are the most realistic. There is little evidence thus far that states have engaged in the zero day trade with one another, though it is not out of the realm of possibility.[38] Deciding which choice is best for a given vulnerability can be complex, as the United States Vulnerabilities Equities Process outlines, because of "competing 'equities' for [United States Government] offensive and defensive mission interests."[39]

Exploiting the zero day presents some appeal for states. The right zero day could open opportunities that would otherwise remain closed. It might enable penetration of particularly hardened targets or permit an intruder to remain undetected for a greater period of time. But the zero day by itself will not radically change the overall intelligence picture. The significance will depend on the particulars of the zero day,[40] on the state's ability to integrate its use into operations, and on the defenses set up by the likely targets. For a capable state, zero days can make meaningful and concrete contributions to intelligence collection operations, even if they are not a panacea. Exploiting the zero day, or having it ready for exploitation if needed, is therefore often of some value.

Reporting the zero day might seem less appealing, at least at first. There are no near-term benefits that accrue uniquely to a state disclosing a zero day. Perhaps, if the state has used the zero day previously in some operations, there could even be some harms.[41] By making the vulnerability known, the state forgoes its opportunity to use the zero day's full value in intelligence operations. Once the software vendor issues a patch to address the zero day, if the state attempts to exploit the vulnerability in a subsequent intrusion, there is at least some chance that its target will have applied the fix and be able to thwart the intrusion. In that case, the state will have sacrificed the prospect of near-term intelligence gains in its decision to disclose the vulnerability. In a public statement, the NSA warned of this possible outcome. The agency said, "Disclosing a vulnerability can mean that we forgo an opportunity to collect crucial foreign intelligence that could thwart a terrorist attack, stop the theft of our nation's intellectual property, or discover even more dangerous vulnerabilities that are being used to exploit our networks."[42] For some, losing capabilities will be deeply concerning. Often there will be other collection methods capable of filling this gap, but not always.

The state that reports a zero day accrues some near-term defensive benefits. Assuming that the vendor issues a patch and that network defenders apply it, the state's computers will in the aggregate become more secure. Foreign actors who might also have discovered and exploited the zero day will have a harder time breaking in. The probability of this sort of independent discovery appears substantial,[43] though there is some debate. As former White House Cybersecurity Coordinator Howard Schmidt said:

> It's pretty naïve to believe that with a newly discovered zero-day, you are the only one in the world that's discovered it ... Whether it's another government, a researcher or someone else who sells exploits, you may have it by yourself for a few hours or for a few days, but you sure are not going to have it alone for long.[44]

But it is not just the state that reports the zero day that benefits defensively. Other states, including its potential adversaries, can also boost their security by applying the vendor's patch.

It is easy to conceive of circumstances in which, even in the short term, it is better for a state to report a vulnerability rather than exploit it. One obvious example occurs when a state finds a vulnerability in software that is used primarily by that state and not by its potential adversaries. In such circumstances, the state will not have much meaningful opportunity to exploit the vulnerability for intelligence gains, since it will not be applicable to its likely targets. Worse, if a potential adversary independently discovers the vulnerability, it could pose serious risks to the first state if no patch exists. Given this, in such circumstances a state has an obvious and immediate interest in reporting the vulnerability to the vendor for remediation. For the NSA's part, it said, "Historically, NSA has released more than 91 percent of vulnerabilities discovered in products that have gone through our internal review process and that are made or used in the U.S." But the statement omits any discussion of when this reporting took place. It appears quite possible that the agency used the vulnerabilities for intrusions before eventually disclosing them.[45]

In the medium and long term, a state may gain other benefits from reporting a zero day vulnerability. Conspicuous and costly action can build trust. A history of turning over zero days to software vendors could have great signaling value. If a state develops a credible reputation for regularly reporting zero day vulnerabilities, other states will have solid reason to think that the state is less likely to be planning sophisticated or powerful intrusions. This is particularly true if the zero days disclosed by the state are not ones that are manifestly in its self-interest to report. If the United States reported a vulnerability in software used primarily by Americans, it would not be too significant a step. If the United States government reported a vulnerability in software used primarily by the Chinese, it would send a strong and costly signal about American intentions.

Conspicuous action in the zero day market is possible. When vendors issue a patch, they often issue commendations or cash prizes, known as bug bounties, to researchers who reported the now-fixed vulnerability. Governments probably do not need the money, which is often in the low-thousands of dollars, but the recognition provided by vendors could be a valuable way to build trust. This has happened already. For example, corporations have formally credited the British signals intelligence agency GCHQ with assistance on vulnerabilities, a recognition touted by a former agency director.[46] In this way, the zero day question is reasonably unusual in international relations: there are credible third parties, software vendors, who can shed light on the intentions of states using a simple mechanism already in place. Credibility-building unilateral action is therefore possible.

A similar dynamic is at work in encryption, meaning that it is also an area in which states can potentially send costly signals. The essence of encryption is straightforward: it permits two parties to communicate with one another in such a way that a third party cannot make sense of the communication.[47] This is true even if the third-party eavesdropper wholly intercepts the message transmitted between the two parties. While the particulars of how this works are beyond the scope of this text,[48] the power that encryption places in the hands of communicators is quite remarkable. Though it is nothing more than math, the concept can seem almost magical to some. It suffices here to say that strong encryption is at the core of many, if not most, meaningful digital activities, including virtually all banking and shopping, many web searches and website visits, and some chat and email conversations.

For this reason, governments have long had an uneasy relationship with encryption. On the one hand, for economically advanced states like the United States, encryption is of enormous value. Encryption undergirds many of the high-tech services exported by leading companies. American intelligence agencies, diplomats, and the military rely on encryption to coordinate global efforts. Citizens, sometimes knowingly and sometimes not, use encryption for security as they go about their activities online. All of these are good things for the United States. With these benefits in mind, the United States government has a program, run by the National Institute for Standards and Technology (NIST), to certify particular implementations of encryption as safe for use. The program verifies that these implementations do not have any weaknesses that might permit others who have intercepted a message to decode what it means.

Encryption can also frustrate policy-makers. Not only can legitimate citizens, industry, and government officials use encryption, but more nefarious actors can as well. The most obvious and widely discussed example in domestic affairs is that criminals might use it to try to keep one step ahead of the police. Whether, in an effort to combat this, the police should have the ability to read any message with a court order is a lively and ongoing debate, but since it is a matter of domestic politics, it is largely outside the scope of this text.[49]

Encryption can also frustrate foreign intelligence officials, a subject that is of relevance to the cybersecurity dilemma. Unlike in the past, when each state had its own secret encryption mechanisms, many methods are now publicly available for use. For a powerful and technologically advanced state, it is quite plausible that some of the foreign intelligence targets of that state—surveyed both through network intrusions and other methods—will in fact employ encryption invented in that state. In such circumstances, the state's own innovations that benefit it economically might hurt it in matters of intelligence. How much difficulty encryption poses for collectors depends on the particulars of the intelligence operation and the encryption.

The easiest response for states is to try to put export controls in place, in the same way that states seek to regulate the shipment and sale of weapons. In theory, this is an ideal solution: the state's citizens, corporations, and government officials can enjoy the cryptography's protection, but foreign actors will not be able to take advantage of it. In practice, however, it is unworkable. Computer code, such as encryption implementations, crosses borders far more easily than physical weapons. Mathematical ideas, which comprise the core of encryption, spread still faster. The United States government attempted to regulate cryptography during the 1990s and failed.[50] Indeed, the period of attempted export control left an enduring negative legacy: several serious cryptographic weaknesses, some discovered as late as 2015, persisted in modern systems as a result of the old mandated standards.[51]

A second possibility emerges: a state can take an active role in verifying cryptography as secure, but then seek surreptitiously to introduce weaknesses into the cryptographic implementations. In theory, only the state will know about these vulnerabilities and only it will be able to take advantage of them. If the state has sufficient clout, other actors will trust its certification of the cryptographic implementations and will use them to secure their own communications. Once other states put the cryptography to use securing important information, the first state can exploit the weakness to intercept and decode the sensitive data.

The United States reportedly did just this. The NSA worked within the United States interagency process to introduce weaknesses into a key part of a cryptographic implementation. NIST certified that implementation as secure.[52] Reportedly, the NSA then secretly paid an American cybersecurity company, RSA, millions of dollars to use the implementation in one of its products.[53] If foreign actors used the product to secure their networks or data, the NSA would likely be able to overcome the obstacle posed by encryption. The United States' position internationally—the general trust in its government and the reach of its corporations—served its intelligence aims.

In sum, with regard to encryption and foreign intelligence, a powerful state has three choices.[54] First, it can attempt to advance encryption that is truly secure, putting the technological might of its government towards increasing the cybersecurity of all actors. The Dutch government took this approach, announcing in 2016 that it would outlaw mandated weaknesses and earmark money for strengthening encryption globally.[55] Second, the state can do nothing, leaving the question for private sector cryptographers to handle. Third, it can seek surreptitiously to influence the system in ways that suit its own advantage, as the United States did. There are several factors that go into this decision, but one consideration, long-term trust, is particularly relevant in light of the cybersecurity dilemma.

Pursuing the first option, strengthening cryptography, can yield long-term gains in trust for the state. A state's attitude towards cryptography can, to some degree, indicate its attitude towards intelligence collection via cyber operations. States that noticeably work in favor of strong cryptography for all actors can increase their trustworthiness in the eyes of other states. Insofar as strong cryptography interferes with intelligence collection, a state's willingness to promote better encryption demonstrates its recognition of limits on its intelligence collection, its willingness to permit information to remain outside of its own reach, and its readiness to make contributions of broad benefit. This choice comes with real costs. As such, a state conspicuously paying them is more likely to gain long-term trust than a state that pursues the second option and does nothing.

Pursuing the final option, stealthily introducing weaknesses, can yield intelligence gains. By verifying deliberately insecure cryptographic implementations as safe, the United States likely increased the power of its signals intelligence efforts. Assuming that the deception is not uncovered, this option can also lead to long-term gains in trust for a state that chooses it. Other states will not know that the verified algorithms are in fact insecure. But if the state's duplicity is discovered, the loss of trust can be severe. When the American deception eventually came to light, it earned widespread condemnation, including strong warnings from NIST's advisory board.[56] In response, a senior NSA official wrote a mathematical journal article calling the failure to withdraw support for the weakened cryptographic system "regrettable" and stating that the "NSA must be much more transparent in its standards work and act according to that transparency."[57] Whether this will be enough to restore long-term trust in the United States' cryptographic verification program remains to be seen.

There is a confounding factor. State-level variables may influence a government's view on cryptography. Authoritarian regimes may be less willing, for instance, to permit their citizens to use truly secure cryptography, for fear that those resistant to the government will use it too. Conversely, some democratic states seeking to protect or encourage dissidents in authoritarian regimes may be more likely to export strong cryptography. Even individual states pursue contradictory policies. For example, while the NSA spends hundreds of millions of dollars annually on weakening encryption used around the world,[58] the United States State Department spends tens of millions of dollars trying to export strong cryptography to dissidents and journalists overseas.[59] All told, most states' relationship with cryptography is too complex to unpack fully. Suffice it to say that the matter of international trust, which is deeply important for the purposes of mitigating the cybersecurity dilemma, is but one part of a broader policy discussion on the issue.

### Establishing a Security Posture

States develop security postures, determining for themselves and for others how they will interpret and respond to certain events. These postures can guide policy internally, but states can also communicate them more widely. If enough states share similar views on appropriate posture, a stable status quo can result. Part of a state's posture in cybersecurity could try to minimize the dangers of the cybersecurity dilemma. These are some possible components of such a posture.

States must first develop a plan for dealing with third-party Counter-Computer Network Exploitation (CCNE) intrusions. These intrusions provide a defensive justification for breaking into a great number of targets: that the intruders are looking to learn about other intruders who have penetrated those targets. Chapter Three outlines how the Five Eyes learned about French capabilities by targeting another state, for example. If these sorts of intrusions are removed from consideration, the cybersecurity dilemma is theoretically much easier to mitigate. Without third-party CCNE intrusions, the only intrusions that are both narrowly defensive[60] for one state yet also threatening to another are intrusions into cyber operations units. This comparatively smaller set of intrusions would still meet the criteria of the cybersecurity dilemma. They would enable the intruding side to collect direct information about another state's cyber operations capabilities while also threatening the state suffering the intrusion.

Third-party CCNE intrusions have the effect, therefore, of broadening the cybersecurity dilemma. When states break into the important networks of third parties to uncover the techniques used by a potential adversary who has also penetrated those networks, states needlessly threaten those third parties. They are also unlikely to constrain themselves much in their targeting, but will instead intrude on networks likely to be of interest to a potential adversary, including economic, political, and critical infrastructure targets. In each case, if the third party discovers the intrusion(s), it risks bringing about the cybersecurity dilemma. The state suffering the intrusion will then, under the dilemma of interpretation, have to determine if the intrusion is threatening and a prelude to future danger, or if it is a defensive-minded third-party CCNE effort. Getting this interpretation wrong by viewing defensive third-party CCNE efforts as threats risks escalation desired by neither side; getting it wrong by interpreting a real threat as a third-party CCNE intrusion risks remaining vulnerable to potentially serious dangers.

States seeking to limit the overall scope of the cybersecurity dilemma must find a way around the third-party CCNE issue. Strong states have at least one course of action available to them. They can, in advance of any particular incident, announce a clear position on third-party CCNE intrusions: when they discover an intrusion in one of their own important networks, but not a network directly associated with their own cyber operations, they will not consider the third-party CCNE possibility as they confront the dilemma of interpretation. In other words, in no circumstance will they assume that other states have penetrated their networks to gather intelligence on other states that might also be in those networks. They will treat each network penetration as its own threat, removing any possible benefit of the doubt for intruders relating to CCNE.

This has a broader mitigating effect. If a state assumes that its potential adversary has active cyber capabilities and uses them in ways that are not narrowly defensive, the state is likely to conclude that its potential adversary has penetrated a substantial number of networks from a wide variety of states. If the state wants to conduct a third-party CCNE intrusion to learn more about these capabilities, it then has some choice in which networks it will target to do so. It can pick any network that its potential adversary has likely targeted. This range of choice is constrained only to the degree that the potential adversary develops and deploys unique capabilities for each of its targets. While there is certainly variance in which capabilities states employ, even sophisticated actors re-use many frameworks and pieces of infrastructure across operations.

If strong states have made clear that they will not give any credence to the possibility of third-party CCNE intrusions, the state seeking to conduct such an intrusion will then have additional incentive to do so instead against a comparatively weaker state with weaker response capabilities. If implemented, this expectation creates a positive feedback loop for strong states with an enforced and clear posture on CCNE: when they do discover an intrusion in their own networks that might otherwise potentially be seen as third-party CCNE, they can have greater confidence that it is something probably more serious and thereby act with greater certainty. If such a forceful treatment of CCNE is credible—which is a challenge, to be sure—it reduces the overall risk of the cybersecurity dilemma among strong states.

This aggressive treatment of potential third-party CCNE intrusions, in which states treat them exactly the same as other intrusions, yields a much thornier strategic problem: states must figure out how to treat intrusions into serious networks in general. The difficulty is straightforward. Even with strong baseline defenses, it seems likely that some intruders will get through into important networks. Analysts may detect some of these intruders before they can establish a presence, but it is likely that even the best defenders will not be able to detect every intrusion right away. On the one hand, this inability to detect all intrusions helps to animate the cybersecurity dilemma, prompting states to go looking in the networks of potential adversaries for information of use in defensive efforts. On the other hand, the fact that states detect some percentage of intrusions, though sometimes too late to stop the intended effect, means that they must determine how to respond.

For a state that wants to mitigate the cybersecurity dilemma but also set out clear consequences for those who intrude on its networks, the following three principles could offer useful starting points. First, states must recognize the limits of their ability to punish and constrain behavior in cyber operations. Below some threshold of intrusion seriousness, they are unlikely to devise appropriate responses to punish intruders.[61] That is, no single retaliatory and deterrent strategy will stop all unwanted behavior. This is especially true for networks of moderate or less importance, where claims of a powerful response are less credible.

Fortunately for the discussion of the cybersecurity dilemma, however, these less important networks are not of primary concern. The dilemma is only relevant on networks of true strategic importance. Thus, for states that worry about the cybersecurity dilemma, the way in which they respond to intrusions above the threshold must be fundamentally different from the way in which they respond to intrusions below it. Recognizing this difference internally—the additional options available and the additional risks that arise—is the first step.[62]

A second principle is that, for networks of true strategic importance, states should reconsider their notion of proportionality. Assuming that a state cannot detect all intrusions into its important networks, a response calibrated just to the intrusions it does uncover is likely to be insufficient. The state will have to scale up its response if it wants to account for the activity it did not detect. In this way, responding to a network intrusion is similar to law enforcement responding to a crime; some percentage of even serious crimes will go undetected or unsolved,[63] but the consequences for most serious crimes are severe.

There are limits on what a state can do to stop a particular individual criminal. A system of strong criminal punishments maxes out its potential responses well before a felon maxes out conceivable serious crimes. For example, in most states the penalty for murdering one hundred people is not likely to be ten times worse than the penalty for murdering ten people. The state has overwhelming power over the individual. When the justice system enacts this maximum punishment, it renders irrelevant the issue of deterring that individual in the future. The criminal will usually either suffer a life sentence behind bars or the death penalty. As a result, aggregation is not useful in determining a punishment. If a criminal has committed a hundred separate murders, there are diminishing returns to the justice system in spending lots of resources prosecuting the criminal for each one, since the maximum sentence will be reached long before that point.[64]

In international affairs, the opposite is true. Everything under consideration in the cybersecurity dilemma falls well short of the maximum kinetic threshold, so there are functionally no limits on what responses are possible. States also have far greater capacity for causing harm than individual criminals do. A state with developed cyber operations capabilities might be able to break into dozens of the important networks of another state. If this occurs, the state suffering the intrusions will be better able to consider their impact and what they mean for the relationship with the intruding state by investigating the incidents individually but then aggregating them together for the purposes of determining a cumulative response. Moving a deterrence paradigm in this direction could make it more effective.[65]

To put this into practice, a state might conduct regular reviews of intrusions into its important networks by a particular actor. It could use these reviews to determine what the intrusions, in the aggregate, reveal about the actor's priorities, its capabilities, and its future actions. If the intrusions are serious or threatening and if they violate whatever status quo a state is trying to establish, the state could use this forum to devise a response that fits the identified pattern of behavior. It is not difficult to imagine such reviews becoming a routine part of government, much in the same way that agencies conduct reviews for potential proliferators, human rights abusers, and state sponsors of terror.

One of the common reasons states cite for not responding to network intrusions is that doing so reveals a state's investigative and attributive capabilities. For example, American officials mentioned this concern both as a reason for withholding information regarding the North Korean attack on Sony and as a reason for not publicly attributing the intrusion at OPM to the Chinese government or affiliated actors.[66] But as states aggregate incidents, this worry diminishes. The state needs only to justify its response by pointing to a pattern of activity. A state may even choose to omit a specific incident from its public justification entirely—treating it as unattributed or providing comparatively less information to the public—but nonetheless increase the severity of its response to account for it. In an anarchic system, states are free to enact whatever seemingly disproportionate responses they can enforce while maintaining both their own capabilities and their credibility.

All this talk of seemingly disproportionate response might seem quite worrying, especially in the context of minimizing a security dilemma and limiting escalation. This is why a third principle is vital: while states' near-term operational responses are likely to relate to cyber operations, states' strategic responses should not be cyber operations. Assuming that the intrusion in question is not a destructive cyber attack equivalent to a major military operation, no response to a network intrusion should directly put lives at risk or should animate any of the specific threats outlined in Chapter Four. States will still have tools available to them to express their displeasure and cause harm to adversaries without escalating in the direction of military conflict. This is true at both the operational and strategic levels, and is known as cross-domain deterrence.[67]

At the operational level, one option states have is to disclose the capabilities of their adversaries, rendering those capabilities less useful in future operations. By distributing information about their adversaries' tools and techniques, states make it easier for other actors to detect and respond to similar intrusions. This makes operations more difficult for the adversary and can impose additional costs, particularly if the adversary must develop new infrastructure. However, because this step relies on forensic information gathered from the network on which the intrusion took place, rather than by penetrating the adversary's strategic networks, it does not unduly threaten the adversary.

Another option is to blunt the unwanted activity as it occurs. For example, the same Presidential Policy Directive 20 that discusses authorizing Offensive Cyber Effects Operations outlines circumstances under which the United States might undertake so-called Defensive Cyber Effects Operations.[68] Although details on these efforts are not provided, they take place at the operational level, seeking to stop an adversary's activity from succeeding. It is not hard to imagine techniques in this category of actions that would thwart sophisticated denial of service attacks or send misleading operational data to an adversary. But these activities are not necessarily intrusions per se, in that they do not develop a persistent presence on the adversary's networks. Instead, they might rely on a presence within the infrastructure of the internet itself. For this reason, the impact of these techniques is more likely to be limited only to their immediate defensive use. As a result, they are also less likely to animate the cybersecurity dilemma.

The strategic response to intrusions ideally does not require intrusion capabilities at all. Instead, states should examine other tools available to them that do not risk animating the cybersecurity dilemma. The most likely candidates are political and economic sanctions. For example, states might use their reviews of aggregated activity by other states to determine which sanctions are appropriate. After such reviews, a state might impose these economic sanctions, enacting limits on trade with certain states or companies deemed to have carried out serious intrusions; it might decide on a fitting political protest or an indictment, seeking to isolate and condemn another state whose actions have crossed a certain threshold.

There is already some precedent for this sort of action. In response to the North Korean attack on Sony, the Obama Administration levied economic sanctions on the country. The administration left itself a small degree of wiggle room, however, contending that the sanctions were in response to both the North Korean cyber activity and the country's oppression of human rights.[69] Likewise, the 2014 indictment of five Chinese People's Liberation Army officers and the 2016 indictment of Iranian operators are law enforcement responses but also political ones. By splashing the intruders' pictures on Wild West-style "Wanted" posters, the United States sought to attract attention to the case and demonstrate its commitment to the issue. A crucial point is evident from these examples: states need not respond in the matter in which they were provoked. Economic sanctions can meet politically-minded attacks and political actions can meet economic espionage.[70]

These sorts of political and economic actions do not animate the cybersecurity dilemma. They do not involve intrusions into an adversary's networks. That said, they should not be taken lightly. Fair international trade and political engagement are increasingly important and, according to most economists, of benefit to all sides. Sanctions are not always effective. They will potentially invite retaliatory sanctions, though these responses will likely also not animate the cybersecurity dilemma. Nevertheless, these tools can be of help when wielded carefully; the American willingness to sanction the Chinese is perhaps due some credit for facilitating the agreement in 2015 on cybersecurity. In critical circumstances, when adversaries penetrate and threaten networks of strategic national importance, states should recognize the value that a firm response can provide, particularly when that response does not risk military or intelligence escalation. To do otherwise is to invite trouble. A state with no red lines is a state ripe for intrusion, and a state fearing serious intrusions is most at risk for the cybersecurity dilemma.

*Conclusion: Old Variables, New Mitigations*

This chapter has tried to chart the beginnings of a possible way around the cybersecurity dilemma. Chapters Five and Six noted that the failure of traditional mitigations to apply to the cybersecurity dilemma did not mean that the variables they attempt to shape—offense–defense balance, offense–defense differentiation, greed, state-level analysis, information distribution, and a shared status quo—lose relevance. On the contrary, the earlier chapters' assessment of these variables indicated that the cybersecurity dilemma could be quite severe. In light of that, it is worth examining how the proposed mitigations in this chapter address the problem.

At the foundation of a multi-pronged approach is the unilateral deployment of baseline defenses. This does not meaningfully affect the offense–defense balance more generally, since, unlike some physical defenses, cyber defenses do not also inhibit offensive action. The defenses' primary value is their ability to keep intruders out and simplify the decisions faced by policy-makers.

The bilateral and unilateral actions outlined in the second and third sections seek to alter the offense–defense balance in a practical and systemic way. By taking zero days off the market, a state reduces its own ability, as well as everyone else's ability (to some degree), to intrude into foreign networks. Likewise, by advancing strong encryption, it indicates a willingness to place other system-wide goals, mostly aligned with defense, ahead of its own intelligence collection. Doing each of these things in a conspicuous and costly way, verified with the passage of time, also sends meaningful signals about a state's greed or lack thereof and its commitment to advancing stability. All told, it is in the areas of offense–defense balance and perceptions of greed where states have the most tools available to them for mitigating the cybersecurity dilemma—tools they have not yet begun to employ significantly.

The actions outlined in the fourth section work towards achieving a more stable status quo. With effort in this area, strong states can take steps to communicate their seriousness on cybersecurity. They can firmly establish their commitment to defense without animating fears in potential adversaries. Cross-domain deterrence provides a possibility for mitigating the cybersecurity dilemma, and a firm posture on

Counter-Computer Network Exploitation intrusions can help to minimize the dilemma. With time, and in combination with some other steps, the unilateral actions discussed in this section can contribute towards a stable multi-lateral baseline of behavior.

Some variables of the cybersecurity dilemma are largely unmoved by all the foregoing possible options. The main problem with offense—defense differentiation—that apparently or even genuinely defensive-minded intrusions can quickly morph into offensive ones—remains unsolved. The primary challenge of information asymmetry—providing verification of other states' capabilities, or lack thereof—is likewise mostly unaddressed, although some of the bilateral possibilities in the second section provide states with means through which they might share some information on capabilities. Similarly, this chapter largely does not tackle the role that state-level factors might play in mitigating the cybersecurity dilemma, mostly because there is not yet enough information available to do justice to that topic. In the future, mitigations shaping these variables might also form key parts of a multi-pronged approach.

# CONCLUSION

## THE DANGERS OF THE CYBERSECURITY DILEMMA

The security dilemma has been called an "old and brilliant concept for new and dangerous times."[1] The long-standing idea demonstrates that, in a variety of circumstances, fears and tensions arise not just between states seeking conflict, but also between two states that only want to assure their own safety. States know their own fear and act to quell it. But they find it difficult or impossible to appreciate the fear their actions cause in others. From the time of Thucydides to the Cold War and beyond, this danger has emerged again and again. The development of new weapons, the deployment of military forces, and the collection of intelligence by intrusive means can all cause the security dilemma.

The dilemma varies in severity based on the technology, geography, and the states involved. The pitfalls are particularly acute when there is a perception of offense-dominance, when offense and defense are hard to differentiate, when states are greedy or not well understood, and when there is no flow of credible information and no stable status quo. The risk of unintentional threats, amplified by these variables, can compound and form a hazardous cycle. The anarchic international system dictates that states must fend for themselves. As a result, they sometimes have good reason to fear the worst.

In cybersecurity, these variables suggest a dilemma that is dangerous. Many policy-makers, up to and including senior Department of

Defense officials and President Obama, have made clear their belief that the offense has significant advantages and that offense and defense are hard to tell apart. Major states, including democracies, are perceived by other states to be greedy in their cyber operations. The international concern about Chinese and Russian intrusions and the outcry following the Snowden revelations shows as much. Some actors have vastly more information than others, partly as a result of more developed intelligence-gathering capabilities, including intrusions. The international norms of behavior are only nascent, even with progress at the United Nations. As such, when it comes to cybersecurity, the structures of the international system and the characteristics of operations encourage fear. This fear, and the escalation that results, does damage in five ways.

First, the cybersecurity dilemma's tendency towards escalation emerges not just in a crisis, but also in anticipation of one. A fearful state is more likely to pursue offensive capabilities for contingencies, deterrence, and retaliation. States concerned about cybersecurity dedicate large amounts of resources to training people and developing technology to build out their forces. The rapidly increasing investments in cyber operations from a large number of governments, including the creation and expansion of military and intelligence cyber units around the world, confirm this. States do much of this groundwork within their own borders, including force development and tool refinement. Just as the security dilemma predicts that traditional military preparations can cause fear, this kind of preparation can cause other states to be afraid.

The cybersecurity dilemma adds an additional important wrinkle. A state that desires offensive options in cyber operations will often need to intrude into the networks of other states in advance of tension to enable its capabilities. The lack of speed and momentum in cyber operations, the value of a pre-existing foothold in foreign networks, and the power of persistence are key factors in cyber operations. All these factors enable or encourage states to set up offensive efforts, or important parts thereof, in advance. Statements from intelligence officials, forensic reports from cybersecurity professionals, and leaked documents demonstrate that a variety of states, including the United States and its potential adversaries, perform these kinds of enabling intrusions. Governed by authorities like Presidential Policy Directive 20, these operations provide options to the intruding state but animate great fear in the state suffering the breach. The perceived and actual need for attack and broad collection capabilities during a crisis, brought on by fear of the crisis, paradoxically makes the crisis more likely.

A second danger is that fear prompts advance escalation on defense, too. Most protective activities will be benign. Organizations set up baseline defenses to secure their networks. Some of these defenses are automated ones, relying on a combination of signatures and heuristics to detect or block malicious code. Organizations with more developed capabilities will likely add human analysts into the mix, actively hunting within their networks for malicious code that might have slipped past the automated sensors. These hunters, when properly trained and equipped, can greatly improve an organization's security posture and are an increasingly appealing investment. For many organizations and some states, the defensive mission ends there.

But a state that fears a potential adversary's cyber capabilities has incentives to get ahead of the problem. Even if the state genuinely does not want offensive options and does not wish to threaten others, it has good reason to intrude into foreign networks so that it can collect intelligence of defensive value. This helps it detect and stop a potential adversary's intrusions as easily as possible. Leaked documents show that the United States and its signals intelligence partners employ this approach. These documents outline the lengths to which the United States goes to gather intelligence on its adversaries' activities in order to build tailored countermeasures. States such as China, Russia, France, Israel, and others have similar or greater structural incentives to launch defensive-minded intrusions, although there is no information on whether they do.

Defensive-minded intrusions are a gamble. If the effort goes undetected and successfully collects information that helps block malicious activity, all is well. In that case, the state has secured itself more effectively without causing further escalation. But if the state suffering the intrusion detects it and responds forcefully, the trouble that the defensive-minded operation tried to avoid becomes more likely. In short, a key component of network defense for strategically important networks, at least as practiced by the United States and its partners, carries risks of its own. If it yields an escalatory response from another state, it can amplify the threat that it seeks to mitigate and thus increase the need for that defense.

Both causes of possible escalation—intrusions to enable offensive action and intrusions that improve defenses—are amplified still further by the potency of breaches. Intrusions can enable targeted and destructive cyber attacks. These powerful attacks sometimes have physical effects, like Stuxnet or the blackout in Ukraine. The intrusions can also provide a beachhead for less-tailored destructive wiping operations of the sort seen against Sony Pictures Entertainment, Sands Casino, and Aramco. More generally, these intrusions can shape future conflict and competition through the wide-ranging collection of intelligence. This includes observation of military capabilities or political decision-making. Lastly, intrusions can cause major counterintelligence trouble, compromising the sources, methods, and knowledge of a penetrated intelligence service. States will desire these capabilities against other states, but fear suffering intrusions in their own networks. The power of cyber operations drives both halves of the cybersecurity dilemma, spurring offensive- and defensive-minded intrusions even before an incident.

This yields the third way in which the escalation of the cybersecurity dilemma can be damaging. When a state detects an intrusion from another state into a strategically important network, it must decide how much danger the intrusion poses. The intrusion could be setting up offensive action, a serious threat. It could be narrowly focused on improving the other state's defensive measures, something of less concern. This assessment of intention is the dilemma of interpretation. States make this determination with imperfect information. The threatening possibilities of network intrusions will weigh on the calculus. With threats looming, decision-makers are more likely to assume the worst. Thus not only does the fear engendered by the cybersecurity dilemma make incidents more likely by increasing the number of offensive and defensive intrusions, but it also makes the incidents themselves potentially more serious.

At a minimum, intrusions into important networks can prompt major concern within a government. One previously discussed example of this is the Solar Sunrise case, in which the activities of independent hackers—mistaken for a time for Iraqi operators—set off alarms throughout key parts of the American military. Another is the Moonlight Maze operation: a sustained series of Russian intrusions into a wide variety of American targets prompted policy-makers to interpret the breaches as battlefield preparation and even cyberwarfare. This latter case also demonstrated how an intrusion yields escalation; in their response to the Russian activity, the United States government launched intrusions of its own against Russian systems. While there has not yet been a case in which network breaches have escalated into sustained conflict between two actors, as cyber operations become more integrated into military operations, the risk will continue to grow.

A fourth danger is that these two pressures—the simultaneous need for better offensive capability and access plus the need for better defensive security and resilience—force states into sometimes contradictory policy positions. Zero day vulnerabilities, which can enable some kinds of intrusions but also leave a state's own systems vulnerable, provide an example. On the one hand, governments have obvious incentives to encourage the patching of zero days, so that the software used in their state is secure. But because of the role that zero days can sometimes play in enabling operations against hard targets, such as foreign intelligence agencies, there are countervailing reasons to preserve the vulnerabilities for use in intrusions. Indeed, their use can reduce the chances of detection and minimize the risk of unintentional threats and escalation. If states did not need intrusions for defense, or if they did not employ intrusions at all, the matter of zero days would be much simpler. But as things stand, there is great potential for damage in trying to optimize this contradictory policy. Preserving too few zero days risks making intrusions against hard targets impossible or more likely to lead to detection and escalation; yet preserving too many or the wrong kind of zero days risks leaving critical software vulnerable to foreign intrusions.

Encryption offers a parallel set of incentives and challenges. Used properly, it can strengthen the security of networks, software, and users. Encryption is therefore vital for statecraft, as well as for a wide variety of other critical parts of society. This prompts some states, such as the Netherlands, to give unequivocal support to strong encryption.[2] But encryption can also confound certain types of intelligence collection against a wide variety of targets, domestically and overseas. When encryption thwarts collection, it frustrates law enforcement and intelligence agencies. The interplay between intrusion and defense at the center of the cybersecurity dilemma emerges once more. On the one hand, states want cryptography to secure their strategically important public and private sector communications from intruders and eavesdroppers. On the other hand, states want to be able to bypass encryption when they are the ones seeking access. The policy balance is once again hard to optimize without doing damage. Weak encryption leaves vital information and systems vulnerable, but strong encryption could sometimes protect a state's adversaries.

Lastly, the cybersecurity dilemma can tempt policy-makers into potentially damaging duplicity. As governments try to navigate their way through the aforementioned policy challenges, they may find deception appealing. Some governments might try to promote encryption as secure, even though they can secretly gain access; or they might condemn certain kinds of intrusions while simultaneously performing them. These actions can give the false impression of sending costly signals. They can win the trust of other states but not actually constrain a state's intelligence capabilities. In this regard, deceptive behavior, such as the United States' certification of a deliberately weakened encryption algorithm, is a policy success if it remains undetected. Most states would happily convince others to adhere to a rules-based system while themselves silently subverting that system when necessary.

A line from Thucydides' Melian Dialogue, quoted previously, provides one view on this course of action: "the strong do what they can, and the weak suffer what they must."[3] From this perspective, duplicity is wise if a state can get away with it. Weaker states will not be able to sustain a duplicitous approach in response to the cybersecurity dilemma. Yet a strong enough state can condemn and punish the actions of another state even when carrying out those same actions itself. The strong state may be able to do so in secret, negating any trouble. Even if its duplicity is detected, however, it might not matter. A true hegemon—the state that is substantially stronger than any other—may be so powerful that it will be capable of enforcing an open double standard. Unless other states are capable enough to resist in some credible manner and care enough about cybersecurity practice to do so, the hegemon has no reason to restrain its own activities. Once its duplicity is uncovered, a mistrusted hegemon can still try to meld the status quo to its own liking, favoring resilience, deterrence, and strength over trust-building and costly signals.

But, from another perspective, detected duplicity does long-run damage. The harms of a hypocritical approach can be significant, even for powerful actors. For a hegemon, constructing an overt system to benefit mostly itself at the expense of other states risks losing the trust of those other states.[4] Over time, a mistrusted hegemon's lack of credibility erodes the stability and functioning of the international system. Even a strong hegemon does not want other states to be perpetually doubting it. Game theoretic models of international relations broadly support this conclusion, as do some interpretations of historical case studies.[5]

Malicious cybersecurity activities can undermine trust. For example, Five Eyes activities have caused even democratic allies to condemn their behavior.[6] Similarly, after information about the NSA's activities became known in 2013, the Chinese government viewed the revelations as evidence of dishonesty on the part of the United States. American officials allege that, in response, Chinese leaders at one point reneged on their commitments to apply international law to cyberspace.[7] This necessitated further American trust-building efforts before the two sides signed an agreement in 2015. While costly signals, credible institutions, and consistency in behavior make overcoming mistrust easier, unexpected duplicity instead breeds damaging suspicion.[8] From this perspective, states are unwise to carry out deceitful policies as a means of managing the cybersecurity dilemma.

All told, the core of the cybersecurity dilemma is about fear and escalation: the fear that causes the dilemma to arise and the escalation that the dilemma potentially brings about. This pattern of fear and escalation shapes policy-makers' decisions. Overcoming the cybersecurity dilemma is no easy task. It will likely require a bigger investment in baseline defenses, an increased readiness for bilateral trust-building, a willingness to send costly signals, and a sustainable security posture. Prospects for mitigation will wane if the price of these actions is more than influential states are willing to pay.

In an anarchic system, it makes some sense for states to be skeptical of other states and of sending costly signals. The need for security is paramount, and cyber operations, for offensive and defensive purposes, have much to contribute. But the cybersecurity dilemma logic shows how misinterpretation can lead to outcomes that no state wants. As cyber operations become more potent and computer networks grow still more important, the dilemma's dangers—already real—will only grow. States will either take action in search of mitigation or they will bear the dilemma's risks. There is no easy way out.

# NOTES

## INTRODUCTION

1. Alexander Mooney, 'Who Has Obama's E-Mail Address?', CNN, 2 February 2009.
2. Michael Schmidt and David Sanger, 'Russian Hackers Read Obama's Unclassified Emails, Officials Say', *New York Times*, April 2015.
3. Carter may have been more open because the case he disclosed was one in which the Pentagon's digital defenses detected the intruders not long after they gained access. Ash Carter, 'Drell Lecture: "Rewiring the Pentagon: Charting a New Path on Innovation and Cybersecurity" (Stanford University)', Department of Defense, 23 April 2015.
4. Shane Smith, 'Cyberspies, Nukes, and the New Cold War: Shane Smith Interviews Ashton Carter (Part 1)', *Vice News*, 15 May 2015, 2:13.
5. The definition of which networks are important enough to meet this threshold will be discussed shortly.
6. John Herz, 'Idealist Internationalism and the Security Dilemma', *World Politics* 2, no. 2 (1950); Herbert Butterfield, *History and Human Relations* (London: Collins, 1951).
7. Robert Jervis, 'Cooperation under the Security Dilemma', *World Politics* 30, no. 2 (1978).
8. Barry Posen, 'The Security Dilemma and Ethnic Conflict', *Survival* 35, no. 1 (1993).
9. Some of these states that do not conduct intrusions ask larger states to share intelligence.
10. The most prominent work is by Robert Jervis. See Jervis, 'Cooperation under the Security Dilemma'. See also Charles Glaser, 'The Security Dilemma Revisited', *World Politics* 50, no. 1 (1997). Chapter Five discusses both articles in much greater detail.
11. For one acknowledgement of the importance of this intersection, see Joseph Nye, 'Cyber Power', Belfer Center for Science and International

Affairs, May 2010. See also Lucas Kello, 'The Meaning of the Cyber Revolution: Perils to Theory and Statecraft', *International Security* 38, no. 2 (2013).

12. This book's formal point of departure is what is known as the "defensive realist" approach, for reasons outlined in the first chapter.

13. For a fuller unpacking of high-quality incident reports, see Thomas Rid and Ben Buchanan, 'Attributing Cyber Attacks', *Journal of Strategic Studies* 39, no. 1 (2015).

14. For one example of a news report that began with a Snowden document, but relied on significant additional reporting, see Barton Gellman and Ashkan Soltani, 'NSA Infiltrates Links to Yahoo, Google Data Centers Worldwide, Snowden Documents Say', *Washington Post*, 30 October 2013.

15. For one example, see Richard Clarke et al., 'Liberty and Security in a Changing World', The President's Review Group on Intelligence and Communications Technologies, 12 December 2013.

16. For one version of this argument, see Robert Lee and Thomas Rid, 'OMG Cyber!', *RUSI Journal* 159, no. 5 (2014).

17. This is most true for the realist school of international relations, in which this work is situated. Other schools have done an admirable job of broadening the analytical focus beyond states.

18. The notion of state responsibility for a network intrusion is a deeply interesting one, but—beyond a certain level—not within the scope of this text. For more on the subject, see Richard Bejtlich, 'What Does Responsibility Mean for Attribution?', TaoSecurity, 22 December 2014; Jason Healey, 'Beyond Attribution: Seeking National Responsibility for Cyber Attacks', Atlantic Council, 2011.

19. For an example of a detailed discussion of the weaponization process integral to attack, see 'The Cyber Warfare Lexicon', United States Strategic Command: National Security Archive, 2016.

20. For a particularly good discussion of the practice of intelligence studies, including the problem of classified information, see John Ferris, 'Coming in from the Cold War: The Historiography of American Intelligence, 1945–1990', *Diplomatic History* 19, no. 1 (1995).

21. This term refers to the intelligence cooperation agreement between the United States, the United Kingdom, Canada, Australia, and New Zealand.

1. THE SECURITY DILEMMA

1. This account of the incident is drawn from Michael Dobbs, 'One Minute to Midnight', National Security Archive, 11 June 2008. For a

more detailed examination, see Michael Dobbs, *One Minute to Midnight* (New York: Knopf, 2008).

2. Thucydides, *The History of the Peloponnesian War*, trans. Richard Crawley (Amazon Digital Services, 2012), 236.

3. The significance of international institutions, such as the United Nations, is debated by various schools of international relations. But even the most powerful institutions, such as military alliances, are in the end made up of states.

4. It is perhaps no surprise that Hobbes' gloomy ideas became most prominent after the violence of the English Civil War. Thomas Hobbes, *Of Man, Being the First Part of Leviathan*, ed. Charles W. Eliot, vol. 34 (New York: P. F. Collier & Son, 1909–14).

5. John Locke, *Two Treatises of Government* (London: Whitmore and Fenn, 1821).

6. In some influential definitions of the state, the ability to overcome anarchy with violence legitimately is a central characteristic. See Max Weber, *Weber's Rationalism and Modern Society*, trans. Tony Waters and Dagmar Waters (London: Palgrave, 2015).

7. For one of the most central articulations of this idea, see Kenneth Waltz, *Man, the State, and War* (New York: Columbia University Press, 1959).

8. Herz and Butterfield are acknowledged as the modern architects of the security dilemma idea and the originators of the term. The bare concept, however, that states might unintentionally threaten one another, also dates back to Thucydides. The Greek historian wrote of the Peloponnesian War, "The growth of the power of Athens, and the alarm which this inspired in Lacedaemon, made war inevitable." Thucydides, *History of the Peloponnesian War*, 10.

9. John Herz, 'Idealist Internationalism and the Security Dilemma', *World Politics* 2, no. 2 (1950): 157.

10. How inevitable this outgrowth is and to what degree internal characteristics matter depends on the school of international relations.

11. John Herz, *Political Realism and Political Idealism* (Chicago: University of Chicago Press, 1951), 3. John Herz, *International Politics in the Atomic Age* (New York: Columbia University Press, 1959), 235.

12. Herz, *Political Realism and Political Idealism*, 15.

13. On this point, Herz provided Nazi Germany as an example. He wrote, "It can hardly be maintained that it was a German security dilemma which lay at the heart of the conflict but rather one man's, or one regime's, ambition to master the world." Herz, *International Politics in the Atomic Age*, 234.

14. Ken Booth and Nicholas J. Wheeler, *The Security Dilemma* (New York: Palgrave Macmillan, 2008), 4.

15. Herbert Butterfield, *History and Human Relations* (London: Collins, 1951), 21.

16. Other misperceptions can similarly drive the security dilemma. Robert Jervis, *Perception and Misperception in International Politics* (Princeton, NJ: Princeton University Press, 1976), 75.

17. David Finlay, Ole Holsti, and Richard Fagen, *Enemies in Politics* (Chicago: Rand McNally, 1967), 26.

18. Ronald Reagan, 'Remarks at the Annual Convention of the National Association of Evangelicals in Orlando, Florida', Ronald Reagan Foundation, 8 March 1983.

19. Herz, 'Idealist Internationalism and the Security Dilemma', 157.

20. Butterfield, *History and Human Relations*, 17. See also Herz, *Political Realism and Political Idealism*, 3.

21. Booth and Wheeler, *The Security Dilemma*, 4.

22. Ibid., 4–5.

23. Ibid. These different approaches map inexactly with different schools of international relations. For a brief overview of the different schools, see Stephen M. Walt, 'International Relations: One World, Many Theories', *Foreign Policy*, no. 110 (1998). See also Jack Snyder, 'One World, Rival Theories', *Foreign Policy*, no. 145 (2004).

24. For discussions of state expansion and conquest, see John J. Mearsheimer, *The Tragedy of Great Power Politics* (New York: W. W. Norton & Co., 2001); Peter Liberman, *Does Conquest Pay? The Exploitation of Occupied Industrial Societies* (Princeton, NJ: Princeton University Press, 1998).

25. For a discussion of security dilemma fatalists throughout history, see Booth and Wheeler, *The Security Dilemma*, 12.

26. Ibid., 9.

27. Ibid., 6–9.

28. Ibid., 15.

29. This group of thinkers is often referred to as defensive realists. Chapter Five discusses two noteworthy examples in great detail: Jervis, 'Cooperation under the Security Dilemma', *World Politics* 30, no. 2 (1978); Glaser, 'The Security Dilemma Revisited', *World Politics* 50, no. 1 (1997).

30. This is a more neoliberal view of international relations. For a noteworthy example of how institutions can have impact, see G. John Ikenberry, *After Victory: Institutions, Strategic Restraint, and the Rebuilding of Order after Major Wars* (Princeton, NJ: Princeton University Press, 2009). See also Robert Keohane, *After Hegemony: Cooperation and Discord in the World Political Economy* (Princeton, NJ: Princeton University Press, 2005). For further sharpening of the distinction between realism and other theories like liberalism, see Robert Keohane, *Neorealism and Its Critics* (New York: Columbia University Press, 1986).

31. Booth and Wheeler, *The Security Dilemma*, 10–17.

32. In general, such an approach is most consistent with the constructivist school of international relations. For a seminal work, see Alexander Wendt, 'Anarchy Is What States Make of It: The Social Construction of Power Politics', *International Organization* 46, no. 2 (1992).

33. An example is the norm of humanitarian intervention, which has strengthened in recent decades. Martha Finnemore, 'Constructing Norms of Humanitarian Intervention', in *The Culture of National Security*, ed. Peter Katzenstein (New York: Columbia University Press, 1996). See also Martha Finnemore and Kathryn Sikkink, 'International Norm Dynamics and Political Change', *International Organization* 52, no. 4 (1998); Michael Barnett and Martha Finnemore, *Rules for the World* (Ithaca, NY: Cornell University Press, 2004); John Gerard Ruggie, 'What Makes the World Hang Together? Neo-Utilitarianism and the Social Constructivist Challenge', *International Organization* 52, no. 4 (1998).

34. Booth and Wheeler, *The Security Dilemma*, 17–18.

35. Michael Herman, *Intelligence Power in Peace and War* (Cambridge: Cambridge University Press, 1996), 368–75. Michael Herman, 'Intelligence as Threats and Reassurance', in *Intelligence in the Cold War: What Difference Did It Make?*, ed. Michael Herman and Gwilym Hughes (New York: Routledge, 2013), 37.

36. The art of preventing surprise attacks is a deeply fascinating one. For an analysis informed by a variety of historical examples, see Richard Posner, *Preventing Surprise Attacks* (Lanham, MD: Rowman and Littlefield, 2005).

37. Michael Handel, 'Intelligence and Military Operations', *Intelligence and National Security* 5, no. 2 (1990): 67.

38. Sherman Kent, one of the most famous writers on intelligence and a former CIA Director of National Estimates, was a prominent defender of the role of intelligence in guarding against ideology-based policymaking. Sherman Kent, *Strategic Intelligence for American World Policy* (Princeton, NJ: Princeton University Press, 1966), 203–6. See also Herman, *Intelligence Power in Peace and War*, 138.

39. Herman, *Intelligence Power in Peace and War*, 192.

40. Ibid., 194.

41. Ibid., 192.

42. Ibid., 198.

43. Ibid., 191.

44. Anna Ringstrom, 'Sweden Security Forces Fear Russian Military Operations', Reuters, 18 March 2015.

45. Benjamin Fischer, 'A Cold War Conundrum: The 1983 Soviet War Scare', Central Intelligence Agency, 1997.

46. Herman, *Intelligence Power in Peace and War*, 188.
47. Ibid. See also Seymour Hersh, *The Target Is Destroyed* (New York: Random House, 1986), 37.
48. Fischer, 'A Cold War Conundrum: The 1983 Soviet War Scare'.
49. Ibid.
50. David Hoffman, *Dead Hand* (New York: Doubleday, 2009), 64.
51. Hersh, *The Target Is Destroyed*, 18–19.
52. George Shultz, *Turmoil and Triumph* (New York: Scribner, 1993), 367.
53. 'Tass Report on a Soviet General's Comments About Airliner', *New York Times*, 5 September 1983. For more on this case, see Herman, *Intelligence Power in Peace and War*, 189–90.
54. Herman, *Intelligence Power in Peace and War*, 190–91. A 1990 document from the President's Foreign Intelligence Advisory Board noted that the intelligence community committed the "especially grave error to assume that since we know the US is not going to start World War III, the next leaders of the Kremlin will also believe that." Quoted in Nate Jones, Tom Blanton, and Lauren Harper, 'The 1983 War Scare Declassified and for Real', National Security Archive, 24 October 2015.
55. Martin Walker, *The Cold War: A History* (New York: Henry Holt, 1995), 286.
56. Shultz, *Turmoil and Triumph*, 464; Charles Glaser, *Analyzing Strategic Nuclear Policy* (Princeton, NJ: Princeton University Press, 1990), 77.
57. Geoffrey Wiseman, *Concepts of Non-Provocative Defence: Ideas and Practices in International Security* (London: Palgrave, 2002), 250.
58. Herman, *Intelligence Power in Peace and War*, 370–72.

## 2. THE INTRUDER'S VIEW

1. For a full account of Stuxnet, see Kim Zetter, *Countdown to Zero Day* (New York: Crown, 2014).
2. Ralph Langner, 'Stuxnet's Secret Twin', *Foreign Policy*, 19 November 2013.
3. In the wake of Stuxnet, the Iranians (quite potentially out of paranoia) accused individuals of spying in furtherance of an "electronic war." Peter Beaumont, 'Iran "Detains Western Spies" after Cyber Attack on Nuclear Plant', *The Guardian*, 2 October 2010. Others have reported, without substantiation, that human assets aided early stages of the operation; see Richard Sale, 'Stuxnet Loaded by Iran Double Agents', Industrial Safety and Security Source, 11 April 2012.
4. This account of NITRO ZEUS draws from David Sanger and Mark Mazzetti, 'U.S. Had Cyberattack Plan if Iran Nuclear Dispute Led to

Conflict', *New York Times*, 16 February 2016; James Ball, 'U.S. Hacked into Iran's Critical Civilian Infrastructure for Massive Cyberattack, New Film Claims', BuzzFeed, 16 February 2016.

5. This model draws on, and is compatible with, more technical or more focused models that are very useful. One of the most notable is "Kill Chain Analysis," which focuses more narrowly, and more technically, on the challenges facing a digital incident responder or forensic analyst; intrusion reports like those from Mandiant have a similar focus. Since the focus of this text is on cyber operations at the state level, it is necessary to include discussion of additional concepts, such as bureaucratic oversight, damage assessment, and internal communication and analysis. See Eric Hutchins, Michael Cloppert, and Rohan Amin, 'Intelligence-Driven Computer Network Defense Informed by Analysis of Adversary Campaigns and Intrusion Kill Chains', Lockheed Martin, 2010; Michael Assante and Robert Lee, 'The Industrial Control System Cyber Kill Chain', SANS Institute, 2015; 'APT1', Mandiant, 18 February 2013; Herbert S. Lin, Kenneth W. Dam, and William A. Owens, *Technology, Policy, Law, and Ethics Regarding US Acquisition and Use of Cyberattack Capabilities* (Washington, DC: National Academies Press, 2009); Matthew Monte, *Network Attacks and Exploitation: A Framework* (Indianapolis, IN: Wiley, 2015).

6. Although there is not the space to explore these mini-cases in depth, they are useful follow-up resources for those who wish to go beyond the concepts and enter into more technical detail.

7. Jason Healey, ed., *A Fierce Domain* (Washington, DC: Cyber Conflict Studies Association, 2012).

8. Clifford Stoll, *The Cuckoo's Egg* (New York: Doubleday, 1989).

9. Thomas Rid, *Rise of the Machines* (New York: W. W. Norton & Co., 2016), 316–39.

10. Legitimate security researchers also perform these scans. For more on this kind of scanning, see Robert Graham, 'From Scratch: Why These Mass Scans Are Important', Errata Security, 31 May 2016.

11. James Eng and Wendy Jones, 'OPM Chief Says Government Agency Thwarts 10 Million Hack Attempts a Month', NBC News, 16 June 2015.

12. Reporting on American special operations activities indicates a convergence as well between signals intelligence collection and ground units. For more, see Sean Naylor, *Relentless Strike: The Secret History of Joint Special Operations Command* (New York: St Martin's Press, 2015); Shane Harris, *@War: The Rise of the Military-Internet Complex* (New York: Eamon Dolan/Houghton Mifflin Harcourt, 2014).

13. Rob Joyce, 'USENIX Enigma 2016—NSA TAO Chief on Disrupting Nation State Hackers', YouTube, 28 January 2016.

14. Sometimes this concept, or a related one, is called weaponization. For an early view on this term and some of its nuances, see a United States military lexicon for cyber operations, declassified in 2016: 'The Cyber Warfare Lexicon', United States Strategic Command, 2016.

15. This was the case with a well-known vulnerability known as Heartbleed that surfaced in 2014. For more, see 'The Heartbleed Bug', Codenomicon, 29 April 2014.

16. As one researcher of cyber operations, Herb Lin, said, "You can make a general-purpose fighter plane and it will function more or less the same in the Pacific as in the Atlantic ... The same is not true for going after a Russian cyber-target versus a Chinese target." Quoted in Ellen Nakashima, 'Pentagon to Fast-Track Cyberweapons Acquisition', *Washington Post*, 9 April 2012.

17. The most popular, Metasploit, is widely used by defenders as well to make sure their networks are secure against a wide range of vulnerabilities. It claims to be the "world's most commonly used penetration test software." For more, see 'Metasploit', Rapid7.

18. Leyla Bilge and Tudor Dumitras, 'Before We Knew It: An Empirical Study of Zero Day Attacks in the Real World', paper presented at 'Conference on Computer and Communication Security', 2012. For additional nuance on this paper's analysis sample, see David Aitel, 'Talking About 0days and Attacks from Weird Datasets', CyberSecPolitics, 6 May 2016.

19. Bilge and Dumitras, 'Before We Knew It: An Empirical Study of Zero Day Attacks in the Real World', 7.

20. Former NSA Director Michael Hayden acknowledges this, as do many others. Michael Hayden, 'The Making of America's Cyberweapons', *Christian Science Monitor*, 24 February 2016.

21. Robert Lee, Michael Assante, and Tim Conway, 'Analysis of the Cyber Attack on the Ukrainian Power Grid', Electricity Information Sharing and Analysis Center, 18 March 2016, 21.

22. William Broad, John Markoff, and David Sanger, 'Israeli Test on Worm Called Crucial in Iran Nuclear Delay', *New York Times*, 15 January 2011.

23. Zetter, *Countdown to Zero Day*, 167.

24. Programmable Logic Controllers are machines that control industrial machinery and processes.

25. Zetter, *Countdown to Zero Day*, 175.

26. Ironically, the Stuxnet worm spread more widely than its operators anticipated, leading to the worm's public examination by private security researchers. Ron Rosenbaum, 'Cassandra Syndrome', *Smithsonian Magazine* 43, no. 1 (2012): 12.

27. The two pieces of malicious code known as Gauss and GrayFish are

examples of this. In such circumstances, encryption hides the payload unless the code is at the target location, making it more difficult for security researchers to figure out the purpose of the malicious code. Kim Zetter, 'Suite of Sophisticated Nation-State Attack Tools Found with Connection to Stuxnet', Wired, 16 February 2015; Nicole Perlroth, 'Unable to Crack Computer Virus, Security Firm Seeks Help', New York Times, 14 August 2012.

28. For more concrete examples, see Brian Grow and Mark Hosenball, 'Special Report: In Cyberspy vs. Cyberspy, China Has the Edge', Reuters, 14 April 2011; 'APT30 and the Mechanics of a Long-Running Cyber Espionage Operation', FireEye, April 2015, 22–5.

29. One major industry survey concluded that around 11 per cent of users open the harmful attachments that come with these emails. '2015 Data Breach Investigations Report', Verizon, April 2015, 12–13.

30. 'ICS-CERT Monitor September 2014–February 2015', National Cyber-security and Communications Integration Center: Department of Homeland Security, 2015.

31. Perhaps most significantly, social engineering substituted for exploits in the 2015 attack on Ukraine's power system. Kim Zetter, 'Inside the Cunning, Unprecedented Hack of Ukraine's Power Grid', Wired, 3 March 2016. Other examples include the Poseidon group, a signif-icant Portuguese-speaking threat actor, which relies heavily on this technique. John Snow, 'The Poseidon's Domain', Kaspersky Lab, 9 Feb-ruary 2016. Bruce Schneier, Liars and Outliers, Indianapolis, IN: John Wiley & Sons, 2012.

32. Intruders used such a method to great effect in notable cases target-ing United States government employees, in which even sites as benign as local Chinese takeout places served as unwitting watering holes. Nicole Perlroth, 'Hackers Lurking in Vents and Soda Machines', New York Times, 7 April 2014.

33. Peter Bright, 'How the Comodo Certificate Fraud Calls CA Trust into Question', Ars Technica, 24 March 2011.

34. 'Quantum Spying: GCHQ Used Fake LinkedIn Pages to Target Engineers', Der Spiegel, 11 November 2013.

35. USB drives can also be useful even if there is not an airgap. Matthew Tischer et al., 'Users Really Do Plug in Usb Drives They Find', University of Illinois Urbana-Champaign, April 2016.

36. William Lynn, 'Defending a New Domain', Foreign Affairs (2010). It is not clear if this attack was a deliberate act by a foreign adversary.

37. Zetter, Countdown to Zero Day, 91.

38. The rest of this chapter will continue to refer to "the intruders" as if they had real-time or semi-real-time control over the malicious code, since that is most often the case.

39. A notable example of this obfuscation effort is known as Operation Poisoned Hurricane, in which seemingly legitimate requests to the Domain Name System of the internet in fact were quietly handling command and control instructions; another example is Duqu 2, which coordinated command and control between machines on an infected network to maximize stealthiness. In still other cases, such as LusyPOS, which targets point of sale systems in retailers, malicious software relies on anonymizing networks to try to hide the communications' true destination. Lastly, another category of malicious code employs multiple-step communications protocols to obfuscate its instructions. Ned Moran, Joshua Homan, and Mike Scott, 'Operation Poisoned Hurricane', FireEye, 6 August 2014; 'The Duqu 2.0: Technical Details', Kaspersky Lab, 11 June 2015, 33–7; Eduard Kovacs, 'New "LusyPOS" Malware Uses Tor for C&C Communications', *Security Week*, 3 December 2014. For example, the protocols used by the so-called APT30 group fall into this category. 'APT30 and the Mechanics of a Long-Running Cyber Espionage Operation', FireEye, 9.
40. 'Moving Data through Disconnected Networks: Delay Tolerant Networking and the IC', National Security Agency: *Der Spiegel*, 2015, 24.
41. David Sanger and Thom Shanker, 'NSA Devises Radio Pathway into Computers', *New York Times*, 14 January 2014.
42. Perhaps the most notable example of this watering hole technique occurred in 2014, when every visitor to the popular Forbes.com website was targeted with malicious code. Jim Finkle, 'Update 2-Hackers Infect Forbes.com to Spy on Visitors—Researchers', Reuters, 10 February 2015.
43. One way to do this is to exfiltrate information about the system's files, such as document names, pass them to analysts for review, and then later only exfiltrate the files of interest. 'APT30 and the Mechanics of a Long-Running Cyber Espionage Operation', FireEye, 17.
44. Zetter, *Countdown to Zero Day*, 145.
45. For one prominent example, see Zetter, 'Inside the Cunning, Unprecedented Hack of Ukraine's Power Grid'; Lee, Assante, and Conway, 'Analysis of the Cyber Attack on the Ukrainian Power Grid'.
46. Peter Bright, 'Anonymous Speaks: The Inside Story of the HBGary Hack', *Ars Technica*, 16 February 2011.
47. The British signals intelligence agency's 2010 guide to operational risk includes this danger. 'What's the Worst That Could Happen?', Government Communications Headquarters: BoingBoing, 2016, 2.
48. Hayden, 'The Making of America's Cyberweapons'.
49. Richard Clarke and Robert Knake, *Cyberwar* (New York: HarperCollins, 2010), 30.

50. Joel Brenner, *Glass Houses* (New York: Penguin, 2014), 199.
51. 'Budget Request for Information Technology and Cyber Operations Programs: Written Testimony of Gen. Keith Alexander', Committee on Armed Services: US House of Representatives, 2012.
52. For more on the status of automation in offensive efforts, see Chris Rohlf, 'Offense at Scale', GitHub, 30 May 2015.
53. For a discussion of how tools enable cyber operations, see thegrugq, 'On Cyber—Power of Community 2015', YouTube, 6 December 2015; Bruce Schneier, 'Attacking Tor: How the NSA Targets Users' Online Anonymity', *The Guardian*, 4 October 2013; 'Quantum Insert Diagrams', National Security Agency: *The Intercept*, 2014. It is unclear how scalable these operations are, however, at least in the QUANTUM INSERT formulation. Nicholas Weaver, 'A Close Look at the NSA's Most Powerful Internet Attack Tool', Wired, 13 March 2014.
54. An operation known as Duqu is a prime example of this. Zetter, *Countdown to Zero Day*, 266.
55. Sometimes, intruders will deliver the payload and not activate it. At other times, they will keep the payload in reserve once they gain access, to lower the risk of detection and preserve operational security. These sorts of efforts are technically achievable, but require many well-trained practitioners to carry out at scale—another sign of how important humans are to cyber operations.
56. For a comparatively early discussion of some of these operations, see 'Dragonfly: Cyberespionage Attacks against Energy Suppliers', Symantec, 7 July 2014.
57. Damian Paletta, 'NSA Chief Says Cyberattack at Pentagon Was Sophisticated, Persistent', *Wall Street Journal*, 8 September 2015.
58. Vassilis Prevelakis and Diomidis Spinellis, 'The Athens Affair', IEEE Spectrum, 29 June 2007. For a more recent piece on the Athens Affair, see James Bamford, 'A Death in Athens', *The Intercept*, 29 September 2015.
59. The RedOctober operation used another approach that was conceptually similar, installing plug-ins on breached computers. 'Cloud Atlas: RedOctober APT is Back in Style', Kaspersky Lab, 10 December 2014.
60. Sometimes multiple layers of malicious code can make it easier to retain access. For example, see 'Operation SMN: Axiom Threat Actor Group Report', Novetta, November 2014.
61. Nicole Perlroth, 'Hackers in China Attacked the Times for Last 4 Months', *New York Times*, 30 January 2013.
62. Duqu 2 achieved a much lighter footprint by using this reinfection technique and minimizing its presence on the hard drive of infected machines. 'The Duqu 2.0: Technical Details', Kaspersky Lab, 33.

63. 'S3285 WikiInfo', National Security Agency: *Der Spiegel*, 2015.
64. Corey Kallenberg and Xeno Kovah, 'How Many Million BIOSes Would You Like to Infect?', Legbacore, 11 June 2015.
65. Bruce Schneier, 'DEITYBOUNCE: NSA Exploit of the Day', Schneier on Security, 20 January 2014.
66. Nicole Perlroth and David Sanger, 'U.S. Embedded Spyware Overseas, Report Claims', *New York Times*, 16 February 2015.
67. 'Equation: The Death Star of Malware Galaxy', Kaspersky Lab, 16 February 2015.
68. Michael Mimoso, 'Inside nls_933w.dll, the Equation APT Persistence Module', ThreatPost, 17 February 2015.
69. Barton Gellman and Ellen Nakashima, 'U.S. Spy Agencies Mounted 231 Offensive Cyber-Operations in 2011, Documents Show', *Washington Post*, 30 August 2013.
70. Ellen Nakashima, 'Meet the Woman in Charge of the FBI's Most Controversial High-Tech Tools', *Washington Post*, 8 December 2015. As discussed in Chapter Eight, the United States sometimes turns these vulnerabilities over to the appropriate software vendor for remediation, but not always—particularly not if the software is primarily used overseas and not used as much by Americans. Michael Daniel, 'Heartbleed: Understanding When We Disclose Cyber Vulnerabilities', The White House Blog, 28 April 2014. A partially redacted document released under the Freedom of Information Act in 2016 provides more details: 'Commercial and Government Information Technology and Industrial Control Product or System Vulnerabilities Equities Policy and Process', United States Government: Electronic Frontier Foundation, 2016.
71. Weaver, 'A Close Look at the NSA's Most Powerful Internet Attack Tool'; 'Quantum Insert Diagrams', National Security Agency, 2014; Schneier, 'Attacking Tor: How the NSA Targets Users' Online Anonymity'.
72. Melanie Newman, 'Encryption Risks Leading to "Ethically Worse" Behaviour by Spies, Says Former GCHQ Chief', Bureau of Investigative Journalism, 23 January 2015.
73. Brian Fung, 'The NSA Hacks Other Countries by Buying Millions of Dollars' Worth of Computer Vulnerabilities', *Washington Post*, 31 August 2013.
74. Kim Zetter, 'Hacking Team Leak Shows How Secretive Zero-Day Exploit Sales Work', Wired, 24 July 2015.
75. For a seminal work on the zero day market, see Charlie Miller, 'The Legitimate Vulnerability Market', Independent Security Evaluators, 6 May 2007. See also Mailyn Fidler, 'Regulating the Zero-Day

Vulnerability Trade: A Preliminary Analysis', *I/S: A Journal of Law and Policy for the Information Society*, no. 11 (2015).

76. Ned Moran and James T. Bennett, 'Supply Chain Analysis: From Quartermaster to Sunshop', FireEye, 11 November 2013.
77. The four operations are Stuxnet, Duqu, Duqu 2 and Flame. 'W32. Duqu, Version 1.4', Symantec, 23 November 2011; 'The Duqu 2.0: Technical Details', Kaspersky Lab. See also Zetter, *Countdown to Zero Day*.
78. 'APT30 and the Mechanics of a Long-Running Cyber Espionage Operation', FireEye.
79. For example, the attack on the *New York Times* used servers at a number of universities as infrastructure. Perlroth, 'Hackers in China Attacked the Times for Last 4 Months'.
80. 'Landmark', Communications Security Establishment Canada: *C'T Magazin*, 2014, 18. This infrastructure-building preparation provides another incentive for launching intrusions in advance, as a means of enabling offensive capabilities. If detected, it is likely to threaten others—though these sorts of intrusions are less likely to be in important networks.
81. This is in addition to the other factors which possibly make cyber operations enticing, such as plausible deniability, lower costs, or the possibility of asymmetric action.
82. Many states might choose not to launch an intrusion to establish a contingency option, but some will. On the general point of contingency plans, former Secretary of Defense Robert McNamara said, "a strategic planner must ... prepare for the worst plausible case and not be content to hope and prepare for the most probable." Lawrence Freedman, *US Intelligence and the Soviet Strategic Threat* (London: Macmillan, 1977), 85.

3. THE DEFENDER'S VIEW

1. Nathan Thornburgh, 'The Invasion of the Chinese Cyberspies (and the Man Who Tried to Stop Them)', *Time*, 5 September 2005.
2. For a partial list, see 'BYZANTINE HADES: An Evolution in Collection', National Security Agency: *Der Spiegel*, 2015, 17. 'BYZANTINE HADES Causes Serious Damage to DoD Interests', National Security Agency, 2015.
3. Ibid.
4. Ibid., 18–20.
5. The number of five computers includes virtual machines. Ibid., 26.
6. Ibid.

7. Just as the intrusion model drew on notable predecessors, so too does this defensive model. Five models of network defense, written by practitioners, are useful. First, the model put forth by the National Institute for Standards and Technology on incident response lays out core concepts in an accessible and very detailed manner. Second, the Kill Chain models mentioned in the last chapter provide value here as well. Third, another model known as the Sliding Scale of Cyber Security provides a useful expansion of important concepts and outlines a spectrum of defensive action, including the penetration of foreign networks for the purposes of collecting threat intelligence. Fourth, the work of network security monitoring practitioners provides great insight on moving beyond more basic detection mechanisms. Fifth, the Diamond Model gives great insight into current defensive practices. 'Computer Security Incident Handling Guide', National Institute of Standards and Technology: Department of Commerce, 2012; Hutchins, Cloppert, and Amin, 'Intelligence-Driven Computer Network Defense Informed by Analysis of Adversary Campaigns and Intrusion Kill Chains', Lockheed Martin; Assante and Lee, 'The Industrial Control System Cyber Kill Chain', SANS Institute; Robert Lee, 'The Sliding Scale of Cyber Security', SANS Institute, August 2015; Richard Bejtlich, *The Practice of Network Security Monitoring* (San Francisco: No Starch Press, 2013); Sergio Caltagirone, Andrew Pendergast, and Christopher Betz, 'The Diamond Model of Intrusion Analysis', Defense Technical Information Center, 5 July 2013.

8. Some computer scientists propose using the attack surface of a piece of software as a means of measuring how secure it is. For more, see Pratyusa Manadhata and Jeannette Wing, 'An Attack Surface Metric', *IEEE Transactions on Software Engineering* 37, no. 3 (2011).

9. Kevin Poulsen, 'Slammer Worm Crashed Ohio Nuke Plant Network', Security Focus, 19 August 2003.

10. Like much else in this chapter, patch management on large networks is a world unto itself. For an overview of useful technologies and concepts, see 'Guide to Enterprise Patch Management Technologies', National Institute of Standards and Technology: Department of Commerce, 2013.

11. 'The Remediation Gap', Kenna Security, September 2015, 3. See also 'Cisco Annual Security Report Reveals Widening Gulf between Perception and Reality of Cybersecurity Readiness', Cisco, 20 January 2015.

12. 'BYZANTINE HADES Causes Serious Damage to DoD Interests', National Security Agency: *Der Spiegel*, 2015.

13. For an example of account compromise in an operation, see the

SendGrid case, in which intruders used user accounts as a means of exfiltrating data. Brian Krebs, 'SendGrid: Employee Account Hacked, Used to Steal Customer Credentials', Krebs on Security, 27 April 2015.

14. One of the most notable efforts in this vein is a massive attempt by the United States federal government to dramatically reduce the number of federal internet connections from tens of thousands to a more centralized fifty. Cory Bennett, '"Please Contribute," White House's Ozment Implores Network Security Crowd', Yahoo, 15 August 2013.

15. Joyce, 'USENIX Enigma 2016—NSA TAO Chief on Disrupting Nation State Hackers'.

16. For more on this, see Richard Bejtlich, 'Army Cyber Institute Cyber Talks: Thinking Strategically About Digital Security', YouTube, September 2015.

17. This external detection figure is usually lower in the case of larger organizations. For a discussion of this topic, with trendlines, see '2016 Data Breach Investigations Report', Verizon, April 2016, 11.

18. For a more detailed overview of detection methods, see Lee, 'The Sliding Scale of Cyber Security', SANS Institute.

19. Hutchins, Cloppert, and Amin, 'Intelligence-Driven Computer Network Defense Informed by Analysis of Adversary Campaigns and Intrusion Kill Chains', Lockheed Martin, 3.

20. One of the most notable reports to do this was the APT1 report. 'APT1', Mandiant.

21. For more on this, see Leo Obrst, Penny Chase, and Richard Markeloff, 'Developing an Ontology of the Cyber Security Domain', paper presented at 'STIDS', 2012, 13. See also Bret Jordan, 'Stix and Taxii: On the Road to Becoming the De Facto Standard', Blue Coat Systems, 26 August 2014.

22. Computer scientists call this polymorphism. For a more detailed study of more than 1.2 million instances of polymorphic code, see Michalis Polychronakis, Kostas G. Anagnostakis, and Evangelos P. Markatos, 'An Empirical Study of Real-World Polymorphic Code Injection Attacks', paper presented at 'Proceedings of the 2nd USENIX Conference on Large Scale Exploits and Emergent Threats', Boston, MA, 21 April 2009.

23. For an overview of threat hunting, see Robert Lee and Rob Lee, 'The Who, What, Where, When, Why, and How of Effective Threat Hunting', SANS Institute, February 2016. Active defense is a fraught term in cybersecurity. Some—in a shrinking minority—use the term to refer to "hacking back," or targeting the intruders with cyber operations. More commonly, it refers to proactively hunting at or within the

perimeter of one's own network to find threats. As Robert Lee points out, the term has had this latter meaning since long before cybersecurity was an issue. Lee, 'The Sliding Scale of Cyber Security', SANS Institute, 9.

24. Jim Garamone, 'Lynn Explains U.S. Cybersecurity Strategy', American Forces Press Service, 15 September 2010.

25. For a brief history of the practice of network security monitoring, see Richard Bejtlich, 'Network Security Monitoring History', TaoSecurity, 11 April 2007. See also Bejtlich, *The Practice of Network Security Monitoring*.

26. Bejtlich, *The Practice of Network Security Monitoring*, 1.

27. Other sources more fully cover this sort of analysis, known as Extrusion Detection. See Richard Bejtlich, *Extrusion Detection: Security Monitoring for Internal Intrusions* (Upper Saddle River, NJ: Addison-Wesley, 2006).

28. Roughly speaking, powering off a machine resets the RAM.

29. For more on memory analysis in malicious code detection efforts, see Michael Hale Ligh et al., *The Art of Memory Forensics: Detecting Malware and Threats in Windows, Linux, and Mac Memory* (Hoboken, NJ: John Wiley & Sons, 2014).

30. Duqu 2 is an example of this kind of malicious code. 'The Duqu 2.0: Technical Details', Kaspersky Lab.

31. For more on penetration testing, see Sugandh Shah and B. M. Mehtre, 'A Modern Approach to Cyber Security Analysis Using Vulnerability Assessment and Penetration Testing', *International Journal of Electronics Communication and Computer Engineering* 4, no. 6 (2013); Anestis Bechtsoudis and Nicolas Sklavos, 'Aiming at Higher Network Security through Extensive Penetration Tests', *Latin America Transactions, IEEE (Revista IEEE America Latina)* 10, no. 3 (2012).

32. 'M-Trends 2016', Mandiant, February 2016, 4.

33. 'Understanding the Cyber Threat and Implications for the 21st Century Economy', Subcommittee on Oversight and Investigations Committee on Energy and Commerce: US House of Representatives, 2015.

34. For further discussion, see Bejtlich, *The Practice of Network Security Monitoring*, ch. 1.

35. In law enforcement cases, investigators must take care that they do this collection in accordance with proper evidence handling and chain-of-custody procedures. In other cases less likely to result in a legal proceeding, such as those involving intelligence agencies, investigators must perform this collection in a rigorous yet expeditious manner.

36. Two prominent models that describe this investigation process in more detail are the Diamond Model and the Q Model. Caltagirone,

Pendergast, and Betz, 'The Diamond Model of Intrusion Analysis', Defense Technical Information Center; Thomas Rid and Ben Buchanan, 'Attributing Cyber Attacks', *Journal of Strategic Studies* 39, no. 1 (2015).

37. For example, when Windows runs a program, it either creates or updates a hidden file. By looking at the time-stamps of this file, analysts can understand the last time Windows executed the program. Similar files provide information on the use of USB drives, the opening of documents, and internet activity. For more on the forensic artifacts in Windows, see Cory Altheide and Harlan Carvey, *Digital Forensics with Open Source Tools* (Waltham, MA: Elsevier, 2011), 69–93.

38. This process, which can often be painstaking and difficult, frequently occurs at a very technical level. By analyzing the software and by running the code in controlled conditions, malicious code reverse-engineers get better insight into its design and functioning. For more on this process, see Michael Sikorski and Andrew Honig, *Practical Malware Analysis* (San Francisco: No Starch, 2012).

39. Snorre Fagerland and Waylon Grange, 'The Inception Framework', Blue Coat Systems, 9 December 2014. See also 'Cloud Atlas: RedOctober APT is Back in Style', Kaspersky Lab.

40. For more on this process, see Bejtlich, *The Practice of Network Security Monitoring*.

41. An example of this is Oak Ridge National Lab in 2011. Kim Zetter, 'Top Federal Lab Hacked in Spear-Phishing Attack', Wired, 20 April 2011.

42. A fuller discussion of the possible interactions between the defenders and the intruders is beyond the scope of this book; it would require exploring a campaign-like model of intrusions rather than the more simplified linear version presented here. Richard Bejtlich has begun this sort of analysis. For example, see Kenneth Geers, ed., *Cyber War in Perspective: Russian Aggression against Ukraine* (Tallinn: NATO Cooperative Cyber Defence Center of Excellence, 2015), ch. 18.

43. These honeypots can also be set up as part of the preparation stage, before the intrusion, which may be the ideal course of action in many situations. However, customizing and deploying a honeypot after the intrusion provides the opportunity to tailor it to the likely interests of that particular intruder. For example, see Thomas Rid, *Rise of the Machines* (New York: W. W. Norton & Co., 2016), 327–8.

44. Ben Elgin and Michael Riley, 'Now at the Sands Casino: An Iranian Hacker in Every Server', Bloomberg, 11 December 2014.

45. As of 2007, the NSA used that system for extracting data from "network infrastructure devices" such as routers—rather than individual computers. 'Analytic Challenges from Active-Passive Integration',

National Security Agency: *Der Spiegel*, 2015, 2. See also, 'The FASHIONCLEFT Protocol', National Security Agency: *Der Spiegel*, 2008.

46. Two examples of interference with the human-machine interface are Stuxnet and Ukraine. The former was much more subtle than the latter. Kim Zetter, *Countdown to Zero Day* (New York: Crown, 2014), 122–5; Lee, Assante, and Conway, 'Analysis of the Cyber Attack on the Ukrainian Power Grid', Electricity Information Sharing and Analysis Center, 18 March 2016,

47. Ellen Nakashima, 'Several Nations Trying to Penetrate U.S. Cyber-Networks, Says Ex-FBI Official', *Washington Post*, 18 April 2012.

48. Justin Fishel and Lee Ferran, 'State Dept. Shuts Down Email after Cyber Attack', ABC News, 13 March 2015.

49. Perlroth, 'Hackers in China Attacked the Times for Last 4 Months'.

50. Leon Panetta, 'Defending the Nation from Cyber Attack', Department of Defense, 11 October 2012.

51. Too often, discussions of cyber deterrence hew too closely to a Cold War worldview, in which deterrence is equated with Mutually Assured Destruction. For more on the necessity of taking a broader view of deterrence, see Ben Buchanan, 'Cyber Deterrence isn't MAD; it's Mosaic', *Georgetown Journal of International Affairs*, International Engagement on Cyber IV (2014). See also Tim Stevens, 'A Cyberwar of Ideas? Deterrence and Norms in Cyberspace', *Contemporary Security Policy* 33, no. 1 (2012).

52. One of the only other works to discuss the idea of a cybersecurity dilemma, by Martin Libicki, acknowledges that states will launch intrusions for defensive purposes, but speculates without much elaboration or evidence that this technique is not effective. This section attempts to bring greater detail to this debate. Martin C. Libicki, 'Is There a Cybersecurity Dilemma?', *Cyber Defense Review* 1, no. 1 (2016).

53. 'Transcript of President Obama's Jan. 17 Speech on NSA Reforms', *Washington Post*, 17 January 2014.

54. Susan Hennessey, 'Good Defense is Good Offense: NSA Myths and the Merger', Lawfare, 9 February 2016.

55. Danny Vinik, 'America's Secret Arsenal', *Politico*, 9 December 2015.

56. 'Case Studies of Integrated Cyber Operations Techniques', National Security Agency: *Der Spiegel*, 2015, 3.

57. Ibid., 4.

58. 'Getting Close to the Adversary: Forward-Based Defense with QFire', National Security Agency: *Der Spiegel*, 2013, 7.

59. Ibid.

60. 'TUTELAGE 411', National Security Agency: *Der Spiegel*, 2015, 4.

61. For a brief separate discussion of this system, and potential ways it

can be overcome by sophisticated actors, see Ross Anderson, 'Meeting Snowden in Princeton', Cambridge University, 2 May 2015.
62. 'TUTELAGE 411', National Security Agency, 2015, 8–14.
63. Ibid., 15–29.
64. Ibid., 26. The code phrase BYZANTINE HADES refers to a large category of Chinese operations, encompassing more than "30,000 incidents and 500 significant intrusions." For more on this, see 'BYZANTINE HADES Causes Serious Damage to DoD Interests', National Security Agency, 2015.
65. 'Homeland Security Seeks Cyber Counterattack System', CNN, 4 October 2008.
66. 'The DHS Role in Federal Cybersecurity and the Recent Compromise at the Office of Personnel Management: Written Testimony of Dr. Andy Ozment', Committee on Oversight and Government Reform: US House of Representatives, 2015.
67. The Five Eyes countries are the United States, the United Kingdom, Canada, Australia, and New Zealand.
68. For one example, see Ryan Gallagher, 'Vodafone-Linked Company Aided British Mass Surveillance', The Intercept, 20 November 2014.
69. 'CSEC SIGINT Cyber Discovery: Summary of the Current Effort', Communications Security Establishment Canada: Der Spiegel, 2015, 13.
70. Kaspersky Lab says that the number is greater than five and includes operations not yet made public, but does not specify how many and does not provide any detail on those operations. 'Equation Group: Questions and Answers', Kaspersky Lab, February 2015, 31–2.
71. 'Pay Attention to That Man Behind the Curtain: Discovering Aliens on CNE Infrastructure', Communications Security Establishment Canada: Der Spiegel, 2010, 27.
72. Ibid., 29.
73. The link between WARRIORPRIDE and Regin has not been officially acknowledged, but there is good evidence that the two are the same, or very closely related. For more on the strong links, from one of the researchers who discovered Regin, see Claudio Guarnieri, 'Everything We Know of NSA and Five Eyes Malware', Nex.sx, 27 January 2015. For more on Regin, see 'Regin: Top-Tier Espionage Tool Enables Stealthy Surveillance', Symantec, 24 November 2014.
74. 'CSEC SIGINT Cyber Discovery: Summary of the Current Effort', Communications Security Establishment Canada, 2015, 8.
75. Other documents outline the possibility of directly interfering with these operations by other states, placing such efforts under the framework for CCNE. For this reason, the rest of the text will distinguish third-party CCNE operations from ones that directly engage the

potential adversary. 'HIMR Data Mining Research Problem Book', Government Communications Headquarters: BoingBoing, 2016, 13.

76. 'CSEC SIGINT Cyber Discovery: Summary of the Current Effort', Communications Security Establishment Canada, 2015, 15–16.

77. Ibid., 9–12. See also 'Pay Attention to That Man Behind the Curtain: Discovering Aliens on CNE Infrastructure', Communications Security Establishment Canada.

78. 'SNOWGLOBE: From Discovery to Attribution', Communications Security Establishment Canada: *Der Spiegel*, 2015, 5.

79. Ibid.

80. It is worth noting that this distinction between public and private sector is relevant for exploitation, too. For example, state-owned companies might benefit from information taken from foreign networks. For states with many private companies in competition with one another and overseas competitors—such as the United States—it is less obvious that such sharing of information is easily possible. For more, see David Sanger, 'Fine Line Seen in U.S. Spying on Companies', *New York Times*, 20 May 2014.

81. For greater discussion of public–private partnerships in cybersecurity, see Madeline Carr, 'Public–Private Partnerships in National Cyber-Security Strategies', *International Affairs* 92, no. 1 (2016).

82. Eamon Javers, 'Silicon Valley, DC at Odds on Security Clearances', CNBC, 6 March 2015.

83. For more on public–private partnerships in cybersecurity, see Carr, 'Public–Private Partnerships in National Cyber-Security Strategies'.

84. Katie Zezima, 'Obama Signs Executive Order on Sharing Cybersecurity Threat Information', *Washington Post*, 12 February 2015.

85. 'The Department of Defense Cyber Strategy', Office of the Secretary of Defense: Department of Defense, 2015, 3.

## 4. HOW NETWORK INTRUSIONS THREATEN

1. Ralph Langner, 'Stuxnet's Secret Twin', *Foreign Policy*, 19 November 2013; Kim Zetter, *Countdown to Zero Day* (New York: Crown, 2014), 167.

2. Zetter, *Countdown to Zero Day*, 145.

3. 'Equation: The Death Star of Malware Galaxy', Kaspersky Lab, 16 February 2015.

4. Kaspersky does not definitely say that the group that produced the code is the NSA, but there is substantial overlap in terminology and code words between the NSA's secret documents and the malicious code revealed by Kaspersky. Zetter, 'Suite of Sophisticated Nation-State

Attack Tools Found with Connection to Stuxnet', Wired, 16 February 2015; Zetter, *Countdown to Zero Day*; 'A Fanny Equation: "I Am Your Father, Stuxnet"', Kaspersky Lab, 17 February 2015; 'Equation: The Death Star of Malware Galaxy', Kaspersky Lab.

5. For one seminal discussion of how threats impact the international system, see Stephen M. Walt, *The Origins of Alliance* (Ithaca, NY: Cornell University Press, 1990). For a more modern take on risk analysis and warfare, see Christopher Coker, *War in the Age of Risk* (Cambridge: Polity Press, 2009).

6. 'Guide for Conducting Risk Assessments (Rev. 1)', National Institute of Standards and Technology: Department of Commerce, 2012.

7. For one articulation of this threat model by a veteran computer incident responder, see Michael Cloppert, 'Security Intelligence: Introduction (Pt 2)', SANS Institute, 23 July 2009.

8. For an overview of risks concerning operations, see GCHQ's 2010 guide: 'What's the Worst That Could Happen?', Government Communications Headquarters, 2016.

9. James Bamford, 'The Most Wanted Man in the World', Wired, 22 August 2015.

10. Ken Booth and Nicholas J. Wheeler, *The Security Dilemma* (New York: Palgrave Macmillan, 2008), 58–9.

11. Thomas Rid and Peter McBurney, 'Cyber-Weapons', *RUSI Journal* 157, no. 1 (2012).

12. Zetter, 'Inside the Cunning, Unprecedented Hack of Ukraine's Power Grid', Wired, 3 March 2016; 'Cyber-Attack against Ukrainian Critical Infrastructure', Industrial Control Systems Emergency Response Team: Department of Homeland Security, 2016; Lee, Assante, and Conway, 'Analysis of the Cyber Attack on the Ukrainian Power Grid', Electricity Information Sharing and Analysis Center, 18 March 2016.

13. Lee, Assante, and Conway, 'Analysis of the Cyber Attack on the Ukrainian Power Grid', Electricity Information Sharing and Analysis Center, 2.

14. Sean Kanuck, 'Sean Kanuck on Deterrence and Arms Control in Cyberspace', YouTube, 30 March 2016, 31:04. Michael Hayden, former Director of the NSA, said, "If you can spy on a network, you can manipulate it. It's already included. The only thing you need is an act of will." *Zero Days*, Alex Gibney, Magnolia Pictures, 2016, 55:50.

15. 'Virtual Criminology Report 2009', McAfee, 2009, 13.

16. A 1997 NSA journal article, later declassified, notes the "synergistic" relationship between intelligence, communications, and information warfare. William Black, 'Thinking Out Loud About Cyberspace', *Cryptolog (National Security Agency)* 23, no. 1 (1997): 4.

215

17. The document defines significant consequences as "loss of life, significant responsive actions against the United States, significant damage to property, serious adverse U.S. foreign policy consequences, or serious economic impact on the United States." 'Presidential Policy Directive 20', The White House: *The Guardian*, 2013, 3.
18. Ibid., 15.
19. Ibid., 9.
20. 'Memorandum: Subject: Joint Terminology for Cyberspace Operations', Vice Chairman of the Joint Chiefs of Staff: Department of Defense, 2010, 7.
21. The C-OPE term is an update to the general concept of using exploitation in preparation of attack, rather than an entirely new concept. As an earlier Department of Defense National Military Strategy for Cyber Operations notes, using the previously more vague language: "DOD will use [computer] network exploitation to gather intelligence and shape the cyberspace environment as necessary to provide integrated offensive and defensive options." 'The National Military Strategy for Cyberspace Operations', Chairman of the Joint Chiefs of Staff: Department of Defense, 2005, 2.
22. 'Memorandum: Subject: Joint Terminology for Cyberspace Operations', Vice Chairman of the Joint Chiefs of Staff, 2010, 7.
23. 'CYBERCOM Announcement Message', United States Cyber Command: National Security Archive, 2016, 2.
24. For more on the interplay of authorities in intelligence and military operations, see Andru E. Wall, 'Demystifying the Title 10-Title 50 Debate: Distinguishing Military Operations, Intelligence Activities & Covert Action', *Harvard National Security Journal* 3, no. 1 (2011).
25. 'Computer Network Exploitation (CNE) Classification Guide', National Security Agency: *Der Spiegel*, 2015, 2.
26. Joe McReynolds, 'China's Evolving Perspectives on Network Warfare: Lessons from the Science of Military Strategy', Center for International Maritime Security, 23 June 2015.
27. 'Defensive Best Practices for Destructive Malware', Information Assurance Directorate: National Security Agency, 2015.
28. Ben Elgin and Michael Riley, 'Now at the Sands Casino: An Iranian Hacker in Every Server', Bloomberg, 11 December 2014.
29. These perpetrators likely also attacked the Qatari natural gas firm Rasgas, though less is known about that case. Dennis Fisher, 'Saudi Aramco Confirms Scope of Malware Attack', ThreatPost, 27 August 2012. 'Shamoon the Wiper—Copycats at Work', Kaspersky Lab, 16 August 2012; Kim Zetter, 'Qatari Gas Company Hit with Virus in Wave of Attacks on Energy Companies', Wired, 30 August 2016.

30. Sean Gallagher, 'Your Hard Drive Will Self-Destruct at 2pm: Inside the South Korean Cyberattack', *Ars Technica*, 21 March 2013.
31. The wiper attacks on the Iranian oil and gas sector are different from the others in important respects. Though their effect was indeed to wipe the targeted systems, they did so in quite a sophisticated manner that targeted below the operating system level of the computer, and may have benefited from more collection operations and more target intelligence than the four attacks mentioned above. For more, see 'What Was That Wiper Thing?', Kaspersky Lab, 29 August 2012.
32. Elgin and Riley, 'Now at the Sands Casino: An Iranian Hacker in Every Server'.
33. Ibid.
34. NSA briefing documents suggest this directly. They also suggest that the Iranians learned from the experience of suffering attacks and used the knowledge to inform their own attacks. Glenn Greenwald, 'NSA Claims Iran Learned from Western Cyberattacks', *The Intercept*, 10 February 2015.
35. Kurt Baumgartner, 'Sony/Destover: Mystery North Korean Actor's Destructive and Past Network Activity', Kaspersky Lab, 4 December 2014.
36. For example, the Shamoon attackers might have hoped to affect Aramco's oil production; had they had better knowledge of the Aramco network and procedures, they might have realized that their efforts at the time of attack would not have been enough to affect the oil operations.
37. Baumgartner, 'Sony/Destover: Mystery North Korean Actor's Destructive and Past Network Activity', Kaspersky Lab, 4 December 2014.
38. John J. Mearsheimer, *The Tragedy of Great Power Politics* (New York: W. W. Norton & Co., 2001), 31.
39. 'Regin: Top-Tier Espionage Tool Enables Stealthy Surveillance', Symantec.
40. Fisher, 'Saudi Aramco Confirms Scope of Malware Attack'.
41. Michael Cieply and Brooks Barnes, 'Sony Hack Reveals Email Crossfire over Angelina Jolie and Steve Jobs Movie', *New York Times*, 10 December 2014.
42. Elgin and Riley, 'Now at the Sands Casino: An Iranian Hacker in Every Server'.
43. It is very difficult to make this determination quickly, particularly if the intruders take steps to obfuscate their code. The next chapter will explore offense-defense differentiation in much more detail.
44. Roughly speaking, joint operations enable different types of military

units or branches of the same state to work together in a unified effort. In a different context, it can refer to coordination between states. The discussion here focuses on integration within one state's military so that cyber operations are more routine.

45. For a broader look at joint operations and emerging technology, see Christopher Coker, *Warrior Geeks* (New York: Columbia University Press, 2013).

46. Jumper mentions a finding, a specific presidential approval reserved for high-stakes covert operations. William M. Arkin, 'A Mouse That Roars?', *Washington Post*, 7 June 1999.

47. For more on this, see Robert Schmidle, Michael Sulmeyer, and Ben Buchanan, 'Non-Lethal Weapons and Cyber Capabilities', in *Understanding Cyberconflict: 16 Analogies*, ed. George Perkovich and Ariel E. Levite, forthcoming.

48. Former NSA Director Michael Hayden also echoed this theme: 'The Making of America's Cyberweapons', *Christian Science Monitor*, 24 February 2016.

49. Fred Kaplan, *Dark Territory* (New York: Simon & Schuster, 2016), 24.

50. Strategy documents from the United States Navy and Air Force were declassified in 2016. They discuss, in a general way, the importance and complexity of integrating cyber capabilities into joint operations. 'Navy Cyber Power 2020', United States Navy: National Security Archive, 2016; 'Air Force Policy Directive 10–17 Cyberspace Operations', United States Air Force: National Security Archive, 2016. The United States Cyber Command vision document states that "We are expected to work closely with other combatant commands to integrate cyber operations into broader military missions. Policymakers and Commanders alike look to us for cyber options in all phases of operations." 'Beyond the Build: Delivering Outcomes through Cyberspace', United States Cyber Command: Department of Defense, 2015, 1. For a history of doctrine in this area, see Michael Warner, 'Notes on Military Doctrine for Cyberspace Operations in the United States, 1992–2014', *Cyber Defense Review*, 27 August 2015.

51. The Pentagon's introduction of Plan X states, with emphasis in the original, "*The Plan X program is explicitly not funding research and development efforts in vulnerability analysis or cyberweapon generation.*" 'Special Notice: Plan X Proposers' Day Workshop', Defense Advanced Research Projects Agency: Department of Defense, 2012.

52. Noah Shachtman, 'DARPA Looks to Make Cyberwar Routine with Secret "Plan X"', Wired, 21 August 2012.

53. Jim Lewis, a widely-quoted commenter on cyber operations, said that the goal of Plan X is "To get [cyber operations] to the point where it's a part of routine military operations." Ibid.

54. Ibid.
55. Ellen Nakashima, 'With Plan X, Pentagon Seeks to Spread U.S. Military Might to Cyberspace', *Washington Post*, 30 May 2012.
56. Noah Shachtman, 'This Pentagon Project Makes Cyberwar as Easy as Angry Birds', Wired, 28 May 2013.
57. Ibid.
58. 'Special Notice: Plan X Proposers' Day Workshop', Defense Advanced Research Projects Agency, 2012, 2.
59. Ibid.
60. 'Press Briefing with DARPA Director Arati Prabhakar from the Pentagon', Department of Defense, 24 April 2013.
61. 'Special Notice: Plan X Proposers' Day Workshop', Defense Advanced Research Projects Agency, 2012, 2.
62. 'Bad Guys Are Everywhere, Good Guys Are Somewhere!', National Security Agency: *Der Spiegel*, 2014, 3–5.
63. Ibid., 4.
64. Ibid., 16.
65. Scott Wilson and Anne Gearan, 'Obama Didn't Know About Surveillance of U.S.-Allied World Leaders until Summer, Officials Say', *Washington Post*, 28 October 2013.
66. Jens Gluesing et al., 'Fresh Leak on US Spying: NSA Accessed Mexican President's Email', *Der Spiegel*, 20 October 2013.
67. Dmitri Alperovitch, 'Bears in the Midst: Intrusion into the Democratic National Committee', CrowdStrike, 15 June 2016.
68. Civilians also used these networks. Sanger, 'Fine Line Seen in U.S. Spying on Companies', *New York Times*, 20 May 2014.
69. Ryan Gallagher, 'Operation Auroragold: How the NSA Hacks Cellphone Networks Worldwide', *The Intercept*, 4 December 2014.
70. Gellman and Nakashima, 'U.S. Spy Agencies Mounted 231 Offensive Cyber-Operations in 2011, Documents Show'.
71. Ellen Nakashima, 'Confidential Report Lists U.S. Weapons System Designs Compromised by Chinese Cyberspies', *Washington Post*, 27 May 2013; Caitlin Dewey, 'The U.S. Weapons Systems That Experts Say Were Hacked by the Chinese', *Washington Post*, 28 May 2013.
72. 'Resilient Military Systems and the Advanced Cyber Threat', Defense Science Board: Department of Defense, 2012, 4.
73. 'FY 2015 Annual Report', Operational Test and Evaluation Office of the Director: Department of Defense, 2016, vi.
74. Bree Feng, 'Among Snowden Leaks, Details of Chinese Cyberespionage', *New York Times*, 20 January 2015.
75. Luis Martinez et al., 'Major U.S. Weapons Compromised by Chinese Hackers, Report Warns', ABC News, 28 May 2013.
76. Dave Majumdar, 'U.S. Pilots Say New Chinese Stealth Fighter Could

Become Equal of F-22, F-35', *US Naval Institute News*, 5 November 2014.

77. Scott Shane, 'No Morsel Too Minuscule for All-Consuming N.S.A.', *New York Times*, 2 September 2013.

78. Mark Hosenball, 'Obama Halted NSA Spying on IMF and World Bank Headquarters', Reuters, 31 October 2013.

79. Shane, 'No Morsel Too Minuscule for All-Consuming N.S.A.'

80. For a case arguing the limits of espionage in gaining competitive advantage, see Thomas Rid, *Cyber War Will Not Take Place* (Oxford/New York: Oxford University Press, 2013), 82–3.

81. Ellen Nakashima, 'Indictment of PLA Hackers Is Part of Broad U.S. Strategy to Curb Chinese Cyberspying', *Washington Post*, 22 May 2014.

82. For example, see Richard Clarke, 'How China Steals Our Secrets', *New York Times*, 2 April 2012.

83. For the first major report of its kind, see 'APT1', Mandiant. Many have since followed, though the corporations are not always named.

84. For example, see Simon Romero, 'N.S.A. Spied on Brazilian Oil Company, Report Says', *New York Times*, 9 September 2013.

85. James Woolsey, 'Why We Spy on Our Allies', *Wall Street Journal*, 17 March 2000.

86. Allen Dulles, *The Craft of Intelligence* (Guilford, CT: Lyons Press, 2006), 117–29.

87. 'The Department of Defense Strategy for Counterintelligence in Cyberspace', Office of the Under Secretary of Defense for Intelligence: Department of Defense, 2016, 14.

88. David Sanger, 'N.S.A. Breached Chinese Servers Seen as Security Threat', *New York Times*, 22 March 2014.

89. The usage of attacks almost certainly refers to scans, not completed intrusions. Lee Davidson, 'Massive Utah Cyberattacks—up to 300 Million Per Day—May Be Aimed at NSA Facility', *Salt Lake Tribune*, 10 February 2015.

90. First-party collection is that carried out by the NSA itself. Second-party collection is that carried out by its Five Eyes partners. Partners outside of the Five Eyes, such as Germany, carry out third-party collection.

91. In addition to the Korean example, another document indicates a similar sequence of events involving Chinese intrusions against the United Nations. The United States, in tracking the Chinese capabilities, penetrated the command and control network which the intruders were using. They were thus able to intercept the Chinese collection against the United Nations and send it to their own analysts for review. 'NSA's

Offensive and Defensive Missions: The Twain Have Met', National Security Agency: *Der Spiegel*, 2015, 2.

92. This contrasts with "passive acquisition," which does not perform an intrusion on the endpoints, but instead collects information from the internet connection itself using the NSA's signals intelligence collection network. The downside to passive collection is that by that point the data is often encrypted or obfuscated. By breaking into the machines carrying the data before it is encrypted, intruders can get unobscured visibility. On the other hand, if the data can be decrypted, passive acquisition is preferred because it is less intrusive and less likely to get noticed. 'Fourth Party Opportunities', National Security Agency: *Der Spiegel*, 2015, 4–5. Other NSA documents provide examples of operations that appear to be passive collection. '"4th Party Collection": Taking Advantage of Non-Partner Computer Network Exploitation Activity', National Security Agency: *Der Spiegel*, 2015.

93. 'Is There "Fifth Party" Collection?', National Security Agency: *Der Spiegel*, 2015, 2.

94. 'Fourth Party Opportunities', National Security Agency, 2015, 6.

95. 'Is There "Fifth Party" Collection?', National Security Agency, 2015, 2.

96. In July 2016, unknown hackers published a cache of NSA exploits, some still working, online. These hackers could have, and perhaps did, use the exploits for their own purposes. Sanger, David, '"Shadow Brokers" Leak Raises Alarming Question: Was the N.S.A. Hacked?', *New York Times*, 16 August 2016.

97. 'Fourth Party Opportunities', National Security Agency, 2015, 7, emphasis in the original.

98. 'Is There "Fifth Party" Collection?', National Security Agency, 2015, 2.

99. Michael Herman, *Intelligence Power in Peace and War* (Cambridge: Cambridge University Press, 1996), 198.

100. In some ways, computer technology has made the disclosure of secrets far easier, whether for espionage or leaking to the media. For more on this, see Andy Greenberg, *This Machine Kills Secrets* (New York: Dutton, 2012). See also Adrian Duncan, Sadie Creese, and Michael Goldsmith, 'An Overview of Insider Attacks in Cloud Computing', *Concurrency and Computation: Practice and Experience* 27, no. 12 (2015).

101. Thomas Rid, *Rise of the Machines* (New York: W. W. Norton & Co., 2016), 315.

102. Ibid., 327.

103. Ibid., 336.

104. 'We're in the Middle of a Cyberwar', *Newsweek*, 19 September 1999. See also Rid, *Rise of the Machines*, 338.
105. Kaplan, *Dark Territory*, 75–85.
106. Chapter Seven specifically outlines and rebuts the argument that cybersecurity does not have high enough stakes to bring about a security dilemma.

## 5. THE FAILURE OF TRADITIONAL MITIGATIONS

1. Roosevelt's assessment was correct. Both German and British source documents indicated a great fear of the other, yet no desire for aggression. Robert Jervis, *Perception and Misperception in International Politics* (Princeton, NJ: Princeton University Press, 1976), 74.
2. Ned Moran and others have made some preliminary attempts at applying the (currently hypothetical) notion of strategic and catastrophic cyber attacks to a famous work on mitigation. See Ned Moran, 'A Historical Perspective on the Cybersecurity Dilemma', *Insecure*, no. 21 (2009). See also Nicholas Rueter, 'The Cybersecurity Dilemma' (Durham, NC: Duke University, 2011).
3. Because so much of the traditional security dilemma writing concerned the fear of invasion and the outcome of battles, it refers to the two sides as the "offense" and the "defense." To avoid confusion, this chapter uses that parlance when discussing the previous works. Nonetheless, when discussing network intrusions, in which penetrating an adversary's network is not necessarily done with offensive intent, the chapter sticks with the formulation used elsewhere in this text of "intruders" and "defenders."
4. Robert Jervis, 'Cooperation under the Security Dilemma', *World Politics* 30, no. 2 (1978): 187.
5. Ibid.
6. Ibid., 190.
7. Other writers have discussed this as well. For example, see Stephen Van Evera, *Causes of War* (Ithaca, NY: Cornell University Press, 1999). See also Jack Snyder, *The Ideology of the Offensive* (Ithaca, NY: Cornell University Press, 1984).
8. While this view has great popularity within international relations, important strands of dissent have started to emerge. For an example that draws on historical research to make the case that German leaders prepared for a long and difficult war, see Keir Lieber, 'The New History of World War I and What It Means for International Relations Theory', *International Security* 32, no. 2 (2007).
9. Jervis, 'Cooperation under the Security Dilemma', 191.

10. This recalls Napoleon's famous (and perhaps apocryphal) claim that "Geography is destiny."
11. For more on points of equilibrium, see Luttwak's example on paradoxical effects in strategy and conflict. Edward Luttwak, *Strategy: The Logic of War and Peace*, enlarged edn (Cambridge, MA: Belknap, 2002).
12. It is also known as the Five-Power Treaty, referring to the United States, Britain, France, Italy, and Japan. Jervis, 'Cooperation under the Security Dilemma', 191–6.
13. Ibid., 194–5.
14. Ibid., 196–8.
15. It would be a mistake to say that geography has no bearing on cyber operations. The geographically important locations of certain states enable some forms of intelligence collection, such as tapping fiber optic cables. The art of manipulating targeted traffic to run by these collection points is potentially relevant, as is using those points to enable man-on-the-side operations. States also have additional investigative capacity against servers, such as command and control nodes, that are within their borders. In addition, some might argue that the variety of protocols that move data are a technical geography of their own. But overall, geography as it is commonly understood has only limited bearing on the cybersecurity dilemma. For more on network traffic shaping, see 'Network Shaping 101', National Security Agency: *The Intercept*, 2016.
16. This is a subject already explored by Ned Moran, who notes, "In the context of cyberspace, natural fortifications like oceans and mountains do not exist." Moran, 'A Historical Perspective on the Cybersecurity Dilemma'.
17. Erik Gartzke, 'The Myth of Cyberwar: Bringing War in Cyberspace Back Down to Earth', *International Security* 38, no. 2 (2013): 53.
18. Paul Senese, 'Territory, Contiguity, and International Conflict: Assessing a New Joint Explanation', *American Journal of Political Science* 49, no. 4 (2005); Paul Hensel, 'Territory: Theory and Evidence on Geography and Conflict', in *What Do We Know About War?*, ed. John Vasquez (New York: Rowman and Littlefield, 2000).
19. Jervis, 'Cooperation under the Security Dilemma', 195.
20. There are reports that the NSA conducts deep packet analysis on at least some of the main internet routing points entering and exiting the United States. But this analysis is not self-limiting. Charlie Savage et al., 'Hunting for Hackers, N.S.A. Secretly Expands Internet Spying at U.S. Border', *New York Times*, 4 June 2015.
21. At a technical level, some additional nuance is useful around the concept of zero days. The criticality and usefulness of a zero day depends on the particulars of how the software in which it is found is deployed.

For more on this, see David Aitel, '0days', CyberSecPolitics, 11 February 2016.

22. Once a state uses exploits and those exploits are discovered, in time they are likely to diffuse to other actors. Ben Buchanan, 'The Life Cycles of Cyber Threats', *Survival* 58, no. 1 (2016). For more on the timing and incentives for cyber conflict, see Robert Axelrod and Rumen Iliev, 'Timing of Cyber Conflict', *Proceedings of the National Academy of Sciences* 111, no. 4 (2014). See also Tyler Moore, Allan Friedman, and Ariel Procaccia, 'Would a "Cyber Warrior" Protect Us? Exploring Trade-Offs between Attack and Defense of Information Systems', paper presented at 'New Security Paradigms Workshop', Concord, MA, 2010.

23. Zetter, *Countdown to Zero Day*.

24. Additional zero days were discovered by actors without malicious intent, such as security researchers and firms, and sent to software vendors for patching. Additional zero days were also likely discovered and either used in undetected attacks or stockpiled for future use. See 'Internet Security Threat Report 2016', Symantec, 12 April 2016.

25. After zero days are publicized and a patch issued, they are functionally in the same category as a known vulnerability, though there is some complexity on this point. As noted below, they can gain additional attention from operators, however, once they become public.

26. Leyla Bilge and Tudor Dumitras, 'Before We Knew It: An Empirical Study of Zero Day Attacks in the Real World', paper presented at 'Conference on Computer and Communication Security', 2012, 1.

27. 'Internet Security Threat Report 2014', Symantec, 2014, 35.

28. Included in this group are many important networks, such as some in the United States Navy, nuclear reactors, and major police forces, many of which have delayed updating systems in an effort to save money. Emil Protalinksi, 'Windows 7 Drops under 50% Market Share, XP Falls Below 10%', VentureBeat, 1 May 2016; Simon Sharwood, 'Fukushima Nuke Plant Owner Told to Upgrade from Windows XP', *The Register*, 23 April 2015; Joseph Cox, 'London's Metropolitan Police has over 35,000 Computers Still Running Windows XP', *Vice News*, 27 April 2015.

29. William Lynn, 'Defending a New Domain', *Foreign Affairs* (2010).

30. Ibid.

31. Overview publications from policy-focused organizations, such as the Council on Foreign Relations and Brookings Institution, reach similar conclusions. Kenneth Lieberthal and Peter W. Singer, 'Cybersecurity and U.S.–China Relations', February 2012, 24; Jonathan Masters, 'Confronting the Cyber Threat', Council on Foreign Relations, 23 May

2011. Many academics also agree. For examples of scholarly works arguing that cyber operations are offense-dominant, see Salma Shaheen, 'Offense–Defense Balance in Cyber Warfare', in *Cyberspace and International Relations*, ed. Jan-Frederik Kremer and Benedikt Muller (New York: Springer, 2014); Andrea Locatelli, 'The Offense/Defense Balance in Cyberspace', *Strategic Studies* 35, no. 1 (2011); Ilai Saltzman, 'Cyber Posturing and the Offense-Defense Balance', *Contemporary Security Policy* 34, no. 1 (2013).

32. Amaani Lyle, 'Obama Discusses National Security During Worldwide Troop Talk', Department of Defense, 11 September 2015.
33. Richard Clarke and Robert Knake, *Cyberwar* (New York: HarperCollins, 2010).
34. Joel Brenner, *Glass Houses* (New York: Penguin, 2014).
35. In addition to the above, see Richard Clarke, 'How China Steals Our Secrets', *New York Times*, 2 April 2012.
36. Dan Goodin, 'Fog of Cyberwar: Internet Always Favors the Offense', *The Register*, 29 July 2010.
37. Dan Geers, 'Cybersecurity as Realpolitik', *Black Hat*, 6 August 2014.
38. Jon Lindsay, 'The Impact of China on Cybersecurity: Fiction and Friction', *International Security* 39, no. 3 (2015): 30. For more, see Jon Lindsay, Tai Ming Cheung, and Derek S. Reveron, eds, *China and Cybersecurity: Espionage, Strategy, and Politics in the Digital Domain* (Oxford/New York: Oxford University Press, 2015).
39. Lindsay argues that this perception, as was the case at the dawn of World War I, is incorrect. Lindsay, 'The Impact of China on Cyber-security: Fiction and Friction', 36.
40. For example, "Current defense measures just simply cannot be prepared for the unknown and seemingly limitless way to penetrate and attack a network." David Fahrenkrug, 'Countering the Offensive Advantage in Cyberspace: An Integrated Defensive Strategy', in *2012 4th International Conference on Cyber Conflict*, ed. C. Crosseck, R. Ottis, and K. Ziolkowski (Talinn: NATO CCD COE Publications, 2012), 205.
41. Richard Bejtlich, 'Threat Advantages', TaoSecurity, 18 April 2007.
42. Ibid. This echoes the sentiments of the head of the NSA's intrusion group. Joyce, 'USENIX Enigma 2016—NSA TAO Chief on Disrupting Nation State Hackers'.
43. Neil McAllister, 'Bruce Schneier: "We're in Early Years of a Cyber Arms Race"', *The Register*, 19 August 2015.
44. It is worth noting that, in a separate discussion from the one outlining offensive advantages, Bejtlich cautions against "offense-envy," assuming all intruders are highly capable and all defenders hapless. He

writes, "If you've never seen advanced defenders at work, and have only seen mediocre or nonexistent defense, you're likely to mythologize the powers of the offense." Richard Bejtlich, 'Don't Envy the Offense', TaoSecurity, 28 December 2014.

45. One general exception is from Gartzke and Lindsay, who take a somewhat different approach, arguing that deception is comparatively easy in cyber operations, but that it is a double-edged sword, and so one should not immediately conclude that cyber operations are offense-dominant. Erik Gartzke and Jon Lindsay, 'Weaving Tangled Webs: Offense, Defense, and Deception in Cyberspace', *Security Studies* 24, no. 2 (2015).

46. Myriam Cavelty, 'Cyber-Terror—Looming Threat or Phantom Menace? The Framing of the US Cyber-Threat Debate', *Journal of Information Technology & Politics* 4, no. 1 (2008); Evgeny Morozov, 'Cyber-Scare: The Exaggerated Fears over Digital Warfare', *Boston Review*, 1 July 2009; Jon Lindsay, 'Stuxnet and the Limits of Cyber Warfare', *Security Studies* 22, no. 3 (2013); Gartzke, 'The Myth of Cyberwar: Bringing War in Cyberspace Back Down to Earth'; Sean Lawson, 'Beyond Cyber-Doom: Assessing the Limits of Hypothetical Scenarios in the Framing of Cyber-Threats', *Journal of Information Technology and Politics* 10, no. 1 (2013).

47. Keir Lieber makes specific reference to the possibility of the security dilemma in cyber operations before quickly dismissing it. He argues that the cyber attacks are not powerful enough to animate such fears and that states are not likely to detect preparations for attack. In addition to the response in the text above about the need to look beyond attacks, this argument is undercut by the fact that states do in fact detect intrusions by other states, and that—for the reasons outlined in Chapter Four—those intrusions can appear quite threatening. Keir Lieber, 'The Offense–Defense Balance and Cyber Warfare', *Cyber Analogies* (2014). See also Chapter Seven on the notion of existential risk in cyber operations.

48. Thomas Rid, *Cyber War Will Not Take Place*, (Oxford/New York: Oxford University Press, 2013), 82–3.

49. The general challenges of such categorization have a literature of their own that has spun off from the original discussion. For more on this, see Sean Lynn-Jones, 'Offense–Defense Theory and its Critics', *Security Studies* 4, no. 4 (1995); Jack S. Levy, 'The Offensive/Defensive Balance of Military Technology: A Theoretical and Historical Analysis', *International Studies Quarterly* (1984); Charles Glaser and Chaim Kaufmann, 'What Is the Offense–Defense Balance and Can We Measure It?', *International Security* 22, no. 4 (1998); James Davis et al., 'Taking

Offense at Offense–Defense Theory', *International Security* 23, no. 3 (1999); Keir Lieber, 'Grasping the Technological Peace: The Offense–Defense Balance and International Security', *International Security* 25, no. 1 (2000); Yoav Gortzak, Yoram Haftel, and Kevin Sweeney, 'Offense–Defense Theory: An Empirical Assessment', *Journal of Conflict Resolution* 49, no. 1 (2005).

50. Jervis, 'Cooperation under the Security Dilemma', 199. It is the "inherently ambiguous" nature of weapons that makes the security dilemma real. Ken Booth and Nicholas J. Wheeler, *The Security Dilemma* (New York: Palgrave Macmillan, 2008), 1.

51. Jervis, 'Cooperation under the Security Dilemma', 200.

52. Merze Tate, *The United States and Armaments* (Cambridge, MA: Harvard University Press, 1948), 108.

53. Jervis, 'Cooperation under the Security Dilemma', 201.

54. Ibid., 201–2.

55. Security researchers can also develop zero day exploit code as a proof of concept, in order to lead to the production of a patch to fix the vulnerability. This does not involve actively using the exploits in an unauthorized way on others' networks.

56. Liz Gannes, 'How Cyber Security Is Like Basketball, According to Barack Obama', Recode, 14 February 2015. Other senior officials agree. Without reference to specific capabilities, the former Director of Operations at United States Cyber Command, Brett Williams, said, "You can't clearly define what is defense and what is offense." David Perera, 'Offense and Defense Not Clearly Separable in Cyberspace, Says CYBERCOM General', FierceGovernmentIT, 25 February 2013.

57. Charles Glaser, 'The Security Dilemma Revisited', *World Politics* 50, no. 1 (1997): 191.

58. For more on this view, see Randall Schweller, 'Neorealism's Status-Quo Bias: What Security Dilemma?', *Security Studies* 5, no. 3 (1996). Though the differences between Glaser and Schweller are significant, they are less relevant for the purposes of the cybersecurity dilemma. Glaser comes to something of a détente with Schweller's argumentation, agreeing that "differences in states' goals matter because they can lead states to choose different policies; a security seeker will sometimes choose cooperation when, under the same circumstances, a greedy state will choose competition." Glaser, 'The Security Dilemma Revisited', 190–91.

59. Chapter Eight will discuss this signaling value in more detail.

60. Glaser, 'The Security Dilemma Revisited', 181.

61. Ibid.

62. Ibid.

63. Glaser notes that Charles Osgood was at the forefront of this approach.

For more, see Charles Osgood, *An Alternative to War or Surrender* (Urbana, IL: University of Illinois, 1962).

64. Glaser, 'The Security Dilemma Revisited', 181.

65. Ibid., 191.

66. Sanger, 'N.S.A. Breached Chinese Servers Seen as Security Threat'. A 2015 agreement at the G20 may mean that other nations will also adopt this practice. For more on early indications of adherence, see 'Redline Drawn', FireEye, June 2016.

67. David Sanger, 'Fine Line Seen in U.S. Spying on Companies', *New York Times*, 20 May 2014.

68. President Obama attempted to respond to this criticism directly by slightly changing the procedures for the storage of data on foreign citizens. David Sanger, 'President Tweaks the Rules on Data Collection', *New York Times*, 3 February 2015.

69. For example, see 'Quantum Spying: GCHQ Used Fake LinkedIn Pages to Target Engineers', *Der Spiegel*, 11 November 2013.

70. This topic is not a recent development. For an early examination of some important issues, see Dorothy Denning, 'Obstacles and Options for Cyber Arms Control', paper presented at 'Arms Control in Cyberspace', Berlin, 29–30 June 2001.

71. Sometimes these non-state actors use tools or exploits originally developed by states that have diffused more broadly. Buchanan, 'The Life Cycles of Cyber Threats'.

72. For more on the different levels, or "images," of international relations, see Kenneth Waltz, *Man, the State, and War* (New York: Columbia University Press, 1959).

73. Glaser, 'The Security Dilemma Revisited'.

74. This is a departure from typical realist thinking. According to the realist school of international relations, states do not typically give much weight to the internal characteristics of other states, since states generally infer motives from actions, not statements or characteristics.

75. Glaser, 'The Security Dilemma Revisited', 192.

76. Ibid., 192–3.

77. Ibid., fn. 76.

78. Ibid., 193. See also the discussion in Chapter One.

79. Sometimes states match these protests with actions, as when the German government severed its relationship with Verizon over fears that the telecommunications company was cooperating with the United States government on intelligence matters. 'German Government Cancels Verizon Contract in Wake of U.S. Spying Row', Reuters, 26 June 2014.

80. Even some within democracies, such as those in the legislative branch,

complain that they are not able to oversee because the executive branch is not sufficiently transparent. For a broader discussion of this issue, see Clarke et al., 'Liberty and Security in a Changing World', The President's Review Group on Intelligence and Communications Technologies.

81. Some of the documents disclosed by Edward Snowden are classified SCI in the United States (for Sensitive Compartmented Information) or Strap One in the United Kingdom, a high level of classification. It is worth noting that the United States declassified some older general strategy documents on cyber operations in 2016 in an effort to shed some additional light. For a broader view on data collection, see Bruce Schneier, *Data and Goliath*, New York: W.W. norton & Co., 2015.

82. This varies by news organization. For more on the process, with input from both a former signals intelligence official and a leading national security reporter, see 'The NSA and Privacy', American University, 3 April 2014.

83. 'Equation: The Death Star of Malware Galaxy', Kaspersky Lab.

## 6. INFORMATION DISTRIBUTION AND THE STATUS QUO

1. Jack Davis, 'Improving CIA Analytic Performance: Strategic Warning', Sherman Kent Center for Intelligence Analysis, September 2002.

2. Robert Jervis, 'Cooperation under the Security Dilemma', *World Politics* 30, no. 2 (1978), 199.

3. For more on this dynamic, see Patrick Morgan, 'The Opportunity for a Strategic Surprise', in *Strategic Military Surprise: Incentives and Opportunities*, ed. Klaus Knorr and Patrick Morgan (New Brunswick, NJ: Transaction Books, 1983).

4. Naturally, the time for development could be years, while the time for deployment could be substantially less. The security dilemma is relativistic and works on both timeframes. Development of a capability by one state is matched, potentially, by development of capabilities by another state, which likely occurs on a similar timeframe. A state's deployment of capabilities to a potentially threatening position (e.g. to a contested border) is met by a countervailing deployment by another state (e.g. massing on the other side of the border), which also likely occurs on a similar timeframe. The development of cyber capabilities, and the speed of decision in cyber operations, may occur at still another time scale, but as long as it is relatively consistent for both sides, the cybersecurity dilemma logic will still apply.

5. More properly, some may prefer to think of this as a two-dimensional graph, putting quality and timeliness on two separate axes, but that is not necessary for the purposes of this discussion.

6. For another discussion of the possibility of surprise cyber attack, see Michael S. Goodman, 'Applying the Historical Lessons of Surprise Attack to the Cyber Domain: The Example of the United Kingdom', in *Cyber Analogies*, ed. Emily Goldman and John Arquilla (Monterey, CA: Naval Postgraduate School, 2014).

7. 'The Department of Defense Cyber Strategy', Office of the Secretary of Defense, 2015.

8. There is no doubt of the *tremendous* variation in level of investment. The number of states that have made significant progress in the cyber-security dilemma being relevant to them is probably much smaller than the figure of one hundred states cited in some pieces. Andrew Osborn and Guy Faulconbridge, 'UK Seeks Full Cyber Warfare Capability, Experts', Reuters, 29 September 2013; Shane Harris, 'China Reveals Its Cyberwar Secrets', *The Daily Beast*, 18 March 2015; Bill Gertz, 'Iranian General: IRGC Cyber Warfare Capabilities Now Equal to Those of Major Global Powers', FlashCritic, 4 January 2014; Michael Crowley and Josh Gerstein, 'No Rules of Cyber War', *Politico*, 23 December 2014.

9. Nicole Perlroth, Jeff Larson, and Scott Shane, 'N.S.A. Able to Foil Basic Safeguards of Privacy on Web', *New York Times*, 5 September 2013.

10. The journalists, possessing incomplete information about American efforts, did not want to name some of the algorithms targeted by the NSA and thus incorrectly implicitly verify other algorithms as secure. An exception is a random number generator that it appears the NSA compromised and encouraged for use in security products. Joseph Menn, 'Exclusive: Secret Contract Tied NSA and Security Industry Pioneer', Reuters, 20 December 2013. Another exception is a program that weakens certain means of encrypting cell phone communications. Craig Timberg and Ashkan Soltani, 'By Cracking the Cellphone Code, NSA Has Ability to to Decode Private Conversations', *Washington Post*, 13 December 2013.

11. Mimoso, 'Inside nls_933w.dll, the Equation APT Persistence Module', ThreatPost.

12. Kim Zetter, 'How the NSA's Firmware Hacking Works and Why It's So Unsettling', Wired, 22 February 2015.

13. 'Unveiling "Careto"—the Masked APT', Kaspersky Lab, 6 February 2014.

14. APT is short for Advanced Persistent Threat. The term usually refers to an organized group of network intruders. 'APT1', Mandiant.

15. 'APT30 and the Mechanics of a Long-Running Cyber Espionage Operation', FireEye.

16. 'Putter Panda', CrowdStrike, 9 June 2014.
17. 'Cloud Atlas: RedOctober APT is Back in Style', Kaspersky Lab.
18. Gavin O'Gorman and Geoff McDonald, 'The Elderwood Project', Symantec, 6 September 2012.
19. 'Equation Group: Questions and Answers', Kaspersky Lab.
20. Thomas Rid and Ben Buchanan, 'Attributing Cyber Attacks', *Journal of Strategic Studies* 39, no. 1 (2015): 29.
21. For example, see Ross Rustici, 'Cyberweapons: Leveling the International Playing Field', *Parameters* 41, no. 3 (2011).
22. 'The Department of Defense Cyber Strategy', Office of the Secretary of Defense, 2015.
23. Glenn Greenwald, 'NSA Claims Iran Learned from Western Cyber-attacks', *The Intercept*, 10 February 2015.
24. 'Operation Cleaver', Cylance, 2014.
25. For a discussion of the Concert of Europe and similar institutions as they relate to the security dilemma, see Ken Booth and Nicholas J. Wheeler, *The Security Dilemma* (New York: Palgrave Macmillan, 2008), 107–14.
26. Jervis, 'Cooperation under the Security Dilemma', 191–6.
27. The use of anti-aircraft weapons in the 1973 conflict between Israel and Egypt is an example of this. Ibid., 202–3.
28. For more on the history, concept, and implementation of the Open Skies Treaty, see 'The Open Skies Treaty', Federation of American Scientists, February 1996.
29. 'The Sveriges Riksbank Prize in Economic Sciences in Memory of Alfred Nobel 2005', Swedish Academy of Sciences, 10 October 2005.
30. It is formally called the William and Katherine Estes Award. 'William and Katherine Estes Award', National Academy of Sciences.
31. For more on the treaty, including its specifications, see 'Treaty between the United States of America and the Union of Soviet Socialist Republics on the Limitation of Anti-Ballistic Missile Systems', Bureau of Arms Control Verification and Compliance: Department of State, 1972. The George W. Bush Administration withdrew from the treaty.
32. Joseph Marks, 'U.S. Makes New Push for Global Rules in Cyberspace', *Politico*, 5 May 2015; 'Group of Governmental Experts on Developments in the Field of Information and Telecommunications in the Context of International Security', United Nations General Assembly, 2015.
33. 'Group of Governmental Experts on Developments in the Field of Information and Telecommunications in the Context of International Security', United Nations General Assembly, 2013.
34. Detlev Wolter, 'The UN Takes a Big Step Forward on Cybersecurity', Arms Control Association, 4 September 2013.

35. International agreements very often have an incremental foundation. For more, see Abram Chayes and Antonia Handler Chayes, *The New Sovereignty* (Cambridge, MA: Harvard University Press, 1998), 15.
36. For recollection of early cyber arms control discussions by one participant, see Richard Clarke and Robert Knake, *Cyberwar* (New York: HarperCollins, 2010), 219–57.
37. Michael N. Schmitt, ed., *Tallinn Manual on the International Law Applicable to Cyber Warfare* (New York: Cambridge University Press, 2013).
38. Sometimes states will recognize in advance which networks of theirs are important, but at other times it will take a breach before that happens. David Aitel, 'Cyber Norms: The Futility of Blacklisting Critical Infrastructure', CyberSecPolitics, 14 March 2016.
39. David Sanger and Mark Mazzetti, 'U.S. Had Cyberattack Plan if Iran Nuclear Dispute Led to Conflict', New York Times, 16 February 2016; *Zero Days*, Alex Gibney, Magnolia Pictures, 2016.
40. The United States and China agreed in late 2015 to bilateral mutual cooperation of this sort, but it is too early to analyze what form that will take. 'Full Text: Outcome List of President Xi Jinping's State Visit to the United States', Xinhua, 26 September 2015; 'Remarks by President Obama and President Xi of the People's Republic of China in Joint Press Conference', The White House, 25 September 2015.

## 7. LIMITATIONS, OBJECTIONS, AND THE FUTURE OF THE CYBER-SECURITY DILEMMA

1. Early contributions include Richard Clayton, *Anonymity and Traceability in Cyberspace*, vol. 653, Technical Report (Cambridge: University of Cambridge Computer Laboratory, 2005); Susan Brenner, '"At Light Speed": Attribution and Response to Cybercrime/Terrorism/Warfare', *Journal of Criminal Law and Criminology* 97, no. 2 (2007). A notable early case study is Clifford Stoll, *The Cuckoo's Egg* (New York: Doubleday, 1989).
2. For example, "Perhaps the most difficult problem is that of attribution." P. W. Singer and Allan Friedman, *Cybersecurity and Cyberwar* (New York, Oxford: Oxford University Press, 2014), 73. See also David Betz and Tim Stevens, *Cyberspace and the State*, Adelphi Series (London: International Institute for Strategic Studies, 2011), 75–6.
3. See for instance W. Earl Boebert, 'A Survey of Challenges in Attribution', paper presented at 'Proceedings of a workshop on Deterring Cyberattacks', 2010; also Martin C. Libicki, *Cyberdeterrence and Cyberwar* (Santa Monica, CA: Rand Corporation, 2009), 43; Mike

McConnell, 'How to Win the Cyber-War We're Losing', *Washington Post*, 28 Feburary 2010. For a contribution on how laws and politics affect the issue, see Jack Goldsmith and Tim Wu, *Who Controls the Internet? Illusions of a Borderless World* (Oxford: Oxford University Press, 2006).

4. Former Secretary of Defense Panetta implied a generalizable, rather than case-specific, view of the attribution problem, saying "the [Department of Defense] has made significant advances in solving a problem that makes deterring cyber adversaries more complex: the difficulty of identifying the origins of an attack." Panetta, 'Defending the Nation from Cyber Attack'.

5. Notable papers on attribution often ignore the challenges in communication of analysis. For example, see Caltagirone, Pendergast, and Betz, 'The Diamond Model of Intrusion Analysis', Defense Technical Information Center. See also Hutchins, Cloppert, and Amin, 'Intelligence-Driven Computer Network Defense Informed by Analysis of Adversary Campaigns and Intrusion Kill Chains', Lockheed Martin. For a broader discussion of this point and of the assumptions in the attribution debate, see Thomas Rid and Ben Buchanan, 'Attributing Cyber Attacks', *Journal of Strategic Studies* 39, no. 1 (2015).

6. Cyber attacks are rarely totally and completely unexpected, but instead often are born of a particular geopolitical climate. For an early articulation of this idea, see Ned Moran, 'A Cyber Early Warning Model', in *Inside Cyber Warfare*, ed. Jeffrey Carr (Sebastopol, CA: O'Reilly Media, 2010).

7. James Niccolai, 'A Security Firm Says Code Used against Sony Has Similarities to Other Malware Linked to North Korea', *Computer World*, 17 February 2015.

8. The company later somewhat softened its conclusions, adding "Likely" to the title of its report. 'Taia Global Linguists Establish Nationality of Sony Hackers as Likely Russian, Not Korean', Taia Global, 8 January 2015.

9. For more on the attribution process in general and the questions asked therein, see Rid and Buchanan, 'Attributing Cyber Attacks'. For a critical perspective, see Jeffrey Carr, 'A Critical Review of Tom Rid and Ben Buchanan's "Attributing Cyber Attacks"', Taia Global, 6 January 2015.

10. Kim Zetter, 'The Evidence That North Korea Hacked Sony Is Flimsy', Wired, 17 December 2014.

11. Michael Schmidt, Nicole Perlroth, and Matthew Goldstein, 'F.B.I. Says Little Doubt North Korea Hit Sony', *New York Times*, 7 January 2015.

12. David Sanger and Martin Fackler, 'N.S.A. Breached North Korean

Networks before Sony Attack, Officials Say', *New York Times*, 18 January 2015.

13. David Sanger and Stewart Baker, 'Steptoe Cyberlaw Podcast—Interview with David Sanger', Steptoe & Johnson, 21 January 2015; Richard Bejtlich, 'Notes on Stewart Baker Podcast with David Sanger', TaoSecurity, 22 January 2015.
14. Rid and Buchanan, 'Attributing Cyber Attacks', 31–2.
15. The factor of time does not appear to be significant for this discussion.
16. 'The Department of Defense Cyber Strategy', Office of the Secretary of Defense, 2015, 11–12.
17. For example, the Iranian attacks on the American financial system, on Aramco, and on Sands Casino were on the whole not well-disguised. The same is somewhat true of the North Korean attack on Sony.
18. Robert Jervis, 'From Balance to Concert: A Study of International Security Cooperation', *World Politics* 38, no. 1 (1985): 69.
19. David Sanger and Mark Mazzetti, 'U.S. Had Cyberattack Plan if Iran Nuclear Dispute Led to Conflict', *New York Times*, 16 February 2016; *Zero Days*, Alex Gibney, Magnolia Pictures, 2016.
20. Tami Abdollah, 'Obama Seeks Cybersecurity Boost to Replace "Ancient" Tech', Associated Press, 9 February 2016; Andrea Shalal and Alina Selyukh, 'Obama Seeks $14 Billion to Boost U.S. Cybersecurity Defenses', Reuters, 2 February 2015.
21. For an argument on this point, see Robert Lee and Thomas Rid, 'OMG Cyber!', *RUSI Journal* 159, no. 5 (2014).
22. For a counterargument, which focuses quite narrowly and exclusively on the number of centrifuges destroyed, see Ivanka Barzashka, 'Are Cyber-Weapons Effective? Assessing Stuxnet's Impact on the Iranian Enrichment Programme', *RUSI Journal* 158, no. 2 (2013).
23. 'Worldwide Threat Assessment of the US Intelligence Community', Office of the Director of National Intelligence: Senate Armed Services Committee, 2016, 1–3.
24. For more, see Ellen Nakashima, 'Indictment of PLA Hackers Is Part of Broad U.S. Strategy to Curb Chinese Cyberspying', *Washington Post*, 22 May 2014.
25. James Coyle, 'Russia Has Complete Information Dominance in Ukraine', Atlantic Council, 12 May 2015; see Kenneth Geers, ed., *Cyber War in Perspective: Russian Aggression against Ukraine* (Tallinn: NATO Cooperative Cyber Defence Center of Excellence, 2015), ch. 18.
26. Bill Marczak et al., 'Hacking Team and the Targeting of Ethiopian Journalists', Citizen Lab, 12 February 2014.
27. Siobhan Gorman and Julian E. Barnes, 'Cyber Combat: Act of War', *Wall Street Journal*, 31 May 2011.

28. Naturally, long-term economic interests do sometimes factor into the decision to go to war; and some tactics, such as blockades, use military capabilities as the means of causing medium-term economic harm.
29. For the United States' view on cyber deterrence, see Scott Maucione, 'White House Finally Acquiesces to Congress on Cyber Deterrence Policy', Federal News Radio, 29 December 2015. For a classic overview, see Lawrence Freedman, *Deterrence* (Cambridge: Polity Press, 2004).
30. Ben Buchanan, 'Cyber Deterrence isn't MAD; it's Mosaic', *Georgetown Journal of International Affairs*, International Engagement on Cyber IV (October 2014): 130–40.
31. Nicole Perlroth and Quentin Hardy, 'Bank Hacking Was the Work of Iranians, Officials Say', *New York Times*, 8 January 2013; David Sanger, 'U.S. Indicts 7 Iranians in Cyberattacks on Banks and a Dam', *New York Times*, 24 March 2016.
32. For example, see Rolf Weber, 'Internet of Things–New Security and Privacy Challenges', *Computer Law and Security Review* 26, no. 1 (2010).
33. Thomas Rid and Peter McBurney, 'Cyber-Weapons', *RUSI Journal* 157, no. 1 (2012).
34. Andy Greenberg, 'Hackers Remotely Kill a Jeep on the Highway—with Me in It', Wired, 21 July 2015.
35. Irwin Lebow, 'The Impact of Computer Security in the Department of Defense', paper presented at 'Proceedings of the Second Seminar on the DOD Computing Security Program', Gaithersburg, Maryland, 15–17 January 1980, C18–19.
36. Shane Harris, *@War: The Rise of the Military-Internet Complex* (New York: Eamon Dolan/Houghton Mifflin Harcourt, 2014).
37. Eric Schmitt and Thom Shanker, 'U.S. Debated Cyberwarfare in Attack Plan on Libya', *New York Times*, 17 October 2011.
38. Jon Lindsay, 'The Impact of China on Cybersecurity: Fiction and Friction', *International Security* 39, no. 3 (2015).
39. Ryan Gallagher, 'Operation Auroragold: How the NSA Hacks Cellphone Networks Worldwide', *The Intercept*, 4 December 2014; Craig Timberg and Ashkan Soltani, 'By Cracking the Cellphone Code, NSA Has Ability to to Decode Private Conversations', *Washington Post*, 13 December 2013.
40. In the aftermath of 9/11, this was the case with the United States and al-Qaeda. American policy-makers, despite a tremendous advantage in resources and military capabilities, greatly fear another catastrophic terrorist attack. For an account of this period, see Peter Baker, *Days of Fire* (New York: Doubleday, 2013).
41. Richard Clarke has made this argument: Richard Clarke and Robert

Knake, *Cyberwar* (New York: HarperCollins, 2010). See also Joel Brenner, *Glass Houses* (New York: Penguin, 2014).

## 8. MITIGATING THE CYBERSECURITY DILEMMA

1. It is outside the scope of this discussion, but better security engineering of software would also make intrusions more difficult.
2. There are many examples. For one, see Robert Falcone and Miller-Osborn Jen, 'Scarlet Mimic: Years-Long Espionage Campaign Targets Minority Activists', Palo Alto Networks, 24 January 2016. See also John Snow, 'The Poseidon's Domain', Kaspersky Lab, 9 February 2016.
3. 'Officials: Second Hack Exposed Military and Intel Data', *New York Times*, 12 June 2015.
4. Kim Zetter and Andy Greenberg, 'Why the OPM Breach is Such a Security and Privacy Debacle', Wired, 11 June 2015.
5. 'Federal Information Security Management Act Audit FY 2014', Office of Inspector General: Office of Personnel Management, 2014, 10.
6. Aliya Sternstein, 'Here's What OPM Told Congress Last Time Hackers Breached its Networks', NextGov, 15 June 2015.
7. For a post-breach update on OPM and other agencies, see 'Agencies Need to Improve Controls over Selected High-Impact Systems', Government Accountability Office, 2016.
8. 'Cross Agency Priority Goal: Cybersecurity', The White House: Performance.gov, 2015, 11.
9. Anthony Cuthbertson, 'Teenage "CIA Hacker" Cracka Arrested in the U.K.', *Newsweek*, 12 February 2016.
10. James Eng and Wendy Jones, 'OPM Chief Says Government Agency Thwarts 10 Million Hack Attempts a Month', NBC News, 16 June 2015.
11. For just one example of Cold War thinking applied to cyber operations, see Joseph Nye, 'Cyber Power', Belfer Center for Science and International Affairs, May 2010.
12. During the Cold War, various advocates on both sides sought to devise similar kinds of "non-provocative defenses." Ken Booth and Nicholas J. Wheeler, *The Security Dilemma* (New York: Palgrave Macmillan, 2008), 141–5. For a more modern perspective, see Geoffrey Wiseman, *Concepts of Non-Provocative Defence: Ideas and Practices in International Security* (London: Palgrave, 2002).
13. There is a reservoir of good scholarship on trust in international relations. This book primarily functions within a realist view of trust, much like the one espoused by Andrew Kydd, which he refers to as Bayesian Realism. Andrew H. Kydd, *Trust and Mistrust in International*

*Relations* (Princeton, NJ: Princeton University Press, 2005). For four other varying perspectives, see Deborah Welch Larson, 'Trust and Missed Opportunities in International Relations', *Political Psychology* 18, no. 3 (1997); Brian C. Rathbun, *Trust in International Cooperation: International Security Institutions, Domestic Politics and American Multilateralism*, vol. 121 (Cambridge University Press, 2011); Torsten Michel, 'Time to Get Emotional: Phronetic Reflections on the Concept of Trust in International Relations', *European Journal of International Relations* 19, no. 4 (2013); Booth and Wheeler, *The Security Dilemma*.

14. Webster Stone, 'Moscow's Still Holding', *New York Times*, 18 September 1988.

15. Ibid.

16. An exception: the Soviets used a hotline conversation initially to deny their invasion of Afghanistan. 'Cold War Hotline Recalled', BBC News, 7 June 2003.

17. Stone, 'Moscow's Still Holding'.

18. The arms control agreements were not negotiated during crises. On one occasion, to underscore the importance of the SALT II negotiations, the Carter Administration sent arms control communications over the hotline—an approach not received well by the Soviets. Ibid.

19. 'Treaty between the United States of America and the Union of Soviet Socialist Republics on the Limitation of Strategic Offensive Arms (SALT II)', Bureau of Arms Control Verification and Compliance: Department of State, 1979.

20. Ellen Nakashima, 'U.S. And Russia Sign Pact to Create Communication Link on Cyber Security', *Washington Post*, 17 June 2013.

21. 'Full Text: Outcome List of President Xi Jinping's State Visit to the United States'; 'Remarks by President Obama and President Xi of the People's Republic of China in Joint Press Conference'.

22. David Sanger, 'U.S. Tries Candor to Assure China on Cyberattacks', *New York Times*, 6 April 2014.

23. Jackie Calmes and Steven Lee Myers, 'Obama and Xi Tackle Cybersecurity as Talks Begin in California', *New York Times*, 7 June 2013; Julie Hirschfeld Davis and David Sanger, 'Obama and Xi Jinping of China Agree to Steps on Cybertheft', *New York Times*, 25 September 2015.

24. Sanger, 'U.S. Tries Candor to Assure China on Cyberattacks'.

25. Ting Shi and Michael Riley, 'China Halts Cybersecurity Cooperation after U.S. Spying Charges', Bloomberg, 20 May 2014.

26. 'Remarks by President Obama and President Xi of the People's Republic of China in Joint Press Conference'; 'Full Text: Outcome List of President Xi Jinping's State Visit to the United States'.

27. Joe Uchill, 'State Department Reverses Course on Cybersecurity Exports', *Christian Science Monitor*, 2 March 2016.

28. Michael Spence, 'Job Market Signaling', *Quarterly Journal of Economics* 87, no. 3 (1973).

29. The cost required to make a signal meaningful depends on a variety of circumstances largely outside the scope of this work. For example, states that are perceived to have less negotiating power in a two-party conflict need to send costlier signals. On the other hand, states that are hegemons still need to signal to other states that they are trustworthy and seek stability, but can do so with less costly signals. For an excellent book-length study of the effects of trust in international relations, including several game theoretic discussions of signaling value, see Kydd, *Trust and Mistrust in International Relations*.

30. Deborah Welch Larson, *Anatomy of Mistrust* (Ithaca, NY: Cornell University Press, 1997), 63.

31. David Finlay, Ole Holsti, and Richard Fagen, *Enemies in Politics* (Chicago: Rand McNally, 1967), 95–6.

32. Booth and Wheeler, *The Security Dilemma*, 155.

33. For a more in-depth discussion of Gorbachev's signals and other actions, and for insight into how they were perceived in the United States, see Kydd, *Trust and Mistrust in International Relations*, ch. 8.

34. 'The End of the Cold War', *Cold War International History Project Bulletin*, no. 12/13 (2001): 24.

35. Raymond Garthoff, *The Great Transition: American–Soviet Relations and the End of the Cold War* (Washington, DC: Brookings Institution, 1994), 354. In Reagan's memoirs, he addressed the gradually changing view of United States–Soviet relations during his second term in office with security dilemma-esque language: "I had come to realize there were people in the Kremlin who had a genuine fear of the United States. I wanted to convince Gorbachev that we wanted peace and they had nothing to fear from us." Ronald Reagan, *An American Life* (New York: Simon & Schuster, 1990), 12.

36. Again, there is complexity around the nuances of defining zero days, but an overall policy approach can be revealing. David Aitel, '0days', CyberSecPolitics, 11 February 2016.

37. Kydd, *Trust and Mistrust in International Relations*, ch. 8.

38. If such trade did occur, it would probably not be for money, but rather as part of relationship building or shared operations. One could imagine Five Eyes states pooling zero days, for example, though not explicitly for cash.

39. The United States' Vulnerabilities Equities Process outlines the process through which various agencies determine a course of action once a vulnerability is discovered. 'Commercial and Government Information Technology and Industrial Control Product or System Vulnerabilities

Equities Policy and Process', United States Government, 2016, 2. This process may have been updated with time. See Daniel, 'Heartbleed: Understanding When We Disclose Cyber Vulnerabilities'. For questions about how frequently the process has been used, see Joseph Menn, 'Apple Says FBI Gave It First Vulnerability Tip on April 14', Reuters, 26 April 2016. For additional proposals on the need to clarify the process, see Ari Schwartz and Robert Knake, 'Government's Role in Vulnerability Disclosure: Creating a Permanent and Accountable Vulnerability Equities Process', Belfer Center for Science and International Affairs, 17 June 2016.

40. Indeed, even the definition of zero day is fuzzier than most policy papers acknowledge. Aitel, '0days'.

41. David Aitel, 'The Value of an 0day Stockpile to the Country Versus the Value of Feeling Self-Rightous', CyberSecPolitics, 12 February 2016.

42. Joseph Menn, 'NSA Says How Often, Not When, It Discloses Software Flaws', Reuters, 6 November 2015.

43. David Aitel and Matt Tait, 'Everything You Know About The Vulnerability Equities Process is Wrong', Lawfare, 18 August 2016. For an empirical study indicating that the rediscovery does occur, see Andy Ozment. "The Likelihood of Vulnerability Rediscovery and the Social Utility of Vulnerability Hunting." In *The Workshop on Economics and Information Security*. Cambridge, MA, 2005.

44. Joseph Menn, 'Special Report: U.S. Cyberwar Strategy Stokes Fear of Blowback', Reuters, 10 May 2013.

45. Menn, 'NSA Says How Often, Not When, It Discloses Software Flaws'.

46. Newman, 'Encryption Risks Leading to "Ethically Worse" Behaviour by Spies, Says Former GCHQ Chief'. See also Joseph Cox, 'GCHQ Has Disclosed over 20 Vulnerabilities This Year, Including Ones in iOS', *Vice News*, 29 April 2016.

47. Encryption can also be used by one party to store a message such that only that party can later read it, such as on a hard drive.

48. For an accessible introduction to encryption, see Simon Singh, *The Code Book* (New York: Doubleday, 1999).

49. Provisionally, it appears that the renewed debate has again been resolved in favor of secure encryption without exceptional access mandates for law enforcement, the same conclusion reached in the 1990s. Ellen Nakashima and Andrea Peterson, 'Obama Administration Opts Not to Force Firms to Decrypt Data—for Now', *Washington Post*, 8 October 2015. For a broader discussion of national regulation and technology, see Ian Brown and Christopher T. Marsden, *Regulating Code: Good Governance and Better Regulation in the Information Age* (Cambridge, MA: MIT Press, 2013).

50. For one full-length recounting, see Steven Levy, *Crypto* (New York: Penguin Books, 2001).
51. Nicole Perlroth and Brian X. Chen, 'Outdated Encryption Keys Leave Phones Vulnerable to Hackers', *New York Times*, 4 March 2015.
52. Jeff Larson, Nicole Perlroth, and Scott Shane, 'Revealed: The NSA's Secret Campaign to Crack, Undermine Internet Security', *Pro Publica*, 5 September 2013.
53. Joseph Menn, 'Exclusive: Secret Contract Tied NSA and Security Industry Pioneer', Reuters, 20 December 2013.
54. A fourth option discussed in domestic politics, overtly requiring weaknesses in encryption to assure law enforcement access, is not workable in foreign affairs, as no state will use encryption that obviously gives access to another state. This option is also likely to be ineffective in a domestic context. For more, see Harold Abelson et al., 'Keys under Doormats', *Massachusetts Institute of Technology Computer Science and Artificial Intelligence Lab Technical Reports* (2015).
55. Glyn Moody, 'Dutch Government: Encryption Good, Backdoors Bad', *Ars Technica*, 6 January 2016.
56. Kate Tummarello, '"Be Careful" Working with NSA, US Tech Security Agency Warned', *The Hill*, 14 July 2014.
57. Michael Wertheimer, 'The Mathematics Community and the NSA', *Notices of the American Mathematical Society* (2015): 166.
58. 'SIGINT Enabling Project', National Security Agency: *Pro Publica*, 2013, 1.
59. Andrea Peterson, 'The NSA is Trying to Crack Tor. The State Department is Helping Pay for It', *Washington Post*, 5 October 2013.
60. It is worth emphasizing again that there are intrusions that might well be construed by one side as "defensive" without being narrowly specific to cybersecurity. For example, a state might argue that its general signals intelligence collection, which will likely involve network intrusions, is defensive in nature. But this collection is likely to go beyond what is narrowly necessary to gather information for increased cybersecurity defenses and is likely to be threatening to the other side. For this reason it was discussed in Chapter Four rather than Chapter Three.
61. For more on this, see Ben Buchanan, 'Cyber Deterrence isn't MAD; it's Mosaic', *Georgetown Journal of International Affairs*, International Engagement on Cyber IV (October 2014).
62. A question worthy of future research is whether this threshold—or red line—can be ambiguous or must be conveyed to other states. On the one hand, ambiguity preserves options for policy-makers and might prompt other states to stay far away from the line, for fear of

unintentionally provoking a response. On the other hand, ambiguity could lead to unintentional escalation, in which a state performs some activity that it thinks will be acceptable, yet which in fact provokes retaliation. Because this question regarding red lines is not particular to cyber operations, it is not discussed in more detail here. As a demonstration of the deterrence and ambiguity discussion in another area, see John Baylis, *Ambiguity and Deterrence: British Nuclear Strategy, 1945–1964* (Oxford/New York: Oxford University Press, 1995).

63. Less than two-thirds of murder cases in the United States, for example, are "cleared" to a resolution. 'Crime in the United States 2014', Federal Bureau of Investigations, 2015.

64. There may be non-punishment related reasons, such as the legal need for completeness, fear of appeals in some previous convictions, or the desire to give closure to the victims' families, which would prompt such prosecutions to continue.

65. For one discussion of this kind of cumulative and restrictive deterrence, see Uri Tor, '"Cumulative Deterrence" as a New Paradigm for Cyber Deterrence', *Journal of Strategic Studies*, 18 December 2015.

66. Ellen Nakashima, 'U.S. Decides against Publicly Blaming China for Data Hack', *Washington Post*, 21 July 2015.

67. For more on cross-domain deterrence, see Vincent Manzo, 'Deterrence and Escalation in Cross-Domain Operations: Where Do Space and Cyberspace Fit?', *Joint Forces Quarterly*, no. 66 (2012); Erik Gartzke and Jon Lindsay, 'Cross-Domain Deterrence: Strategy in an Era of Complexity', University of San Diego, 15 July 2014; Martin C. Libicki, *Cyberdeterrence and Cyberwar* (Santa Monica, CA: Rand Corporation, 2009); James Lewis, 'Cross-Domain Deterrence and Credible Threat', Center for Strategic and International Studies, July 2010.

68. 'Presidential Policy Directive 20', The White House, 2013, 3–14.

69. David Sanger and Michael Schmidt, 'More Sanctions on North Korea after Sony Case', *New York Times*, 2 January 2015.

70. To be clear, for the purposes of the cybersecurity dilemma, most economic espionage intrusions will fall below the threshold of response; only intrusions into truly strategic economic targets, like national stock exchanges, will prompt cybersecurity dilemma worries. Other intrusions may be serious, and may merit a response, but not due to concerns about minimizing the cybersecurity dilemma.

## CONCLUSION: THE DANGERS OF THE CYBERSECURITY DILEMMA

1. Ken Booth and Nicholas J. Wheeler, *The Security Dilemma* (New York: Palgrave Macmillan, 2008), 261.

2. Glyn Moody, 'Dutch Government: Encryption Good, Backdoors Bad', *Ars Technica*, 6 January 2016.
3. Thucydides, *The History of the Peloponnesian War*, trans. Richard Crawley (Amazon Digital Services, 2012), 236.
4. This is a matter of degree. To some degree, it is natural to expect systems led by strong actors to benefit those actors.
5. Andrew H. Kydd, *Trust and Mistrust in International Relations* (Princeton, NJ: Princeton University Press, 2005), ch. 5–6.
6. For two examples, see Gregor Peter Schmitz, 'Belgians Angered by British Spying', *Der Spiegel*, 20 September 2013; 'German Government Cancels Verizon Contract in Wake of U.S. Spying Row', Reuters, 26 June 2014.
7. Joseph Marks, 'U.S. Makes New Push for Global Rules in Cyberspace', *Politico*, 5 May 2015.
8. Different schools of international relations scholarship place emphasis on different trust-building tactics. See Joseph Nye, 'Neorealism and Neoliberalism', *World Politics* 40, no. 2 (1988).

# BIBLIOGRAPHY

*Books and Book Sections*

Altheide, Cory, and Harlan Carvey, *Digital Forensics with Open Source Tools*, Waltham, MA: Elsevier, 2011.

Baker, Peter, *Days of Fire*, New York: Doubleday, 2013.

Barnett, Michael, and Martha Finnemore, *Rules for the World*, Ithaca, NY: Cornell University Press, 2004.

Baylis, John, *Ambiguity and Deterrence: British Nuclear Strategy, 1945–1964*, Oxford/New York: Oxford University Press, 1995.

Bejtlich, Richard, *Extrusion Detection: Security Monitoring for Internal Intrusions*, Upper Saddle River, NJ: Addison-Wesley, 2006.

————, *The Practice of Network Security Monitoring*, San Francisco: No Starch Press, 2013.

Betz, David, and Tim Stevens, *Cyberspace and the State*, Adelphi Series, London: International Institute for Strategic Studies, 2011.

Booth, Ken, and Nicholas J. Wheeler, *The Security Dilemma*, New York: Palgrave Macmillan, 2008.

Brenner, Joel, *Glass Houses*, New York: Penguin, 2014.

Brown, Ian, and Christopher T. Marsden, *Regulating Code: Good Governance and Better Regulation in the Information Age*: Cambridge, MA: MIT Press, 2013.

Butterfield, Herbert, *History and Human Relations*, London: Collins, 1951.

Chayes, Abram, and Antonia Handler Chayes, *The New Sovereignty*, Cambridge, MA: Harvard University Press, 1998.

Clarke, Richard, and Robert Knake, *Cyberwar*, New York: HarperCollins, 2010.

Clayton, Richard, *Anonymity and Traceability in Cyberspace*, Technical Report, Vol. 653, Cambridge: University of Cambridge Computer Laboratory, 2005.

Coker, Christopher, *War in the Age of Risk*, Cambridge: Polity Press, 2009.

————, *Warrior Geeks*, New York: Columbia University Press, 2013.

Dobbs, Michael, *One Minute to Midnight*, New York: Knopf, 2008.

Dulles, Allen, *The Craft of Intelligence*, Guilford, CT: Lyons Press, 2006.

Fahrenkrug, David, 'Countering the Offensive Advantage in Cyberspace: An Integrated Defensive Strategy', in *2012 4th International Conference on Cyber Conflict*, ed. C. Crosseck, R. Ottis, and K. Ziolkowski, pp. 197–207, Talinn: NATO CCD COE Publications, 2012.

Finlay, David, Ole Holsti, and Richard Fagen, *Enemies in Politics*, Chicago: Rand McNally, 1967.

Finnemore, Martha, 'Constructing Norms of Humanitarian Intervention', in *The Culture of National Security*, ed.Peter Katzenstein, New York: Columbia University Press, 1996.

Freedman, Lawrence, *Deterrence*, Cambridge: Polity Press, 2004.

————, *US Intelligence and the Soviet Strategic Threat*, London: Macmillan, 1977.

Garthoff, Raymond, *The Great Transition: American—Soviet Relations and the End of the Cold War*, Washington, DC: Brookings Institution, 1994.

Geers, Kenneth, ed., *Cyber War in Perspective: Russian Aggression against Ukraine*, Tallinn: NATO Cooperative Cyber Defence Center of Excellence, 2015.

Glaser, Charles, *Analyzing Strategic Nuclear Policy*, Princeton, NJ: Princeton University Press, 1990.

Goldsmith, Jack, and Tim Wu, *Who Controls the Internet? Illusions of a Borderless World*, Oxford: Oxford University Press, 2006.

Goodman, Michael S., 'Applying the Historical Lessons of Surprise Attack to the Cyber Domain: The Example of the United Kingdom', in *Cyber Analogies*, ed.Emily Goldman and John Arquilla, Monterey, CA: Naval Postgraduate School, 2014.

Greenberg, Andy, *This Machine Kills Secrets*, New York: Dutton, 2012.

Harris, Shane, *@War: The Rise of the Military-Internet Complex*, New York: Eamon Dolan/Houghton Mifflin Harcourt, 2014.

Healey, Jason, ed., *A Fierce Domain*, Washington, DC: Cyber Conflict Studies Association, 2012.

Hensel, Paul, 'Territory: Theory and Evidence on Geography and Conflict', in *What Do We Know About War?*, ed. John Vasquez, pp. 57–84, New York: Rowman and Littlefield, 2000.

Herman, Michael, 'Intelligence as Threats and Reassurance', in *Intelligence in the Cold War: What Difference Did It Make?*, ed.Michael Herman and Gwilym Hughes, New York: Routledge, 2013.

————, *Intelligence Power in Peace and War*, Cambridge: Cambridge University Press, 1996.

Hersh, Seymour, *The Target Is Destroyed*, New York: Random House, 1986.

Herz, John, *International Politics in the Atomic Age*, New York: Columbia University Press, 1959.

————, *Political Realism and Political Idealism*, Chicago: University of Chicago Press, 1951.

Hobbes, Thomas, *Of Man, Being the First Part of Leviathan*, ed. Charles W. Eliot, Vol. 34, New York: P. F. Collier & Son, 1909–14.

Hoffman, David, *Dead Hand*, New York: Doubleday, 2009.

Ikenberry, G. John, *After Victory: Institutions, Strategic Restraint, and the Rebuilding of Order after Major Wars*, Princeton, NJ: Princeton University Press, 2009.

Jervis, Robert, *Perception and Misperception in International Politics*, Princeton, NJ: Princeton University Press, 1976.

Kaplan, Fred, *Dark Territory*, New York: Simon & Schuster, 2016.

Kent, Sherman, *Strategic Intelligence for American World Policy*, Princeton, NJ: Princeton University Press, 1966.

Keohane, Robert, *After Hegemony: Cooperation and Discord in the World Political Economy*, Princeton, NJ: Princeton University Press, 2005.

————, *Neorealism and Its Critics*: New York: Columbia University Press, 1986.

Kydd, Andrew H., *Trust and Mistrust in International Relations*, Princeton, NJ: Princeton University Press, 2005.

Larson, Deborah Welch, *Anatomy of Mistrust*, Ithaca, NY: Cornell University Press, 1997.

Levy, Steven, *Crypto*, New York: Penguin Books, 2001.

Liberman, Peter, *Does Conquest Pay? The Exploitation of Occupied Industrial Societies*, Princeton, NJ: Princeton University Press, 1998.

Libicki, Martin C., *Cyberdeterrence and Cyberwar*, Santa Monica, CA: Rand Corporation, 2009.

Lieber, Keir, 'The Offense—Defense Balance and Cyber Warfare', in *Cyber Analogies*, ed. Emily Goldman and John Arquilla, pp. 96–107, Monterey, CA: Naval Postgraduate School, 2014.

Ligh, Michael Hale, Andrew Case, Jamie Levy, and Aaron Walters, *The Art of Memory Forensics: Detecting Malware and Threats in Windows, Linux, and Mac Memory*, Hoboken, NJ: John Wiley & Sons, 2014.

Lin, Herbert S., Kenneth W. Dam, and William A. Owens, *Technology, Policy, Law, and Ethics Regarding US Acquisition and Use of Cyberattack Capabilities*, Washington, DC: National Academies Press, 2009.

Lindsay, Jon, Tai Ming Cheung, and Derek S. Reveron, eds, *China and Cybersecurity: Espionage, Strategy, and Politics in the Digital Domain*, Oxford/ New York: Oxford University Press, 2015.

Locke, John, *Two Treatises of Government*, London: Whitmore and Fenn, 1821.

Luttwak, Edward, *Strategy: The Logic of War and Peace*, enlarged edn, Cambridge, MA: Belknap, 2002.

Mearsheimer, John J., *The Tragedy of Great Power Politics*, New York: W. W. Norton & Co., 2001.

# BIBLIOGRAPHY

Monte, Matthew, *Network Attacks and Exploitation: A Framework*, Indianapolis, IN: Wiley, 2015.

Moran, Ned, 'A Cyber Early Warning Model', ch. 11 in *Inside Cyber Warfare*, ed. Jeffrey Carr, p. 200, Sebastopol, CA: O'Reilly Media, 2010.

Morgan, Patrick, 'The Opportunity for a Strategic Surprise', in *Strategic Military Surprise: Incentives and Opportunities*, ed. Klaus Knorr and Patrick Morgan, p. 200, New Brunswick, NJ: Transaction Books, 1983.

Naylor, Sean, *Relentless Strike: The Secret History of Joint Special Operations Command*, New York: St Martin's Press, 2015.

Osgood, Charles, *An Alternative to War or Surrender*, Urbana, IL: University of Illinois, 1962.

Posner, Richard, *Preventing Surprise Attacks*, Lanham, MD: Rowman and Littlefield, 2005.

Rathbun, Brian C., *Trust in International Cooperation: International Security Institutions, Domestic Politics and American Multilateralism*, Vol. 121, Cambridge: Cambridge University Press, 2011.

Reagan, Ronald, *An American Life*, New York: Simon & Schuster, 1990.

Rid, Thomas, *Cyber War Will Not Take Place*, Oxford/New York: Oxford University Press, 2013.

———, *Rise of the Machines*, New York: W. W. Norton & Co., 2016.

Rueter, Nicholas, 'The Cybersecurity Dilemma', Durham, NC: Duke University, 2011.

Schmidle, Robert, Michael Sulmeyer, and Ben Buchanan, 'Understanding Cyberconflict: 16 Analogies', ed. George Perkovich and Ariel E. Levite, forthcoming.

Schmitt, Michael N., ed., *Tallinn Manual on the International Law Applicable to Cyber Warfare*. New York: Cambridge University Press, 2013.

Schneier, Bruce, *Data and Goliath*, New York: W.W. Norton & Co., 2015.

———, *Liars and Outliers*, Indianapolis, IN: John Wiley & Sons, 2012.

Shaheen, Salma, 'Offense–Defense Balance in Cyber Warfare', in *Cyberspace and International Relations*, ed. Jan-Frederik Kremer and Benedikt Muller, pp. 77–93, New York: Springer, 2014.

Shultz, George, *Turmoil and Triumph*, New York: Scribner, 1993.

Sikorski, Michael, and Andrew Honig, *Practical Malware Analysis*, San Francisco: No Starch, 2012.

Singer, P. W., and Allan Friedman, *Cybersecurity and Cyberwar*, New York, Oxford: Oxford University Press, 2014.

Singh, Simon, *The Code Book*, New York: Doubleday, 1999.

Snyder, Jack, *The Ideology of the Offensive*, Ithaca, NY: Cornell University Press, 1984.

Stoll, Clifford, *The Cuckoo's Egg*, New York: Doubleday, 1989.

Tate, Merze, *The United States and Armaments*, Cambridge, MA: Harvard University Press, 1948.

# BIBLIOGRAPHY

Thucydides, *The History of the Peloponnesian War*,trans. Richard Crawley, Amazon Digital Services, 2012.

Van Evera, Stephen, *Causes of War*, Ithaca, NY: Cornell University Press, 1999.

Walker, Martin, *The Cold War: A History*, New York: Henry Holt, 1995.

Walt, Stephen M., *The Origins of Alliance*, Ithaca, NY: Cornell University Press, 1990.

Waltz, Kenneth, *Man, the State, and War*, New York: Columbia University Press, 1959.

Weber, Max, *Weber's Rationalism and Modern Society*, trans.Tony Waters and Dagmar Waters, London: Palgrave, 2015.

Wiseman, Geoffrey, *Concepts of Non-Provocative Defence: Ideas and Practices in International Security*, London: Palgrave, 2002.

Zetter, Kim, *Countdown to Zero Day*, New York: Crown, 2014.


*Journal Articles*

Abelson, Harold, Ross Anderson, Steven M. Bellovin, Josh Benaloh, Matthew Blaze, Whitfield Diffie, John Gilmore, et al., 'Keys under Doormats', *Massachusetts Institute of Technology Computer Science and Artificial Intelligence Lab Technical Reports* (2015).

Axelrod, Robert, and Rumen Iliev, 'Timing of Cyber Conflict', *Proceedings of the National Academy of Sciences* 111, no. 4 (2014): 1298–303.

Barzashka, Ivanka, 'Are Cyber-Weapons Effective? Assessing Stuxnet's Impact on the Iranian Enrichment Programme', *RUSI Journal* 158, no. 2 (2013).

Bechtsoudis, Anestis, and Nicolas Sklavos, 'Aiming at Higher Network Security through Extensive Penetration Tests', *Latin America Transactions, IEEE (Revista IEEE America Latina)* 10, no. 3 (2012): 1752–6.

Black, William, 'Thinking Out Loud About Cyberspace', *Cryptolog (National Security Agency)* 23, no. 1 (1997).

Brenner, Susan, '"At Light Speed": Attribution and Response to Cybercrime / Terrorism / Warfare', *Journal of Criminal Law and Criminology* 97, no. 2 (2007): 379–475.

Buchanan, Ben, 'Cyber Deterrence isn't MAD; it's Mosaic', *Georgetown Journal of International Affairs*, International Engagement on Cyber IV (October 2014): 130–40.

———, 'The Life Cycles of Cyber Threats', *Survival* 58, no. 1 (2016).

Carr, Madeline, 'Public–Private Partnerships in National Cyber-Security Strategies', *International Affairs* 92, no. 1 (2016): 43–62.

Cavelty, Myriam, 'Cyber-Terror—Looming Threat or Phantom Menace? The Framing of the US Cyber-Threat Debate', *Journal of Information Technology and Politics* 4, no. 1 (2008): 19–36.

Davis, James, Bernard Finel, Stacie Goddard, Stephen Van Evera, Charles

# BIBLIOGRAPHY

Glaser, and Chaim Kaufmann, 'Taking Offense at Offense-Defense Theory', *International Security* 23, no. 3 (1999): 179–206.

Duncan, Adrian, Sadie Creese, and Michael Goldsmith, 'An Overview of Insider Attacks in Cloud Computing', *Concurrency and Computation: Practice and Experience* 27, no. 12 (2015): 2964–81.

'The End of the Cold War', *Cold War International History Project Bulletin*, no. 12/13 (2001).

Ferris, John, 'Coming in from the Cold War: The Historiography of American Intelligence, 1945–1990', *Diplomatic History* 19, no. 1 (1995): 87–115.

Fidler, Mailyn, 'Regulating the Zero-Day Vulnerability Trade: A Preliminary Analysis', *I/S: A Journal of Law and Policy for the Information Society*, no. 11 (2015).

Finnemore, Martha, and Kathryn Sikkink, 'International Norm Dynamics and Political Change', *International Organization* 52, no. 4 (1998): 887–917.

Gartzke, Erik, 'The Myth of Cyberwar: Bringing War in Cyberspace Back Down to Earth', *International Security* 38, no. 2 (2013): 41–73.

———, and Jon Lindsay, 'Weaving Tangled Webs: Offense, Defense, and Deception in Cyberspace', *Security Studies* 24, no. 2 (2015).

Glaser, Charles, 'The Security Dilemma Revisited', *World Politics* 50, no. 1 (1997): 171–201.

———, and Chaim Kaufmann, 'What Is the Offense—Defense Balance and Can We Measure It?', *International Security* 22, no. 4 (1998): 44–82.

Gortzak, Yoav, Yoram Haftel, and Kevin Sweeney, 'Offense—Defense Theory: An Empirical Assessment', *Journal of Conflict Resolution* 49, no. 1 (2005): 67–89.

Handel, Michael, 'Intelligence and Military Operations', *Intelligence and National Security* 5, no. 2 (1990): 1–95.

Herz, John, 'Idealist Internationalism and the Security Dilemma', *World Politics* 2, no. 2 (1950): 157–80.

Jervis, Robert, 'Cooperation under the Security Dilemma', *World Politics* 30, no. 2 (1978): 167–214.

———, 'From Balance to Concert: A Study of International Security Cooperation', *World Politics* 38, no. 1 (1985): 58–79.

Kello, Lucas, 'The Meaning of the Cyber Revolution: Perils to Theory and Statecraft', *International Security* 38, no. 2 (2013): 7–40.

Larson, Deborah Welch, 'Trust and Missed Opportunities in International Relations', *Political Psychology* 18, no. 3 (1997): 701–34.

Lawson, Sean, 'Beyond Cyber-Doom: Assessing the Limits of Hypothetical Scenarios in the Framing of Cyber-Threats', *Journal of Information Technology and Politics* 10, no. 1 (2013): 86–103.

Lee, Robert, and Thomas Rid, 'OMG Cyber!', *RUSI Journal* 159, no. 5 (2014): 4–12.

Levy, Jack S., 'The Offensive/Defensive Balance of Military Technology: A

Theoretical and Historical Analysis', *International Studies Quarterly* 28, no. 2 (1984): 219–38.

Libicki, Martin C., 'Is There a Cybersecurity Dilemma?', *Cyber Defense Review* 1, no. 1 (2016).

Lieber, Keir, 'Grasping the Technological Peace: The Offense—Defense Balance and International Security', *International Security* 25, no. 1 (2000): 71–104.

———, 'The New History of World War I and What It Means for International Relations Theory', *International Security* 32, no. 2 (2007): 155–91.

Lindsay, Jon, 'The Impact of China on Cybersecurity: Fiction and Friction', *International Security* 39, no. 3 (2015): 7–47.

———, 'Stuxnet and the Limits of Cyber Warfare', *Security Studies* 22, no. 3 (2013): 365–404.

Locatelli, Andrea, 'The Offense/Defense Balance in Cyberspace', *Strategic Studies* 35, no. 1 (2011).

Lynn, William, 'Defending a New Domain', *Foreign Affairs* (Sept./Oct. 2010).

Lynn-Jones, Sean, 'Offense—Defense Theory and its Critics', *Security Studies* 4, no. 4 (1995): 660–91.

Manadhata, Pratyusa, and Jeannette Wing, 'An Attack Surface Metric', *IEEE Transactions on Software Engineering* 37, no. 3 (2011).

Manzo, Vincent, 'Deterrence and Escalation in Cross-Domain Operations: Where Do Space and Cyberspace Fit?', *Joint Forces Quarterly*, no. 66 (2012).

Michel, Torsten, 'Time to Get Emotional: Phronetic Reflections on the Concept of Trust in International Relations', *European Journal of International Relations* 19, no. 4 (2013): 869–90.

Moran, Ned, 'A Historical Perspective on the Cybersecurity Dilemma', *Insecure*, no. 21 (June 2009): 112–16.

Nye, Joseph, 'Neorealism and Neoliberalism', *World Politics* 40, no. 2 (1988): 235–51.

Posen, Barry, 'The Security Dilemma and Ethnic Conflict', *Survival* 35, no. 1 (1993): 27–47.

Rid, Thomas, and Ben Buchanan, 'Attributing Cyber Attacks', *Journal of Strategic Studies* 39, no. 1 (2015): 4–37.

Rid, Thomas, and Peter McBurney, 'Cyber-Weapons', *RUSI Journal* 157, no. 1 (2012): 6–13.

Rosenbaum, Ron, 'Cassandra Syndrome', *Smithsonian Magazine* 43, no. 1 (April 2012).

Ruggie, John Gerard, 'What Makes the World Hang Together? Neo-Utilitarianism and the Social Constructivist Challenge', *International Organization* 52, no. 4 (1998): 855–85.

Rustici, Ross, 'Cyberweapons: Leveling the International Playing Field', *Parameters* 41, no. 3 (2011): 32–42.

# BIBLIOGRAPHY

Saltzman, Ilai, 'Cyber Posturing and the Offense—Defense Balance', *Contemporary Security Policy* 34, no. 1 (2013): 40–63.

Schweller, Randall, 'Neorealism's Status-Quo Bias: What Security Dilemma?', *Security Studies* 5, no. 3 (1996): 90–121.

Senese, Paul, 'Territory, Contiguity, and International Conflict: Assessing a New Joint Explanation', *American Journal of Political Science* 49, no. 4 (2005): 769–79.

Shah, Sugandh, and B. M. Mehtre, 'A Modern Approach to Cyber Security Analysis Using Vulnerability Assessment and Penetration Testing', *International Journal of Electronics Communication and Computer Engineering* 4, no. 6 (2013).

Snyder, Jack, 'One World, Rival Theories', *Foreign Policy*, no. 145 (2004): 52.

Spence, Michael, 'Job Market Signaling', *Quarterly Journal of Economics* 87, no. 3 (1973): 355–74.

Stevens, Tim, 'A Cyberwar of Ideas? Deterrence and Norms in Cyberspace', *Contemporary Security Policy* 33, no. 1 (2012): 148–70.

Wall, Andru E., 'Demystifying the Title 10-Title 50 Debate: Distinguishing Military Operations, Intelligence Activities and Covert Action', *Harvard National Security Journal* 3, no. 1 (2011).

Walt, Stephen M., 'International Relations: One World, Many Theories', *Foreign Policy*, no. 110 (1998): 29–46.

Weber, Rolf, 'Internet of Things–New Security and Privacy Challenges', *Computer Law and Security Review* 26, no. 1 (2010): 23–30.

Wendt, Alexander, 'Anarchy Is What States Make of It: The Social Construction of Power Politics', *International Organization* 46, no. 2 (1992): 391–425.

Wertheimer, Michael, 'The Mathematics Community and the NSA', *Notices of the American Mathematical Society* (February 2015).


*Government Documents*

In the case of leaked documents, the publication date is when the document was published; both the original agency and the publisher are provided.

'"4th Party Collection": Taking Advantage of Non-Partner Computer Network Exploitation Activity', National Security Agency: *Der Spiegel*, 2015, http://www.spiegel.de/media/media-35680.pdf

'Agencies Need to Improve Controls over Selected High-Impact Systems', Government Accountability Office, 2016, http://www.gao.gov/assets/680/677293.pdf

'Air Force Policy Directive 10–17 Cyberspace Operations', United States Air Force: National Security Archive, 2016, http://nsarchive.gwu.edu/dc.html?doc=2692123-Document-15

'Analytic Challenges from Active-Passive Integration', National Security

Agency: Der Spiegel, 2015, http://www.spiegel.de/media/media-35672. pdf

'Bad Guys Are Everywhere, Good Guys Are Somewhere!', National Security Agency: *Der Spiegel*, 2014, http://www.spiegel.de/media/media-34757. pdf

'Beyond the Build: Delivering Outcomes through Cyberspace', United States Cyber Command: Department of Defense, 2015, http://www.defense. gov/Portals/1/features/2015/0415_cyber-strategy/docs/US-Cyber-Command-Commanders-Vision.pdf

'Budget Request for Information Technology and Cyber Operations Programs: Written Testimony of Gen. Keith Alexander', Committee on Armed Services: US House of Representatives, 2012

'BYZANTINE HADES Causes Serious Damage to DoD Interests', National Security Agency: *Der Spiegel*, 2015, http://www.spiegel.de/media/media-35687.pdf

'BYZANTINE HADES: An Evolution in Collection', National Security Agency: *Der Spiegel*, 2015, http://www.spiegel.de/media/media-35686. pdf

'Case Studies of Integrated Cyber Operations Techniques', National Security Agency: *Der Spiegel*, 2015, http://www.spiegel.de/media/media-35658. pdf

'Commercial and Government Information Technology and Industrial Control Product or System Vulnerabilities Equities Policy and Process', United States Government: Electronic Frontier Foundation, 2016, https:// www.eff.org/files/2016/01/18/37–3_vep_2016.pdf

'Computer Network Exploitation (CNE) Classification Guide', National Security Agency: *Der Spiegel*, 2015, http://www.spiegel.de/media/media-35656.pdf

'Computer Security Incident Handling Guide', National Institute of Standards and Technology: Department of Commerce, 2012, http://nvl-pubs.nist.gov/nistpubs/SpecialPublications/NIST.SP.800–61r2.pdf

'Cross Agency Priority Goal: Cybersecurity', The White House: Performance.gov, 2015, http://www.performance.gov/sites/default/files/ Cybersecurity FY 15 Q1 CLEARANCE READY FINAL A.pdf

'CSEC SIGINT Cyber Discovery: Summary of the Current Effort', Communications Security Establishment Canada: *Der Spiegel*, 2015, http://www. spiegel.de/media/media-35665.pdf

'Cyber-Attack against Ukrainian Critical Infrastructure', Industrial Control Systems Emergency Response Team: Department of Homeland Security, 2016, https://ics-cert.us-cert.gov/alerts/IR-ALERT-H-16–056–01

'CYBERCOM Announcement Message', United States Cyber Command: National Security Archive, 2016, http://nsarchive.gwu.edu/dc.html? doc=2692108-Document-6

# BIBLIOGRAPHY

'The Cyber Warfare Lexicon', United States Strategic Command: National Security Archive, 2016, http://nsarchive.gwu.edu/dc.html?doc=269 2102-Document-1

'Defensive Best Practices for Destructive Malware', Information Assurance Directorate: National Security Agency, 2015, https://www.nsa.gov/ia/_files/factsheets/Defending_Against_Destructive_Malware.pdf

'The Department of Defense Cyber Strategy', Office of the Secretary of Defense: Department of Defense, 2015, http://www.defense.gov/home/features/2015/0415_cyber-strategy/Final_2015_DoD_CYBER_STRATEGY_for_web.pdf

'The Department of Defense Strategy for Counterintelligence in Cyberspace', Office of the Under Secretary of Defense for Intelligence: Department of Defense, 2016, http://nsarchive.gwu.edu/dc.html?doc=269 2104-Document-3

'The DHS Role in Federal Cybersecurity and the Recent Compromise at the Office of Personnel Management: Written Testimony of Dr. Andy Ozment', Committee on Oversight and Government Reform: US House of Representatives, 2015, https://oversight.house.gov/wp-content/uploads/2015/06/Ozment-DHS-Statement-6-16-Data-Breach.pdf

'The FASHIONCLEFT Protocol', National Security Agency: *Der Spiegel*, 2008, http://www.spiegel.de/media/media-35673.pdf

'Federal Information Security Management Act Audit FY 2014', Office of Inspector General: Office of Personnel Management, 2014, https://www.opm.gov/our-inspector-general/reports/2014/federal-information-security-management-act-audit-fy-2014–4a-ci-00–14–016.pdf

'Fourth Party Opportunities', National Security Agency: *Der Spiegel*, 2015, http://www.spiegel.de/media/media-35684.pdf

'FY 2015 Annual Report', Operational Test and Evaluation Office of the Director: Department of Defense, 2016, http://www.dote.osd.mil/pub/reports/FY2015/pdf/other/2015dirintro.pdf

'Getting Close to the Adversary: Forward-Based Defense with QFire', National Security Agency: *Der Spiegel*, 2013, http://www.spiegel.de/fotostrecke/qfire-die-vorwaertsverteidigng-der-nsa-fotostrecke-105358.html

'Guide for Conducting Risk Assessments (Rev. 1)', National Institute of Standards and Technology: Department of Commerce, 2012, http://nvl-pubs.nist.gov/nistpubs/Legacy/SP/nistspecialpublication800–30r1.pdf

'Guide to Enterprise Patch Management Technologies', National Institute of Standards and Technology: Department of Commerce, 2013, http://nvl-pubs.nist.gov/nistpubs/SpecialPublications/NIST.SP.800–40r3.pdf

'HIMR Data Mining Research Problem Book', Government Communications Headquarters: BoingBoing, 2016, https://www.documentcloud.org/documents/2702948-Problem-Book-Redacted.html

# BIBLIOGRAPHY

'ICS-CERT Monitor September 2014–February 2015', National Cyber-security and Communications Integration Center: Department of Homeland Security, 2015, https://ics-cert.us-cert.gov/sites/default/files/Monitors/ICS-CERT_Monitor_Sep2014-Feb2015.pdf

'Is There "Fifth Party" Collection?', National Security Agency: *Der Spiegel*, 2015, http://www.spiegel.de/media/media-35679.pdf

'Landmark', Communications Security Establishment Canada: *C'T Magazin*, 2014, http://www.heise.de/ct/artikel/NSA-GCHQ-The-HACIENDA-Program-for-Internet-Colonization-2292681.html?hg=1&hgi=17&hgf=false

'Memorandum: Subject: Joint Terminology for Cyberspace Operations', Vice Chairman of the Joint Chiefs of Staff: Department of Defense, 2010, http://www.nsci-va.org/CyberReferenceLib/2010–11-joint Terminology for Cyberspace Operations.pdf

'Moving Data through Disconnected Networks: Delay Tolerant Networking and the IC', National Security Agency: *Der Spiegel*, 2015, http://www.spiegel.de/media/media-35674.pdf

'The National Military Strategy for Cyberspace Operations', Chairman of the Joint Chiefs of Staff: Department of Defense, 2005, http://nsarchive.gwu.edu/NSAEBB/NSAEBB424/docs/Cyber-023.pdf

'Navy Cyber Power 2020', United States Navy: National Security Archive, 2016, http://nsarchive.gwu.edu/dc.html?doc=2692124-Document-16

'Network Shaping 101', National Security Agency: *The Intercept*, 2016, https://www.documentcloud.org/documents/2919677-Network-Shaping-101.html

'NSA's Offensive and Defensive Missions: The Twain Have Met', National Security Agency: *Der Spiegel*, 2015, http://www.spiegel.de/media/media-35681.pdf

'Pay Attention to That Man Behind the Curtain: Discovering Aliens on CNE Infrastructure', Communications Security Establishment Canada: *Der Spiegel*, 2010, http://www.spiegel.de/media/media-35688.pdf

'Presidential Policy Directive 20', The White House: *The Guardian*, 2013, http://www.theguardian.com/world/interactive/2013/jun/07/obama-cyber-directive-full-text

'Quantum Insert Diagrams', National Security Agency: *The Intercept*, 2014, https://firstlook.org/theintercept/document/2014/03/12/quantum-insert-diagrams/

'Resilient Military Systems and the Advanced Cyber Threat', Defense Science Board: Department of Defense, 2012, http://www.acq.osd.mil/dsb/reports/ResilientMilitarySystems.CyberThreat.pdf

'S3285 WikiInfo', National Security Agency: *Der Spiegel*, 2015, http://www.spiegel.de/media/media-35661.pdf

# BIBLIOGRAPHY

'SIGINT Enabling Project', National Security Agency: *Pro Publica*, 2013, http://www.propublica.org/documents/item/784280-sigint-enabling-project

'SNOWGLOBE: From Discovery to Attribution', Communications Security Establishment Canada: *Der Spiegel*, 2015, http://www.spiegel.de/media/media-35683.pdf

'Special Notice: Plan X Proposers' Day Workshop', Defense Advanced Research Projects Agency: Department of Defense, 2012, https://www.fbo.gov/utils/view?id=f69bba51a9047620f2e5c3a6857e6f6b

'Treaty between the United States of America and the Union of Soviet Socialist Republics on the Limitation of Anti-Ballistic Missile Systems', Bureau of Arms Control Verification and Compliance: Department of State, 1972, http://www.state.gov/www/global/arms/treaties/abm/abm2.html

'Treaty between the United States of America and the Union of Soviet Socialist Republics on the Limitation of Strategic Offensive Arms (SALT II)', Bureau of Arms Control Verification and Compliance: Department of State, 1979, http://www.state.gov/t/isn/5195.htm

'TUTELAGE 411', National Security Agency: *Der Spiegel*, 2015, http://www.spiegel.de/media/media-35685.pdf

'Understanding the Cyber Threat and Implications for the 21st Century Economy', Subcommittee on Oversight and Investigations Committee on Energy and Commerce: US House of Representatives, 2015, http://democrats.energycommerce.house.gov/sites/default/files/documents/Testimony-Bejtlich-OI-Cybsecurity-2015–3–3.pdf

'What's the Worst That Could Happen?', Government Communications Headquarters: BoingBoing, 2016, https://www.documentcloud.org/documents/2699620-What-Is-the-Worst-That-Can-Happen-March–2010.html

'Worldwide Threat Assessment of the US Intelligence Community', Office of the Director of National Intelligence: Senate Armed Services Committee, 2016, http://www.armed-services.senate.gov/imo/media/doc/Clapper_02–09–16.pdf

*Technical Reports and Analyses*

'2015 Data Breach Investigations Report', Verizon, April 2015, http://www.verizonenterprise.com/resources/rp_data-breach-investigation-report-2015_en_xg.pdf

'2016 Data Breach Investigations Report', Verizon, April 2016, http://news.verizonenterprise.com/2016/04/2016-data-breach-report-info/

Alperovitch, Dmitri, 'Bears in the Midst: Intrusion into the Democratic

# BIBLIOGRAPHY

National Committee', CrowdStrike, 15 June 2016, https://www.crowd-strike.com/blog/bears-midst-intrusion-democratic-national-committee/

'APT1', Mandiant, 18 February 2013, http://intelreport.mandiant.com/Mandiant_APT1_Report.pdf

'APT30 and the Mechanics of a Long-Running Cyber Espionage Operation', FireEye, April 2015, https://www2.fireeye.com/rs/fireye/images/rpt-apt30.pdf

Assante, Michael, and Robert Lee, 'The Industrial Control System Cyber Kill Chain', SANS Institute, 2015, https://www.sans.org/reading-room/whitepapers/ICS/industrial-control-system-cyber-kill-chain-36297

Baumgartner, Kurt, 'Sony/Destover: Mystery North Korean Actor's Destructive and Past Network Activity', Kaspersky Lab, 4 December 2014, http://securelist.com/blog/research/67985/destover/

Caltagirone, Sergio, Andrew Pendergast, and Christopher Betz, 'The Diamond Model of Intrusion Analysis', Defense Technical Information Center, 5 July 2013, http://www.dtic.mil/get-tr-doc/pdf?AD=ADA58 6960

Clarke, Richard, Michael Morell, Geoffrey Stone, Cass Sunstein, and Peter Swire, 'Liberty and Security in a Changing World', The President's Review Group on Intelligence and Communications Technologies, 12 December 2013, https://www.whitehouse.gov/sites/default/files/docs/2013–12–12_rg_final_report.pdf

Cloppert, Michael, 'Security Intelligence: Introduction (Pt 2)', SANS Institute, 23 July 2009, http://digital-forensics.sans.org/blog/2009/07/23/security-intelligence-introduction-pt-2/

'Cloud Atlas: RedOctober APT is Back in Style', Kaspersky Lab, 10 December 2014, https://securelist.com/blog/research/68083/cloud-atlas-redoctober-apt-is-back-in-style/

'Dragonfly: Cyberespionage Attacks against Energy Suppliers', Symantec, 7 July 2014, http://www.symantec.com/content/en/us/enterprise/media/security_response/whitepapers/Dragonfly_Threat_Against_Western_Energy_Suppliers.pdf

'The Duqu 2.0: Technical Details', Kaspersky Lab, 11 June 2015, https://securelist.com/files/2015/06/The_Mystery_of_Duqu_2_0_a_sophisti-cated_cyberespionage_actor_returns.pdf

'Equation Group: Questions and Answers', Kaspersky Lab, February 2015, http://cdn.securelist.com/files/2015/02/Equation_group_questions_and_answers.pdf

'Equation: The Death Star of Malware Galaxy', Kaspersky Lab, 16 February 2015, http://securelist.com/blog/research/68750/equation-the-death-star-of-malware-galaxy/

Fagerland, Snorre, and Waylon Grange, 'The Inception Framework', Blue Coat Systems, 9 December 2014.

# BIBLIOGRAPHY

'A Fanny Equation: "I Am Your Father, Stuxnet"', Kaspersky Lab, 17 February 2015, https://securelist.com/blog/research/68787/a-fanny-equation-i-am-your-father-stuxnet/

'Group of Governmental Experts on Developments in the Field of Information and Telecommunications in the Context of International Security', United Nations General Assembly, 2013, http://www.un.org/ga/search/view_doc.asp?symbol=A/68/98

————, United Nations General Assembly, 2015, http://www.un.org/ga/search/view_doc.asp?symbol=A/70/174

Hutchins, Eric, Michael Cloppert, and Rohan Amin, 'Intelligence-Driven Computer Network Defense Informed by Analysis of Adversary Campaigns and Intrusion Kill Chains', Lockheed Martin, 2010, http://www.ciosummits.com/LM-White-Paper-Intel-Driven-Defense.pdf

'Internet Security Threat Report 2014', Symantec, 2014, https://www.symantec.com/content/en/us/enterprise/other_resources/b-istr_main_report_v19_21291018.en-us.pdf

'Internet Security Threat Report 2016', Symantec, 12 April 2016, https://www.symantec.com/security-center/threat-report

Jordan, Bret, 'Stix and Taxii: On the Road to Becoming the De Facto Standard', Blue Coat Systems, 26 August 2014, https://www.bluecoat.com/security-blog/2014–08–26/stix-and-taxii-road-becoming-de-facto-standard

Kallenberg, Corey, and Xeno Kovah, 'How Many Million BIOSes Would You Like to Infect?', Legbacore, 11 June 2015, http://www.legbacore.com/News_files/HowManyMillionBIOSesWouldYouLikeToInfect_White-paper_v1.pdf

Lee, Robert, 'The Sliding Scale of Cyber Security', SANS Institute, August 2015, https://www.sans.org/reading-room/whitepapers/analyst/sliding-scale-cyber-security-36240?

Lee, Robert, Michael Assante, and Tim Conway, 'Analysis of the Cyber Attack on the Ukrainian Power Grid', Electricity Information Sharing and Analysis Center, 18 March 2016, https://ics.sans.org/media/E-ISAC_SANS_Ukraine_DUC_5.pdf

Lee, Robert, and Rob Lee, 'The Who, What, Where, When, Why, and How of Effective Threat Hunting', SANS Institute, February 2016, https://www.sans.org/reading-room/whitepapers/analyst/who-what-where-when-effective-threat-hunting-36785

Lieberthal, Kenneth, and Peter W. Singer, 'Cybersecurity and U.S.-China Relations', February 2012, http://www.brookings.edu/~/media/Research/Files/Papers/2012/2/23 cybersecurity china us singer lieberthal/0223_cybersecurity_china_us_lieberthal_singer_pdf_english.PDF

'M-Trends 2016', Mandiant, February 2016, https://www2.fireeye.com/rs/848-DID-242/images/Mtrends2016.pdf

# BIBLIOGRAPHY

Marczak, Bill, Claudio Guarnieri, Morgan Marquis-Boire, and John Scott-Railton, 'Hacking Team and the Targeting of Ethiopian Journalists', Citizen Lab, 12 February 2014, https://citizenlab.org/2014/02/hacking-team-targeting-ethiopian-journalists/

Mimoso, Michael, 'Inside nls_933w.dll, the Equation APT Persistence Module', ThreatPost, 17 February 2015, https://threatpost.com/inside-nls_933w-dll-the-equation-apt-persistence-module/111128

Moran, Ned, and James T. Bennett, 'Supply Chain Analysis: From Quartermaster to Sunshop', FireEye, 11 November 2013, https://www.fireeye.com/content/dam/legacy/resources/pdfs/fireeye-malware-supply-chain.pdf

Moran, Ned, Joshua Homan, and Mike Scott, 'Operation Poisoned Hurricane', FireEye, 6 August 2014, http://www.fireeye.com/blog/technical/targeted-attack/2014/08/operation-poisoned-hurricane.html

O'Gorman, Gavin, and Geoff McDonald, 'The Elderwood Project', Symantec, 6 September 2012,

'Operation Cleaver', Cylance, 2014, http://www.cylance.com/assets/Cleaver/Cylance_Operation_Cleaver_Report.pdf

'Operation SMN: Axiom Threat Actor Group Report', Novetta, November 2014, https://www.novetta.com/wp-content/uploads/2014/11/Executive_Summary-Final_1.pdf

'Putter Panda', CrowdStrike, 9 June 2014, http://cdn0.vox-cdn.com/assets/4589853/crowdstrike-intelligence-report-putter-panda.original.pdf

'Redline Drawn', FireEye, June 2016, https://www.fireeye.com/content/dam/fireeye-www/current-threats/pdfs/rpt-china-espionage.pdf

'Regin: Top-Tier Espionage Tool Enables Stealthy Surveillance', Symantec, 24 November 2014, http://www.symantec.com/content/en/us/enterprise/media/security_response/whitepapers/regin-analysis.pdf

'The Remediation Gap', Kenna Security, September 2015, http://pages.kennasecurity.com/rs/958-PRK-049/images/Kenna-NonTargetedAttacks Report.pdf

'Shamoon the Wiper—Copycats at Work', Kaspersky Lab, 16 August 2012, http://securelist.com/blog/incidents/57854/shamoon-the-wiper-copycats-at-work/

'Unveiling 'Careto'—the Masked APT', Kaspersky Lab, 6 February 2014, http://kasperskycontenthub.com/wp-content/uploads/sites/43/vlpdfs/unveilingthemask_v1.0.pdf

'Virtual Criminology Report 2009', McAfee, 2009, http://img.en25.com/Web/McAfee/VCR_2009_EN_VIRTUAL_CRIMINOLOGY_RPT_NOREG.pdf

'W32.Duqu, Version 1.4', Symantec, 23 November 2011, http://www.

symantec.com/content/en/us/enterprise/media/security_response/
whitepapers/w32_duqu_the_precursor_to_the_next_stuxnet.pdf
'What Was That Wiper Thing?', Kaspersky Lab, 29 August 2012, http://
securelist.com/blog/34088/what-was-that-wiper-thing-48/

*Conference Proceedings*

Bilge, Leyla, and Tudor Dumitras, 'Before We Knew It: An Empirical Study of
Zero Day Attacks in the Real World', Paper presented at 'Conference on
Computer and Communication Security', 2012, https://users.ece.cmu.
edu/~tdumitra/public_documents/bilge12_zero_day.pdf

Boebert, W. Earl, 'A Survey of Challenges in Attribution', Paper presented at
'Proceedings of a workshop on Deterring Cyberattacks', 2010, http://
www.nap.edu/read/12997/chapter/5

Denning, Dorothy, 'Obstacles and Options for Cyber Arms Control', Paper
presented at 'Arms Control in Cyberspace', Berlin, 29–30 June 2001,
http://faculty.nps.edu/dedennin/publications/berlin.pdf

Lebow, Irwin, 'The Impact of Computer Security in the Department of
Defense', Paper presented at 'Proceedings of the Second Seminar on the
DOD Computing Security Program', Gaithersburg, MD, 15–17 January
1980, http://csrc.nist.gov/publications/history/nissc/1980–2nd-semi-
nar-proceedings.pdf.

Moore, Tyler, Allan Friedman, and Ariel Procaccia, 'Would a "Cyber Warrior"
Protect Us? Exploring Trade-Offs between Attack and Defense of
Information Systems', Paper presented at 'New Security Paradigms
Workshop', Concord, MA, 2010, http://tylermoore.ens.utulsa.edu/
nspw10.pdf

Obrst, Leo, Penny Chase, and Richard Markeloff, 'Developing an Ontology
of the Cyber Security Domain', Paper presented at 'STIDS', 2012, http://
stids.c4i.gmu.edu/papers/STIDSPapers/STIDS2012_T06_ObrstEtAl_
CyberOntology.pdf

Ozment, Andy. "The Likelihood of Vulnerability Rediscovery and the Social
Utility of Vulnerability Hunting." In *The Workshop on Economics and Information
Security*. Cambridge, MA, 2005.

Polychronakis, Michalis, Kostas G. Anagnostakis, and Evangelos P. Markatos,
'An Empirical Study of Real-World Polymorphic Code Injection Attacks',
Paper presented at 'Proceedings of the 2nd USENIX conference on Large-
scale exploits and emergent threats', Boston, MA, 21 April 2009, https://
www.usenix.org/legacy/events/leet09/tech/full_papers/polychronakis/
polychronakis.pdf?CFID=646919657&CFTOKEN=71225737

# BIBLIOGRAPHY

*News Articles and Web Pages*

Abdollah, Tami, 'Obama Seeks Cybersecurity Boost to Replace "Ancient" Tech', Associated Press, 9 February 2016, http://www.pbs.org/newshour/rundown/obama-seeks-cybersecurity-boost-to-replace-ancient-tech/

Aitel, David, '0days', CyberSecPolitics, 11 February 2016, http://cybersecpolitics.blogspot.com/2016/02/0days.html

————, 'Cyber Norms: The Futility of Blacklisting Critical Infrastructure', CyberSecPolitics, 14 March 2016, http://cybersecpolitics.blogspot.com/2016/03/cyber-norms-futility-of-blacklisting.html

————, 'Talking About 0days and Attacks from Weird Datasets', CyberSecPolitics, 6 May 2016, http://cybersecpolitics.blogspot.com/2016/05/talking-about-0days-and-attacks-from.html

————, 'The Value of an 0day Stockpile to the Country Versus the Value of Feeling Self-Rightous', CyberSecPolitics, 12 February 2016, http://cybersecpolitics.blogspot.com/2016/02/the-value-of-0day-stockpile-to-country.html

Aitel, David, and Matt Tait, 'Everything You Know About the Vulnerability Equities Process Is Wrong', Lawfare, 18 August 2016, https://www.lawfareblog.com/everything-you-know-about-vulnerability-equities-process-wrong

Anderson, Ross, 'Meeting Snowden in Princeton', Cambridge University, 2 May 2015, https://www.lightbluetouchpaper.org/2015/05/02/meeting-snowden-in-princeton/

Arkin, William M., 'A Mouse That Roars?', *Washington Post*, 7 June 1999, http://www.washingtonpost.com/wp-srv/national/dotmil/arkin060799.htm

Ball, James, 'U.S. Hacked into Iran's Critical Civilian Infrastructure for Massive Cyberattack, New Film Claims', BuzzFeed, 16 February 2016, http://www.buzzfeed.com/jamesball/us-hacked-into-irans-critical-civilian-infrastructure-for-ma-.isj6lekW8

Bamford, James, 'A Death in Athens', *The Intercept*, 29 September 2015, https://theintercept.com/2015/09/28/death-athens-rogue-nsa-operation/

————, 'The Most Wanted Man in the World', Wired, 22 August 2015, http://www.wired.com/2014/08/edward-snowden/

Beaumont, Peter, 'Iran "Detains Western Spies" after Cyber Attack on Nuclear Plant', *The Guardian*, 2 October 2010, http://www.theguardian.com/world/2010/oct/02/iran-western-spies-cyber-attack

Bejtlich, Richard, 'Army Cyber Institute Cyber Talks: Thinking Strategically About Digital Security', YouTube, September 2015, https://www.youtube.com/watch?v=ICtg7D3sPJw&app=desktop

————, 'Don't Envy the Offense', TaoSecurity, 28 December 2014, http://taosecurity.blogspot.com/2014/12/dont-envy-offense.html

————, 'Network Security Monitoring History', TaoSecurity, 11 April 2007, http://taosecurity.blogspot.com/2007/04/network-security-monitoring-history.html

————, 'Notes on Stewart Baker Podcast with David Sanger', TaoSecurity, 22 January 2015, http://taosecurity.blogspot.co.uk/2015/01/notes-on-stewart-baker-podcast-with.html

————, 'Threat Advantages', TaoSecurity, 18 April 2007, http://taosecurity.blogspot.com/2007/04/threat-advantages.html

————, 'What Does Responsibility Mean for Attribution?', TaoSecurity, 22 December 2014, http://taosecurity.blogspot.com/2014/12/what-does-responsibility-mean-for.html

Bennett, Cory, '"Please Contribute", White House's Ozment Implores Network Security Crowd', Yahoo, 15 August 2013, http://fedscoop.com/please-contribute-white-houses-ozment-implores-network-security-crowd/

Bright, Peter, 'Anonymous Speaks: The Inside Story of the HBGary Hack', *Ars Technica*, 16 February 2011, http://arstechnica.com/tech-policy/2011/02/anonymous-speaks-the-inside-story-of-the-hbgary-hack/

————, 'How the Comodo Certificate Fraud Calls CA Trust into Question', *Ars Technica*, 24 March 2011, http://arstechnica.com/security/2011/03/how-the-comodo-certificate-fraud-calls-ca-trust-into-question/

Broad, William, John Markoff, and David Sanger, 'Israeli Test on Worm Called Crucial in Iran Nuclear Delay', *New York Times*, 15 January 2011, http://www.nytimes.com/2011/01/16/world/middleeast/16stuxnet.html?pagewanted=all

Calmes, Jackie, and Steven Lee Myers, 'Obama and Xi Tackle Cybersecurity as Talks Begin in California', *New York Times*, 7 June 2013, http://www.nytimes.com/2013/06/08/us%C3%A5/politics/obama-and-xi-open-informal-meetings-in-california.html

Carr, Jeffrey, 'A Critical Review of Tom Rid and Ben Buchanan's "Attributing Cyber Attacks"', Taia Global, 6 January 2015, http://jeffreycarr.blogspot.com/2015/01/a-critical-review-of-tom-rid-and-ben.html

Carter, Ash, 'Drell Lecture: "Rewiring the Pentagon: Charting a New Path on Innovation and Cybersecurity" (Stanford University)', Department of Defense, 23 April 2015, http://www.defense.gov/News/Speeches/Speech-View/Article/606666/drell-lecture-rewiring-the-pentagon-charting-a-new-path-on-innovation-and-cyber

Cieply, Michael, and Brooks Barnes, 'Sony Hack Reveals Email Crossfire over Angelina Jolie and Steve Jobs Movie', *New York Times*, 10 December 2014, http://www.nytimes.com/2014/12/11/business/media/emails-from-hacking-reveal-sonys-dirty-laundry.html

# BIBLIOGRAPHY

'Cisco Annual Security Report Reveals Widening Gulf between Perception and Reality of Cybersecurity Readiness', Cisco, 20 January 2015, http://investor.cisco.com/investor-relations/news-and-events/news/news-details/2015/Cisco-Annual-Security-Report-Reveals-Widening-Gulf-Between-Perception-and-Reality-of-Cybersecurity-Readiness/default.aspx

Clarke, Richard, 'How China Steals Our Secrets', New York Times, 2 April 2012, http://www.nytimes.com/2012/04/03/opinion/how-china-steals-our-secrets.html

'Cold War Hotline Recalled', BBC News, 7 June 2003, http://news.bbc.co.uk/1/hi/world/europe/2971558.stm

Cox, Joseph, 'GCHQ Has Disclosed over 20 Vulnerabilities This Year, Including Ones in iOS', Vice News, 29 April 2016, https://motherboard.vice.com/read/gchq-vulnerabilities-mozilla-apple

————, 'London's Metropolitan Police has over 35,000 Computers Still Running Windows XP', Vice News, 27 April 2015, http://motherboard.vice.com/en_us/tag/machines?trk_source=nav

Coyle, James, 'Russia Has Complete Information Dominance in Ukraine', Atlantic Council, 12 May 2015, http://www.atlanticcouncil.org/blogs/new-atlanticist/russia-has-complete-informational-dominance-in-ukraine

'Crime in the United States 2014', Federal Bureau of Investigations, 2015, https://www.fbi.gov/about-us/cjis/ucr/crime-in-the-u.s/2014/crime-in-the-u.s.-2014/offenses-known-to-law-enforcement/clearances/main/clearances.pdf

Crowley, Michael, and Josh Gerstein, 'No Rules of Cyber War', Politico, 23 December 2014, http://www.politico.com/story/2014/12/no-rules-of-cyber-war-113785.html

Cuthbertson, Anthony, 'Teenage "CIA Hacker" Cracka Arrested in the U.K.', Newsweek, 12 February 2016, http://www.newsweek.com/teenage-cia-hacker-cracka-arrested-uk-425969?rx=us

Daniel, Michael, 'Heartbleed: Understanding When We Disclose Cyber Vulnerabilities', The White House Blog, 28 April 2014, http://www.whitehouse.gov/blog/2014/04/28/heartbleed-understanding-when-we-disclose-cyber-vulnerabilities

Davidson, Lee, 'Massive Utah Cyberattacks—up to 300 Million Per Day—May Be Aimed at NSA Facility', Salt Lake Tribune, 10 February 2015, http://www.sltrib.com/news/2135491-155/massive-utah-cyber-attacks-may-be

Davis, Jack, 'Improving CIA Analytic Performance: Strategic Warning', Sherman Kent Center for Intelligence Analysis, September 2002, https://www.cia.gov/library/kent-center-occasional-papers/vol1no1.htm

Davis, Julie Hirschfeld, and David Sanger, 'Obama and Xi Jinping of China Agree to Steps on Cybertheft', New York Times, 25 September 2015, http://

www.nytimes.com/2015/09/26/world/asia/xi-jinping-white-house.html

Dewey, Caitlin, 'The U.S. Weapons Systems That Experts Say Were Hacked by the Chinese', *Washington Post*, 28 May 2013, http://www.washingtonpost.com/blogs/worldviews/wp/2013/05/28/the-u-s-weapons-systems-that-experts-say-were-hacked-by-the-chinese

Dobbs, Michael, 'One Minute to Midnight', National Security Archive, 11 June 2008, http://nsarchive.gwu.edu/nsa/cuba_mis_cri/dobbs/maultsby.htm

Elgin, Ben, and Michael Riley, 'Now at the Sands Casino: An Iranian Hacker in Every Server', Bloomberg, 11 December 2014, http://www.bloomberg.com/bw/articles/2014-12-11/iranian-hackers-hit-sheldon-adelsons-sands-casino-in-las-vegas

Eng, James, and Wendy Jones, 'OPM Chief Says Government Agency Thwarts 10 Million Hack Attempts a Month', NBC News, 16 June 2015, http://www.nbcnews.com/tech/security/opm-chief-says-government-agency-thwarts-10-million-hack-attempts-n376476

Falcone, Robert, and Miller-Osborn Jen, 'Scarlet Mimic: Years-Long Espionage Campaign Targets Minority Activists', Palo Alto Networks, 24 January 2016, http://researchcenter.paloaltonetworks.com/2016/01/scarlet-mimic-years-long-espionage-targets-minority-activists/

Feng, Bree, 'Among Snowden Leaks, Details of Chinese Cyberespionage', *New York Times*, 20 January 2015, http://sinosphere.blogs.nytimes.com/2015/01/20/among-snowden-leaks-details-of-chinese-cyberespionage/

Finkle, Jim, 'Update 2-Hackers Infect Forbes.Com to Spy on Visitors—Researchers', Reuters, 10 February 2015, http://www.reuters.com/article/2015/02/10/forbes-cybersecurity-idUSL1N0VK21020150210

Fischer, Benjamin, 'A Cold War Conundrum: The 1983 Soviet War Scare', Central Intelligence Agency, 1997, https://www.cia.gov/library/center-for-the-study-of-intelligence/csi-publications/books-and-monographs/a-cold-war-conundrum/source.htm

Fishel, Justin, and Lee Ferran, 'State Dept. Shuts Down Email after Cyber Attack', ABC News, 13 March 2015, http://abcnews.go.com/US/state-dept-shuts-email-cyber-attack/story?id=29624866

Fisher, Dennis, 'Saudi Aramco Confirms Scope of Malware Attack', ThreatPost, 27 August 2012, threatpost.com/saudi-aramco-confirms-scope-malware-attack-082712/76954

'Full Text: Outcome List of President Xi Jinping's State Visit to the United States', Xinhua, 26 September 2015, http://news.xinhuanet.com/english/2015-09/26/c_134661037_4.htm

Fung, Brian, 'The NSA Hacks Other Countries by Buying Millions of Dollars' Worth of Computer Vulnerabilities', *Washington Post*, 31 August 2013,

BIBLIOGRAPHY

http://www.washingtonpost.com/blogs/the-switch/wp/2013/08/31/
the-nsa-hacks-other-countries-by-buying-millions-of-dollars-worth-of-
computer-vulnerabilities/

Gallagher, Ryan, 'Operation Auroragold: How the NSA Hacks Cellphone
Networks Worldwide', *The Intercept*, 4 December 2014, https://firstlook.
org/theintercept/2014/12/04/nsa-auroragold-hack-cellphones/

————, 'Vodafone-Linked Company Aided British Mass Surveillance', *The
Intercept*, 20 November 2014, https://theintercept.com/2014/11/20/
vodafone-surveillance-gchq-snowden/

Gallagher, Sean, 'Your Hard Drive Will Self-Destruct at 2pm: Inside the South
Korean Cyberattack', *Ars Technica*, 21 March 2013, http://arstechnica.
com/security/2013/03/your-hard-drive-will-self-destruct-at-2pm-inside-
the-south-korean-cyber-attack/

Gannes, Liz, 'How Cyber Security Is Like Basketball, According to Barack
Obama', Recode, 14 February 2015, http://www.recode.net/2015/2/
14/11559050 how-cyber-security-is-like-basketball-according-to-barack-
obama

Garamone, Jim, 'Lynn Explains U.S. Cybersecurity Strategy', American
Forces Press Service, 15 September 2010, http://www.defense.gov/
news/newsarticle.aspx?id=60869

Gartzke, Erik, and Jon Lindsay, 'Cross-Domain Deterrence: Strategy in an
Era of Complexity', University of San Diego, 15 July 2014, https://quote.
ucsd.edu/deterrence/files/2014/12/EGLindsay_CDDOverview_
20140715.pdf

Geers, Dan, 'Cybersecurity as Realpolitik', Black Hat, 6 August 2014,
http://geer.tinho.net/geer.blackhat.6viii14.txt

Gellman, Barton, and Ellen Nakashima, 'U.S. Spy Agencies Mounted 231
Offensive Cyber-Operations in 2011, Documents Show', *Washington Post*,
30 August 2013, http://www.washingtonpost.com/world/national-secu-
rity/us-spy-agencies-mounted-231-offensive-cyber-operations-in-2011-
documents-show/2013/08/30/d090a6ae-119e-11e3-b4cb-fd7ce041d
814_story.html

Gellman, Barton, and Ashkan Soltani, 'NSA Infiltrates Links to Yahoo, Google
Data Centers Worldwide, Snowden Documents Say', *Washington Post*,
30 October 2013, http://www.washingtonpost.com/world/national-
security/nsa-infiltrates-links-to-yahoo-google-data-centers-worldwide-
snowden-documents-say/2013/10/30/e51d661e-4166–11e3–8b74-
d89d714ca4dd_story.html

'German Government Cancels Verizon Contract in Wake of U.S. Spying
Row', Reuters, 26 June 2014, http://www.reuters.com/article/2014/
06/26/us-germany-security-verizon-idUSKBN0F11WJ20140626

Gertz, Bill, 'Iranian General: IRGC Cyber Warfare Capabilities Now Equal to

Those of Major Global Powers', FlashCritic, 4 January 2014, http://flash-critic.com/iranian-general-irgc-cyber-war-capabilities-now-equal-those-of-major-world-powers/

Gluesing, Jens, Laura Poitras, Marcel Rosenbach, and Holger Stark, 'Fresh Leak on US Spying: NSA Accessed Mexican President's Email', Der Spiegel, 20 October 2013, http://www.spiegel.de/international/world/nsa-hacked-email-account-of-mexican-president-a-928817.html

Goodin, Dan, 'Fog of Cyberwar: Internet Always Favors the Offense', The Register, 29 July 2010, http://www.theregister.co.uk/2010/07/29/internet_warfare_keynote

Gorman, Siobhan, and Julian E. Barnes, 'Cyber Combat: Act of War', Wall Street Journal, 31 May 2011, http://www.wsj.com/articles/SB10001424 05270230456310457635562313578271 8

Graham, Robert, 'From Scratch: Why These Mass Scans Are Important', Errata Security, 31 May 2016, http://blog.erratasec.com/2016/05/from-scratch-why-these-mass-scans-are.html

Greenberg, Andy, 'Hackers Remotely Kill a Jeep on the Highway—with Me in It', Wired, 21 July 2015, http://www.wired.com/2015/07/hackers-remotely-kill-jeep-highway/

Greenwald, Glenn, 'NSA Claims Iran Learned from Western Cyberattacks', The Intercept, 10 February 2015, https://firstlook.org/theintercept/2015/02/10/nsa-iran-developing-sophisticated-cyber-attacks-learning-attacks/

Grow, Brian, and Mark Hosenball, 'Special Report: In Cyberspy vs. Cyberspy, China Has the Edge', Reuters, 14 April 2011, http://www.reuters.com/article/2011/04/14/us-china-usa-cyberespionage-idUSTRE73D242201 10414

Guarnieri, Claudio, 'Everything We Know of NSA and Five Eyes Malware', Nex.sx, 27 January 2015, https://nex.sx/blog/2015-01-27-everything-we-know-of-nsa-and-five-eyes-malware.html

Harris, Shane, 'China Reveals Its Cyberwar Secrets', The Daily Beast, 18 March 2015, http://www.thedailybeast.com/articles/2015/03/18/china-reveals-its-cyber-war-secrets.html

Hayden, Michael, 'The Making of America's Cyberweapons', Christian Science Monitor, 24 February 2016, http://www.csmonitor.com/World/Pass-code/Passcode-Voices/2016/0224/The-making-of-America-s-cyberweapons

Healey, Jason, 'Beyond Attribution: Seeking National Responsibility for Cyber Attacks', Atlantic Council, 2011, https://www.fbiic.gov/public/2012/mar/National_Responsibility_for_CyberAttacks,_2012.pdf

'The Heartbleed Bug', Codenomicon, 29 April 2014, http://heartbleed.com

Hennessey, Susan, 'Good Defense is Good Offense: NSA Myths and the

Merger', Lawfare, 9 February 2016, https://www.lawfareblog.com/good-defense-good-offense-nsa-myths-and-merger

'Homeland Security Seeks Cyber Counterattack System', CNN, 4 October 2008, http://www.cnn.com/2008/TECH/10/04/chertoff.cyber.security/

Hosenball, Mark, 'Obama Halted NSA Spying on IMF and World Bank Headquarters', Reuters, 31 October 2013, http://www.reuters.com/article/2013/10/31/usa-security-imf-idUSL1N0IL19I20131031

Javers, Eamon, 'Silicon Valley, DC at Odds on Security Clearances', CNBC, 6 March 2015, http://www.cnbc.com/id/102483901

Jones, Nate, Tom Blanton, and Lauren Harper, 'The 1983 War Scare Declassified and for Real', National Security Archive, 24 October 2015, http://nsarchive.gwu.edu/nukevault/ebb533-The-Able-Archer-War-Scare-Declassified-PFIAB-Report-Released/

Joyce, Rob, 'USENIX Enigma 2016—NSA TAO Chief on Disrupting Nation State Hackers', YouTube, 28 January 2016, https://www.youtube.com/watch?v=bDJb8WOJYdA

Kanuck, Sean, 'Sean Kanuck on Deterrence and Arms Control in Cyberspace', YouTube, 30 March 2016, https://www.youtube.com/watch?v=N7VgvPB-3DU

Kovacs, Eduard, 'New "LusyPOS" Malware Uses Tor for C&C Communications', Security Week, 3 December 2014, http://www.securityweek.com/new-lusypos-malware-uses-tor-cc-communications

Krebs, Brian, 'SendGrid: Employee Account Hacked, Used to Steal Customer Credentials', Krebs on Security, 27 April 2015, http://krebsonsecurity.com/2015/04/sendgrid-employee-account-hacked-used-to-steal-customer-credentials/

Langner, Ralph, 'Stuxnet's Secret Twin', Foreign Policy, 19 November 2013, http://www.foreignpolicy.com/articles/2013/11/19/stuxnets_secret_twin_iran_nukes_cyber_attack

Larson, Jeff, Nicole Perlroth, and Scott Shane, 'Revealed: The NSA's Secret Campaign to Crack, Undermine Internet Security', Pro Publica, 5 September 2013, http://www.propublica.org/article/the-nsas-secret-campaign-to-crack-undermine-internet-encryption

Lewis, James, 'Cross-Domain Deterrence and Credible Threat', Center for Strategic and International Studies, July 2010, https://csis.org/files/publication/100701_Cross_Domain_Deterrence.pdf

Lyle, Amaani, 'Obama Discusses National Security During Worldwide Troop Talk', Department of Defense, 11 September 2015, http://www.defense.gov/News-Article-View/Article/616987/obama-discusses-national-security-during-worldwide-troop-talk

Majumdar, Dave, 'U.S. Pilots Say New Chinese Stealth Fighter Could Become Equal of F-22, F-35', US Naval Institute News, 5 November 2014, http://

news.usni.org/2014/11/05/u-s-pilots-say-new-chinese-stealth-fighter-become-equal-f-22-f-35

Marks, Joseph, 'U.S. Makes New Push for Global Rules in Cyberspace', *Politico*, 5 May 2015, http://www.politico.com/story/2015/05/us-makes-new-push-for-global-rules-in-cyberspace-117632.html

Martinez, Luis, James Gordon Meek, Brian Ross, and Lee Ferran, 'Major U.S. Weapons Compromised by Chinese Hackers, Report Warns', ABC News, 28 May 2013, http://abcnews.go.com/Blotter/major-us-weapons-compromised-chinese-hackers-report-warns/story?id=19271995

Masters, Jonathan, 'Confronting the Cyber Threat', Council on Foreign Relations, 23 May 2011, http://www.cfr.org/technology-and-foreign-policy/confronting-cyber-threat/p15577

Maucione, Scott, 'White House Finally Acquiesces to Congress on Cyber Deterrence Policy', Federal News Radio, 29 December 2015, http://federalnewsradio.com/cybersecurity/2015/12/white-house-finally-acquiesces-congress-cyber-deterrence-policy/

McAllister, Neil, 'Bruce Schneier: "We're in Early Years of a Cyber Arms Race"', *The Register*, 19 August 2015, http://www.theregister.co.uk/2015/08/19/bruce_schneier_linuxcon/?mt=1440022640250

McConnell, Mike, 'How to Win the Cyber-War We're Losing', *Washington Post*, 28 Feburary 2010, http://www.washingtonpost.com/wp-dyn/content/article/2010/02/25/AR2010022502493.html

McReynolds, Joe, 'China's Evolving Perspectives on Network Warfare: Lessons from the Science of Military Strategy', Center for International Maritime Security, 23 June 2015, http://cimsec.org/chinas-evolving-perspectives-on-network-warfare-lessons-from-the-science-of-military-strategy/16965

Menn, Joseph, 'Apple Says FBI Gave It First Vulnerability Tip on April 14', Reuters, 26 April 2016, http://www.reuters.com/article/us-apple-encryption-fbi-disclosure-idUSKCN0XO00T

————, 'Exclusive: Secret Contract Tied NSA and Security Industry Pioneer', Reuters, 20 December 2013, http://www.reuters.com/article/2013/12/20/us-usa-security-rsa-idUSBRE9BJ1C220131220

————, 'NSA Says How Often, Not When, It Discloses Software Flaws', Reuters, 6 November 2015, http://www.reuters.com/article/us-cybersecurity-nsa-flaws-insight-idUSKCN0SV2XQ20151107

————, 'Special Report: U.S. Cyberwar Strategy Stokes Fear of Blowback', Reuters, 10 May 2013, http://uk.reuters.com/article/2013/05/10/us-usa-cyberweapons-specialreport-idUSBRE9490EL20130510

'Metasploit', Rapid7, http://www.metasploit.com/

Miller, Charlie, 'The Legitimate Vulnerability Market', Independent Security Evaluators, 6 May 2007, http://weis2007.econinfosec.org/papers/29.pdf

Moody, Glyn, 'Dutch Government: Encryption Good, Backdoors Bad', *Ars*

# BIBLIOGRAPHY

*Technica*, 6 January 2016, http://arstechnica.com/tech-policy/2016/01/dutch-government-encryption-good-backdoors-bad/

Mooney, Alexander, 'Who Has Obama's E-Mail Address?', CNN, 2 February 2009, http://politicalticker.blogs.cnn.com/2009/02/02/who-has-obamas-e-mail-address/

Morozov, Evgeny, 'Cyber-Scare: The Exaggerated Fears over Digital Warfare', *Boston Review*, 1 July 2009, https://bostonreview.net/us/cyber-scare-evgeny-morozov

Nakashima, Ellen, 'Confidential Report Lists U.S. Weapons System Designs Compromised by Chinese Cyberspies', *Washington Post*, 27 May 2013, http://www.washingtonpost.com/world/national-security/confidential-report-lists-us-weapons-system-designs-compromised-by-chinese-cyber-spies/2013/05/27/a42c3e1c-c2dd-11e2–8c3b-0b5e9247e8ca_story.html

———, 'Indictment of PLA Hackers Is Part of Broad U.S. Strategy to Curb Chinese Cyberspying', *Washington Post*, 22 May 2014, http://www.washingtonpost.com/world/national-security/indictment-of-pla-hackers-is-part-of-broad-us-strategy-to-curb-chinese-cyberspying/2014/05/22/a66cf26a-e1b4–11e3–9743-bb9b59cde7b9_story.html

———, 'Meet the Woman in Charge of the FBI's Most Controversial High-Tech Tools', *Washington Post*, 8 December 2015, https://www.washingtonpost.com/world/national-security/meet-the-woman-in-charge-of-the-fbis-most-contentious-high-tech-tools/2015/12/08/15adb35e-9860–11e5–8917–653b65c809eb_story.html

———, 'Pentagon to Fast-Track Cyberweapons Acquisition', *Washington Post*, 9 April 2012, http://www.washingtonpost.com/world/national-security/pentagon-to-fast-track-cyberweapons-acquisition/2012/04/09/gIQAuwb76S_story.html

———, 'Several Nations Trying to Penetrate U.S. Cyber-Networks, Says Ex-FBI Official', *Washington Post*, 18 April 2012, http://www.washingtonpost.com/world/national-security/several-nations-trying-to-penetrate-us-cyber-networks-says-ex-fbi-official/2012/04/17/gIQAFAGUPT_story.html

———, 'U.S. And Russia Sign Pact to Create Communication Link on Cyber Security', *Washington Post*, 17 June 2013, https://www.washingtonpost.com/world/national-security/us-and-russia-sign-pact-to-create-communication-link-on-cyber-security/2013/06/17/ca57ea04-d788–11e2–9df4–895344c13c30_story.html

———, 'U.S. Decides against Publicly Blaming China for Data Hack', *Washington Post*, 21 July 2015, https://www.washingtonpost.com/world/national-security/us-avoids-blaming-china-in-data-theft-seen-as-fair-game-in-espionage/2015/07/21/03779096–2eee-11e5–8353–1215475949f4_story.html?hpid=z1

———, 'With Plan X, Pentagon Seeks to Spread U.S. Military Might to Cyberspace', *Washington Post*, 30 May 2012, http://www.washingtonpost.com/world/national-security/with-plan-x-pentagon-seeks-to-spread-us-military-might-to-cyberspace/2012/05/30/gJQAEca71U_story.html

Nakashima, Ellen, and Andrea Peterson, 'Obama Administration Opts Not to Force Firms to Decrypt Data—for Now', *Washington Post*, 8 October 2015, https://www.washingtonpost.com/world/national-security/obama-administration-opts-not-to-force-firms-to-decrypt-data—for-now/2015/10/08/1d6a6012–6dca-11e5-aa5b-f78a98956699_story.html

Newman, Melanie, 'Encryption Risks Leading to 'Ethically Worse' Behaviour by Spies, Says Former GCHQ Chief', Bureau of Investigative Journalism, 23 January 2015, https://www.thebureauinvestigates.com/2015/01/23/encryption-will-lead-to-ethically-worse-behaviour-by-spies-says-former-gchq-chief/

Niccolai, James, 'A Security Firm Says Code Used against Sony Has Similarities to Other Malware Linked to North Korea', *Computer World*, 17 February 2015, http://www.computerworld.com/article/2885534/code-typo-helps-tie-north-korea-to-the-sony-hack.html

'The NSA and Privacy', American University, 3 April 2014, http://www.american.edu/spa/pti/nsa-privacy-janus-2014.cfm

Nye, Joseph, 'Cyber Power', Belfer Center for Science and International Affairs, May 2010, http://belfercenter.ksg.harvard.edu/files/cyber-power.pdf

'Officials: Second Hack Exposed Military and Intel Data', *New York Times*, 12 June 2015, http://www.nytimes.com/aponline/2015/06/12/us/politics/ap-us-government-hacked-.html?_r=0

'The Open Skies Treaty', Federation of American Scientists, February 1996, http://fas.org/nuke/control/os/news/ost-96.htm

Osborn, Andrew, and Guy Faulconbridge, 'UK Seeks Full Cyber Warfare Capability, Experts', Reuters, 29 September 2013, http://www.reuters.com/article/2013/09/29/us-britain-cyber-warfare-idUSBRE98S0GO20130929

Paletta, Damian, 'NSA Chief Says Cyberattack at Pentagon Was Sophisticated, Persistent', *Wall Street Journal*, 8 September 2015, http://www.wsj.com/articles/nsa-chief-says-cyberattack-at-pentagon-was-sophisticated-persistent-1441761541

Panetta, Leon, 'Defending the Nation from Cyber Attack', Department of Defense, 11 October 2012, http://www.defense.gov/Speeches/Speech.aspx?SpeechID=1728

Perera, David, 'Offense and Defense Not Clearly Separable in Cyberspace, Says CYBERCOM General', FierceGovernmentIT, 25 February 2013, http://www.fiercegovernmentit.com/story/offense-and-defense-not-clearly-separable-cyberspace-says-cybercom-general/2013-02-25

# BIBLIOGRAPHY

Perlroth, Nicole, 'Hackers in China Attacked the Times for Last 4 Months', *New York Times*, 30 January 2013, http://www.nytimes.com/2013/01/31/technology/chinese-hackers-infiltrate-new-york-times-computers.html?pagewanted=all

———, 'Hackers Lurking in Vents and Soda Machines', *New York Times*, 7 April 2014, http://www.nytimes.com/2014/04/08/technology/the-spy-in-the-soda-machine.html

———, 'Unable to Crack Computer Virus, Security Firm Seeks Help', *New York Times*, 14 August 2012, http://bits.blogs.nytimes.com/2012/08/14/unable-to-crack-computer-virus-security-researchers-issue-cry-for-help/

Perlroth, Nicole, and Brian X. Chen, 'Outdated Encryption Keys Leave Phones Vulnerable to Hackers', *New York Times*, 4 March 2015, http://www.nytimes.com/2015/03/05/business/outdated-encryption-leaves-phones-vulnerable-to-hackers.html

Perlroth, Nicole, and Quentin Hardy, 'Bank Hacking Was the Work of Iranians, Officials Say', *New York Times*, 8 January 2013, http://www.nytimes.com/2013/01/09/technology/online-banking-attacks-were-work-of-iran-us-officials-say.html?_r=0

Perlroth, Nicole, Jeff Larson, and Scott Shane, 'N.S.A. Able to Foil Basic Safeguards of Privacy on Web', *New York Times*, 5 September 2013, http://www.nytimes.com/2013/09/06/us/nsa-foils-much-internet-encryption.html?pagewanted=all

Perlroth, Nicole, and David Sanger, 'U.S. Embedded Spyware Overseas, Report Claims', *New York Times*, 16 February 2015, http://www.nytimes.com/2015/02/17/technology/spyware-embedded-by-us-in-foreign-networks-security-firm-says.html

Peterson, Andrea, 'The NSA is Trying to Crack Tor. The State Department is Helping Pay for It.', *Washington Post*, 5 October 2013, http://www.washingtonpost.com/blogs/the-switch/wp/2013/10/05/the-nsa-is-trying-to-crack-tor-the-state-department-is-helping-pay-for-it/

Poulsen, Kevin, 'Slammer Worm Crashed Ohio Nuke Plant Network', Security Focus, 19 August 2003, http://www.securityfocus.com/news/6767

'Press Briefing with DARPA Director Arati Prabhakar from the Pentagon', Department of Defense, 24 April 2013, http://www.defense.gov/transcripts/transcript.aspx?transcriptid=5227

Prevelakis, Vassilis, and Diomidis Spinellis, 'The Athens Affair', IEEE Spectum, 29 June 2007, http://spectrum.ieee.org/telecom/security/the-athens-affair

Protalinksi, Emil, 'Windows 7 Drops under 50% Market Share, XP Falls Below 10%', VentureBeat, 1 May 2016, http://venturebeat.com/2016/05/01/windows-7-drops-under-50-market-share-xp-falls-below-10/

# BIBLIOGRAPHY

'Quantum Spying: GCHQ Used Fake LinkedIn Pages to Target Engineers', *Der Spiegel*, 11 November 2013, http://www.spiegel.de/international/world/ghcq-targets-engineers-with-fake-linkedin-pages-a-932821.html

Reagan, Ronald, 'Remarks at the Annual Convention of the National Association of Evangelicals in Orlando, Florida', Ronald Reagan Foundation, 8 March 1983, http://www.reaganfoundation.org/pdf/Remarks_Annual_Convention_National_Association_Evangelicals_030883.pdf

'Remarks by President Obama and President Xi of the People's Republic of China in Joint Press Conference', The White House, 25 September https://www.whitehouse.gov/the-press-office/2015/09/25/remarks-president-obama-and-president-xi-peoples-republic-china-joint

Ringstrom, Anna, 'Sweden Security Forces Fear Russian Military Operations', Reuters, 18 March 2015, http://www.reuters.com/article/us-sweden-espionnage-russia-idUSKBN0ME1H620150318

Rohlf, Chris, 'Offense at Scale', GitHub, 30 May 2015, https://github.com/struct/research/blob/master/BSidesNola_Offense_At_Scale.pdf

Romero, Simon, 'N.S.A. Spied on Brazilian Oil Company, Report Says', *New York Times*, 9 September 2013, http://www.nytimes.com/2013/09/09/world/americas/nsa-spied-on-brazilian-oil-company-report-says.html

Sale, Richard, 'Stuxnet Loaded by Iran Double Agents', Industrial Safety and Security Source, 11 April 2012, http://www.isssource.com/stuxnet-loaded-by-iran-double-agents/

Sanger, David, 'Fine Line Seen in U.S. Spying on Companies', *New York Times*, 20 May 2014, http://www.nytimes.com/2014/05/21/business/us-snooping-on-companies-cited-by-china.html?_r=0

———, 'N.S.A. Breached Chinese Servers Seen as Security Threat', *New York Times*, 22 March 2014, http://www.nytimes.com/2014/03/23/world/asia/nsa-breached-chinese-servers-seen-as-spy-peril.html

———, 'President Tweaks the Rules on Data Collection', *New York Times*, 3 February 2015, http://www.nytimes.com/2015/02/03/world/president-tweaks-the-rules-on-data-collection.html

———, '"Shadow Brokers" Leak Raises Alarming Question: Was the N.S.A. Hacked?', New York Times, 16 August 2016, http://www.nytimes.com/2016/08/17/us/shadow-brokers-leak-raises-alarming-question-was-the-nsa-hacked.html?_r=0

———, 'U.S. Indicts 7 Iranians in Cyberattacks on Banks and a Dam', *New York Times*, 24 March 2016, http://www.nytimes.com/2016/03/25/world/middleeast/us-indicts-iranians-in-cyberattacks-on-banks-and-a-dam.html?_r=0

———, 'U.S. Tries Candor to Assure China on Cyberattacks', *New York Times*, 6 April 2014, http://www.nytimes.com/2014/04/07/world/us-tries-candor-to-assure-china-on-cyberattacks.html?hp&_r=0

Sanger, David, and Stewart Baker, 'Steptoe Cyberlaw Podcast—Interview with David Sanger', Steptoe & Johnson, 21 January 2015, http://www.steptoe.com/resources-detail-10137.html

Sanger, David, and Martin Fackler, 'N.S.A. Breached North Korean Networks before Sony Attack, Officials Say', New York Times, 18 January 2015, http://www.nytimes.com/2015/01/19/world/asia/nsa-tapped-into-north-korean-networks-before-sony-attack-officials-say.html

Sanger, David, and Mark Mazzetti, 'U.S. Had Cyberattack Plan if Iran Nuclear Dispute Led to Conflict', New York Times, 16 February 2016, http://www.nytimes.com/2016/02/17/world/middleeast/us-had-cyberattack-planned-if-iran-nuclear-negotiations-failed.html

Sanger, David, and Michael Schmidt, 'More Sanctions on North Korea after Sony Case', New York Times, 2 January 2015, http://www.nytimes.com/2015/01/03/us/in-response-to-sony-attack-us-levies-sanctions-on-10-north-koreans.html?_r=0

Sanger, David, and Thom Shanker, 'NSA Devises Radio Pathway into Computers', New York Times, 14 January 2014, http://www.nytimes.com/2014/01/15/us/nsa-effort-pries-open-computers-not-connected-to-internet.html

Savage, Charlie, Julia Angwin, Jeff Larson, and Henrik Moltke, 'Hunting for Hackers, N.S.A. Secretly Expands Internet Spying at U.S. Border', New York Times, 4 June 2015, http://www.nytimes.com/2015/06/05/us/hunting-for-hackers-nsa-secretly-expands-internet-spying-at-us-border.html?_r=0

Schmidt, Michael, Nicole Perlroth, and Matthew Goldstein, 'F.B.I. Says Little Doubt North Korea Hit Sony', New York Times, 7 January 2015, http://www.nytimes.com/2015/01/08/business/chief-says-fbi-has-no-doubt-that-north-korea-attacked-sony.html?_r=0

Schmidt, Michael, and David Sanger, 'Russian Hackers Read Obama's Unclassified Emails, Officials Say', New York Times, 25 April 2015, http://www.nytimes.com/2015/04/26/us/russian-hackers-read-obamas-unclassified-emails-officials-say.html

Schmitt, Eric, and Thom Shanker, 'U.S. Debated Cyberwarfare in Attack Plan on Libya', New York Times, 17 October 2011, http://www.nytimes.com/2011/10/18/world/africa/cyber-warfare-against-libya-was-debated-by-us.html

Schmitz, Gregor Peter, 'Belgians Angered by British Spying', Der Spiegel, 20 September 2013, http://www.spiegel.de/international/europe/belgian-prime-minister-angry-at-claims-of-british-spying-a-923583.html

Schneier, Bruce, 'Attacking Tor: How the NSA Targets Users' Online Anonymity', The Guardian, 4 October 2013, http://www.theguardian.com/world/2013/oct/04/tor-attacks-nsa-users-online-anonymity

# BIBLIOGRAPHY

————, 'DEITYBOUNCE: NSA Exploit of the Day', Schneier on Security, 20 January 2014, https://www.schneier.com/blog/archives/2014/01/nsa_exploit_of.html

Schwartz, Ari, and Robert Knake, 'Government's Role in Vulnerability Disclosure: Creating a Permanent and Accountable Vulnerability Equities Process', Belfer Center for Science and International Affairs, 17 June 2016, http://belfercenter.ksg.harvard.edu/files/vulnerability-disclosure-web-final3.pdf

Shachtman, Noah, 'DARPA Looks to Make Cyberwar Routine with Secret "Plan X"', Wired, 21 August 2012, http://www.wired.com/2012/08/plan-x/

————, 'This Pentagon Project Makes Cyberwar as Easy as Angry Birds', Wired, 28 May 2013, http://www.wired.com/2013/05/pentagon-cyberwar-angry-birds/all/

Shalal, Andrea, and Alina Selyukh, 'Obama Seeks $14 Billion to Boost U.S. Cybersecurity Defenses', Reuters, 2 February 2015, http://www.reuters.com/article/2015/02/02/us-usa-budget-cybersecurity-idUSKBN0L61WQ20150202

Shane, Scott, 'No Morsel Too Minuscule for All-Consuming N.S.A.', New York Times, 2 September 2013, http://www.nytimes.com/2013/11/03/world/no-morsel-too-minuscule-for-all-consuming-nsa.html?pagewanted=all&_r=1

Sharwood, Simon, 'Fukushima Nuke Plant Owner Told to Upgrade from Windows XP', The Register, 23 April 2015, http://www.theregister.co.uk/2015/04/23/fukushima_nuke_plant_owner_told_to_upgrade_from_windows_xp/

Shi, Ting, and Michael Riley, 'China Halts Cybersecurity Cooperation after U.S. Spying Charges', Bloomberg, 20 May 2014, http://www.bloomberg.com/news/2014-05-20/china-suspends-cybersecurity-cooperation-with-u-s-after-charges.html

Smith, Shane, 'Cyberspies, Nukes, and the New Cold War: Shane Smith Interviews Ashton Carter (Part 1)', Vice News, 15 May 2015, https://news.vice.com/video/cyberspies-nukes-and-the-new-cold-war-shane-smith-interviews-ashton-carter-part-1

Snow, John, 'The Poseidon's Domain', Kaspersky Lab, 9 February 2016, https://usblog.kaspersky.com/poseidon-apt-boutique/6664/

Sternstein, Aliya, 'Here's What OPM Told Congress Last Time Hackers Breached its Networks', NextGov, 15 June 2015, http://www.nextgov.com/cybersecurity/2015/06/while-being-hacked-opm-tech-chief-testified-agencys-strong-leadership-and-it-defenses/115357/

Stone, Webster, 'Moscow's Still Holding', New York Times, 18 September 1988, http://www.nytimes.com/1988/09/18/magazine/moscow-s-still-holding.html?pagewanted=all&pagewanted=print

# BIBLIOGRAPHY

'The Sveriges Riksbank Prize in Economic Sciences in Memory of Alfred Nobel 2005', Swedish Academy of Sciences, 10 October 2005, http://www.nobelprize.org/nobel_prizes/economic-sciences/laureates/2005/press.html

'Taia Global Linguists Establish Nationality of Sony Hackers as Likely Russian, Not Korean', Taia Global, 8 January 2015, https://taia.global/2014/12/taia-global-linguists-establish-nationality-of-sony-hackers-as-russian-not-korean/

'Tass Report on a Soviet General's Comments About Airliner', New York Times, 5 September 1983 http://www.nytimes.com/1983/09/05/world/tass-report-on-a-soviet-general-s-comments-about-airliner.html

thegrugq, 'On Cyber—Power of Community 2015', YouTube, 6 December 2015, https://www.youtube.com/watch?v=qlk4JDOiivM&feature=youtu.be

Thornburgh, Nathan, 'The Invasion of the Chinese Cyberspies (and the Man Who Tried to Stop Them)', Time, 5 September 2005, http://courses.cs.washington.edu/courses/csep590/05au/readings/titan.rain.htm

Timberg, Craig, and Ashkan Soltani, 'By Cracking the Cellphone Code, NSA Has Ability to to Decode Private Conversations', Washington Post, 13 December 2013, http://www.washingtonpost.com/business/technology/by-cracking-cellphone-code-nsa-has-capacity-for-decoding-private-conversations/2013/12/13/e119b598–612f-11e3-bf45–61f69f54fc5f_story.html

Tischer, Matthew, Zakir Durumeric, Sam Foster, Sunny Duan, Alec Mori, Elie Bursztein, and Michael Bailey, 'Users Really Do Plug in Usb Drives They Find', University of Illinois Urbana-Champaign, April 2016, https://zakird.com/papers/usb.pdf

Tor, Uri, '"Cumulative Deterrence" as a New Paradigm for Cyber Deterrence', Journal of Strategic Studies, 18 December 2015, http://www.tandfonline.com/doi/abs/10.1080/01402390.2015.1115975?journalCode=fjss20

'Transcript of President Obama's Jan. 17 Speech on NSA Reforms', Washington Post, 17 January 2014, https://www.washingtonpost.com/politics/full-text-of-president-obamas-jan-17-speech-on-nsa-reforms/2014/01/17/fa33590a-7f8c-11e3–9556–4a4bf7bcbd84_story.html

Tummarello, Kate, '"Be Careful" Working with NSA, US Tech Security Agency Warned', The Hill, 14 July 2014, http://thehill.com/policy/technology/212526-us-tech-agency-told-to-be-very-careful-with-nsa

Uchill, Joe, 'State Department Reverses Course on Cybersecurity Exports', Christian Science Monitor, 2 March 2016, http://www.csmonitor.com/World/Passcode/2016/0302/State-Department-reverses-course-on-cybersecurity-exports

# BIBLIOGRAPHY

Vinik, Danny, 'America's Secret Arsenal', *Politico*, 9 December 2015, http://www.politico.com/agenda/story/2015/12/defense-department-cyber-offense-strategy-000331

Warner, Michael, 'Notes on Military Doctrine for Cyberspace Operations in the United States, 1992–2014', *Cyber Defense Review*, 27 August 2015, http://www.cyberdefensereview.org/2015/08/27/notes-on-military-doctrine-for-cyberspace/

'"We're in the Middle of a Cyberwar"', *Newsweek*, 19 September 1999, http://www.newsweek.com/were-middle-cyerwar-166196

Weaver, Nicholas, 'A Close Look at the NSA's Most Powerful Internet Attack Tool', Wired, 13 March 2014, http://www.wired.com/2014/03/quantum/

'William and Katherine Estes Award', National Academy of Sciences, http://www.nasonline.org/about-nas/awards/behavioral-research.html

Wilson, Scott, and Anne Gearan, 'Obama Didn't Know About Surveillance of U.S.-Allied World Leaders until Summer, Officials Say', *Washington Post*, 28 October 2013, http://www.washingtonpost.com/politics/obama-didnt-know-about-surveillance-of-us-allied-world-leaders-until-summer-officials-say/2013/10/28/0cbacefa-4009-11e3-a751-f032898f2dbc_story.html

Wolter, Detlev, 'The UN Takes a Big Step Forward on Cybersecurity', Arms Control Association, 4 September 2013, https://www.armscontrol.org/act/2013_09/The-UN-Takes-a-Big-Step-Forward-on-Cybersecurity

Woolsey, James, 'Why We Spy on Our Allies', *Wall Street Journal*, 17 March 2000, http://online.wsj.com/news/articles/SB95326824311657269

Zetter, Kim, 'The Evidence That North Korea Hacked Sony Is Flimsy', Wired, 17 December 2014, http://www.wired.com/2014/12/evidence-of-north-korea-hack-is-thin/

———, 'Hacking Team Leak Shows How Secretive Zero-Day Exploit Sales Work', Wired, 24 July 2015, http://www.wired.com/2015/07/hacking-team-leak-shows-secretive-zero-day-exploit-sales-work/

———, 'How the NSA's Firmware Hacking Works and Why It's So Unsettling', Wired, 22 February 2015, http://www.wired.com/2015/02/nsa-firmware-hacking/

———, 'Inside the Cunning, Unprecedented Hack of Ukraine's Power Grid', Wired, 3 March 2016, http://www.wired.com/2016/03/inside-cunning-unprecedented-hack-ukraines-power-grid/

———, 'Qatari Gas Company Hit with Virus in Wave of Attacks on Energy Companies', Wired, 30 August 2016, https://www.wired.com/2012/08/hack-attack-strikes-rasgas/

———, 'Suite of Sophisticated Nation-State Attack Tools Found with Connection to Stuxnet', Wired, 16 February 2015, http://www.wired.com/2015/02/kapersky-discovers-equation-group/

# BIBLIOGRAPHY

———, 'Top Federal Lab Hacked in Spear-Phishing Attack', Wired, 20 April 2011, http://www.wired.com/2011/04/oak-ridge-lab-hack/

Zetter, Kim, and Andy Greenberg, 'Why the OPM Breach is Such a Security and Privacy Debacle', Wired, 11 June 2015, http://www.wired.com/2015/06/opm-breach-security-privacy-debacle/

Zezima, Katie, 'Obama Signs Executive Order on Sharing Cybersecurity Threat Information', *Washington Post*, 12 February 2015, http://www.washingtonpost.com/blogs/post-politics/wp/2015/02/12/obama-to-sign-executive-order-on-cybersecurity-threats/

*Films*

*Zero Days*, Alex Gibney, Magnolia Pictures, 2016.

# ACKNOWLEDGMENTS

This book is based in part on research I did while I was a PhD student in War Studies at King's College London. I am quite sure I enjoyed, even loved, this PhD experience substantially more than one is supposed to. In many ways this was due to the efforts of Thomas Rid, my PhD supervisor. Thomas's genuine care for his students, his intellectual honesty, and his insights on cybersecurity are major reasons why I look back very fondly on my time as a graduate student (and why I have the degree that I do). It goes without saying that this project and a great deal else are much stronger as a result of working with him.

I am deeply grateful for the Marshall Scholarship I received, courtesy of the United Kingdom's government, which funded my PhD. My time as a Marshall Scholar was one of the most enjoyable periods of my life. Without this scholarship, I certainly would not have pursued a PhD at all. I consider myself deeply lucky to have met Marshall administrators and friends, too many to list here. Two previous Marshall Scholars, Andy Ozment and Michael Sulmeyer, repeatedly gave generously of their time and insights, despite at the time holding enormously demanding jobs in public service. I am indebted to a lifetime of teachers who made this scholarship, book, and so much else possible. In particular, Regis High School and Georgetown University were wonderful past intellectual homes for me. At Georgetown University, John Glavin and Lauren Tuckley encouraged me to apply for the Marshall, and I am immensely grateful that they did.

My fellow PhD students made this work much better and made my time at King's much more enjoyable. Richard Bejtlich, Robert M. Lee,

ACKNOWLEDGMENTS

and Danny Moore may have been spread out across the world, but they are nonetheless invaluable friends and colleagues.

I am grateful as well for my current fellowship at the Cybersecurity Project at Harvard University's Belfer Center for Science and International Affairs. Thanks are due to the aforementioned Michael Sulmeyer, Annie Boustead, Trey Herr, Kate Miller, Scott Shackelford, Bruce Schneier, and Jessica Malekos Smith for being terrific friends and colleagues. Before coming to Harvard, I spent time at the Woodrow Wilson International Center for Scholars in Washington, DC. My deep thanks go to Meg King and Grayson Clary of the Digital Futures Project for making this period possible, productive, and fun. This book benefited from seminars at Columbia University and Oxford University. Thanks to Jason Healey, Robert Jervis, and Florian Egloff for organizing, and thanks to all attendees.

A number of individuals provided feedback on all or parts of this work, or indulged me in conversations about cybersecurity and more over the years. Among those not mentioned above are James Allen, Alex Baron, Will Berdanier, David Betz, Robert Black, Ian Brown, Matthew Carnes, Christopher Coker, Jerod Coker, Teddy Collins, Paul Farina, Michael Goodman, Ramon Gonzalez, Alex Guyton, Matthew Harries, Shea Houlihan, Hilary Hurd, Kevin Keogh, Derek Leebaert, Jon Lindsay, Dillon Liu, Antonio Loccisano, Alex Loomis, Taylor Miller, Ned Moran, Sir David Omand, Casey Quinn, Rahul Rekhi, Mark Rom, Brian Ross, Colin Ross, David Sanger, Rich Schroeder, Rhonda Schwartz, Tim Stevens, Michael Thomas, Jessica Tisch, Bryan Vadheim, Lauren Van Wazer, John Weidinger, and Heather Williams. At Hurst, Michael Dwyer, Jon de Peyer, Alasdair Craig, Kathleen May, Daisy Leitch, and Alison Alexanian believed in this book and helped guide it to market.

In addition, this project—and my thinking on cybersecurity matters generally—has benefited from my interactions with those in the military and intelligence communities on both sides of the Atlantic. While these individuals cannot be thanked publicly, I hope they know how much I value their friendship and perspective. All errors remain mine alone.

Kelly Krohn has heard more about cybersecurity than anyone should reasonably have to. Nonetheless, her love, patience, and inexhaustible willingness to make transatlantic flights have all been wonderful, and far more than I could have reasonably asked for.

## ACKNOWLEDGMENTS

Family comes last but not least. Mitty, Gerard, and Annie have shown me unconditional love for many years. Mary Buchanan is a loving and patient younger sister who provided exceptionally helpful edits on this manuscript in between bird censuses. But my greatest gratitude goes to my parents, Bruce and Laura. Their love for Mary and me seems to know no bounds. It is a debt I will never be able to repay. This book is dedicated to them.

# INDEX

# INDEX

NITRO ZEUS, 32–3, 40, 43, 75, 99, 121–2, 136, 190
Nobel Prize, 101, 133
non-state actors, 11, 48, 67, 98, 116, 119, 153, 161, 167, 168, 169, 190
North Atlantic Treaty Organization (NATO), 21, 90, 171
North Korea, 83, 84, 95, 144, 153, 182, 184, 234
nuclear power/weapons, 3, 15–16, 25, 54, 132–3, 162, 165–7, 212, 224
  Stuxnet, 31, 36–8, 40–2, 46, 75–8, 99, 107, 121–2, 148, 153, 190, 200, 202, 212
Nuclear Risk Reduction Center, 164–5

Obama, Barack, 1, 32, 66, 72, 79–80, 91, 109, 112, 166, 188, 228, 232
objections
  attribution objection, 143–7
  existential threat objection, 147–51
  uneven distribution objection, 151–5
offense–defense
  balance, 103–10, 117, 119, 137, 185
  differentiation, 110–13, 117, 119, 124, 137, 167, 185, 186
Office of Personnel Management (OPM), 34, 159–62, 182
Ohio, United States, 54
Open Skies Treaty, 132, 165
operating systems, 40, 45, 46, 59, 83, 211
Operation Poisoned Hurricane, 204
operational incentives, 41–9

Pacific Ocean, 105
pacifism, 22
Panetta, Leon, 64, 233
passive collection, 68, 221
patches, 54, 62, 111, 191, 227
pattern-matching, 56–8, 128–9, 158–60, 189
payload activation, 40, 82, 83–4, 136, 203, 205
Pearl Harbor attack (1941), 23, 124
Peloponnesian War (431–404 BC), 17–18, 187, 192, 197
penetration testing, 59
Pentagon, 1, 2, 91, 160
People's Liberation Army (PLA), 92, 167, 184
persistence, 44–6, 48, 63
Persistence Division, 45
pivoting, 39–40, 45, 61, 79, 83
Plan X, 87–9
plausible deniability, 48, 97, 137, 168
political sanctions, 184
polymorphism, 209
Poseidon group, 203
Prabhakar, Arati, 88
Presidential Policy Directive 20 (2012), 79–80, 118, 183, 189
private sector, 71–2, 126–7, 145, 214
Putter Panda, 127

Qatar, 216
quartermasters, 47

railroad standard, 105, 106
Random Access Memory (RAM), 58–9
Reagan, Ronald, 19, 28, 163, 164, 171, 238
reconnaissance, 6, 34, 36, 40, 75, 76, 79–81, 82, 87–9

# INDEX

# INDEX

Washington Naval Treaty, 105, 132
*Washington Post*, 88
watering hole attacks, 38, 39, 203
web browsers, 35, 38, 46
Weinberger, Casper, 28
White House, Washington, DC,
 1–2, 37, 42, 52, 101, 160, 173
Windows, 40, 83, 211
wiping code/data, 46, 62, 79, 82,
 83, 190
World War I (1914–18), 104–5,
 109, 222, 225

World War II (1939–45), 22–3,
 24, 132

Xi Jinping, 167, 232

Yom Kippur War (1973), 164

zero days, 36, 42, 47, 58–9, 66,
 101, 107–8, 128, 159, 163,
 167–8, 171–4, 185, 191, 206,
 223–4, 227
Zetter, Kim, 37